D1377863

Also by Michael Freedland

Jolson
Irving Berlin
James Cagney
Fred Astaire
Sophie, the Story of Sophie Tucker
The Two Lives of Errol Flynn
Gregory Peck
The Secret Life of Danny Kaye
Maurice Chevalier
Peter O'Toole
Jack Lemmon
Shirley MacLaine
Jerome Kern
Jane Fonda
The Warner Brothers
The Goldwyn Touch
Liza with a "Z"
Katharine Hepburn
So Let's Hear The Applause, the story of the Jewish Entertainer
Dino, the Dean Martin Story
Dustin
Leonard Bernstein
Kenneth Williams
Sean Connery
André Previn
Music Man
Bob Hope
Bing Crosby
All The Way – a Biography of Frank Sinatra
With Morecambe and Wise: There's No Answer To That
With Walter Scharf: Composed and Conducted

Michael
Caine

Michael Caine

MICHAEL FREEDLAND

First published in 1999 by
Orion Media
an imprint of Orion Books Ltd
Orion House
5 Upper St Martin's Lane, London, WC2H 9EA

A CIP catalogue record for this book is available from the British Library

ISBN 0 75281 801 5

Typeset by Selwood Systems, Midsomer Norton

Printed and bound in Great Britain by
Butler & Tanner Ltd, Frome and London

PICTURE ACKNOWLEDGEMENTS

Pictures kindly supplied by Pictorial Press Ltd., The Kobal Collection, Rex Features London, Weidenfeld Picture Archive.

FOR MY GRANDCHILDREN

Beth, Elinor, Ben and Jamie

If love represents hope and hope,
as I pray, means happiness,
what a wonderful life is ahead for you.

Contents

	Acknowledgements	ix
	Introduction	1
ONE	Peeper	5
TWO	The Battle of Britain	16
THREE	Victory	18
FOUR	Gambit	27
FIVE	A Hill in Korea	37
SIX	Sweet Liberty	43
SEVEN	A Shock to the System	57
EIGHT	Beyond the Limit	68
NINE	Surrender	71
TEN	Zulu	80
ELEVEN	The Ipcress File	89
TWELVE	Alfie	99
THIRTEEN	Bullseye!	109
FOURTEEN	Woman Times Seven	114
FIFTEEN	Billion Dollar Brain	130
SIXTEEN	Too Late, the Hero	141
SEVENTEEN	The Male of the Species	155

EIGHTEEN	Get Carter	164
NINETEEN	Tonight, let's all make love in London	170
TWENTY	Sleuth	174
TWENTY-ONE	The Romantic Englishwoman	183
TWENTY-TWO	The Man Who Would be King	188
TWENTY-THREE	California Suite	194
TWENTY-FOUR	Deathtrap	199
TWENTY-FIVE	Educating Rita	212
TWENTY-SIX	Noises Off	225
TWENTY-SEVEN	Little Voice – and beyond	236
	Filmography	239
	Index	242

Acknowledgements

Thanking people for help with a biography is one of the most enjoyable features of working on a subject like Michael Caine. They take pleasure in their reminiscences and the joy is transmitted to the author – and hopefully then to the reader. Even if the memories are not totally happy, their perspectives are always incisive. These are the witnesses to the events told in the book. Their evidence makes the case for telling the story of a remarkable personality. For what they are able to relate are memories that form the crucial bricks and mortar of a story all the more remarkable because they are the really decisive events in the Caine story.

There was, for instance, June Wyndham Davies, who talked marvellously about working with Caine in repertory, a period that does not automatically come to mind when discussing his career. Then there's his publicist Jerry Pam who put me in touch with so many people in Hollywood who have worked with Caine and enjoy his friendship.

There were just a few who didn't want their names used – like the old boy of the Grocers School who put so much into perspective by talking about the Maurice Micklewhite he knew in the days when he sat at his school desk. Others who were extraordinarily helpful include:

Joss Ackland; Army Archard; the late Lionel Bart; Don Black; Simon Brett; Barry Brown; Jackie Collins; Betty Comden; Michael Constantine; Angie Dickinson; Alf Fogel; Richard Fleischer; Bryan Forbes; Lewis Gilbert; Jack Gold; the late Lord Grade; Saeed Jaffrey; Andrew Klaven; Ruta Lee; Maureen Lipman; Virginia McKenna; Karl Malden; Wolf Mankowitz; Walter Matthau; Sir John Mills; Ron Moody; Ossie Morris; the late Lord Olivier (during a BBC interview on *Sleuth*); Bernard Pentol; Anthony Quinn; the late Dennis Selinger; the late Johnny

Speight; Janet Suzman; the late Sam Wannamaker; Billy Wilder; Michael Winner; the late Fred Zinnemann.

Also, I must thank Sue Krisman for her invaluable help in London.

And, as always, Merle Kessler was impeccable in the research she conducted from afar.

Lastly, to my wife Sara, my everlasting love.

Michael Freedland, London, 1999.

Introduction

You could call Michael Caine the rule breaker. Not a thing he has done, not a stance he has adopted, fitted in with what most people thought they knew about that strange breed, the Hollywood film star.

'They never make these cars big enough, do they?' he asks as he emerges from the kind of activity previously only hinted at in movies – while Millicent Martin tries to adjust her underclothing (in *Alfie*).

'We men are stuck with courtship rituals. I don't have time for it,' he tells Sigourney Weaver.

'Am I still an arsehole?' he asks Maggie Smith (in *California Suite*).

And above all his own protestations of self doubts:

'I said to myself, "Michael, you're never going to be a star. You've not got much personality. So what you've got to do is learn how to act." '

That's one of the comforting things about Michael Caine. He has always been ready with advice. Which is probably why he has given up time in recent years to acting master-classes and writing books on the subject.

As he has said: 'If you want to be a success, you must first of all invent yourself. I haven't got the face to try to manipulate. They take one look into my eyes and say, "Forget it." Hollywood always has created its own monsters and then screamed all the way to the bank. I, on the other hand, am a normal person.'

If he were that normal – either as a man or as an actor – nobody would be interested in him. Ian Jack once wrote in *The Observer:* 'His voice sounds as though it comes from a London taxi driver who has seen too many fares. And yet the voice, the spectacles, the laconic manner, and a slightly trimmer version of the physique all helped establish him as the closest England ever gets to a sex symbol.'

That accent would always haunt him, which is perhaps why he has never tried to change it. 'You don't have to change,' he has said, 'but you do have to learn how to speak other accents if you're an actor. In a land where accents denote not only who you are, but also your character, I have jammed my accent down people's throats.'

Perhaps his real triumph has been that those people haven't choked at the experience.

Born into a world where the cinema offered the only possible escape from a drudgery few could now imagine, male film stars had widow's peaks like Robert Taylor, impossibly handsome features like Cary Grant or the suave sophisticated voice of Ronald Colman. They didn't look or sound like Michael Caine.

The film star was there to make love to beautiful women who never put their hands in cold water. They never kissed for more than three or four seconds and they could be seen to have at least one foot on the floor at all times.

Domestic activity was confined to putting on a frilly apron in a comedy movie and helping with the washing up. It never got beyond helping, and then only for an odd minute or two before the comedy wore off.

But then before Michael Caine, the idea of an actor, – no, let's say it, a film star – owning a chain of up-market restaurants would have been pretty rare, too. As for actually producing food before the cameras . . . impossible, darling.

Yet Michael Caine is the man who proved he could cook a meal on screen. A man cooking? The nearest most films got to showing that was when Jack Lemmon burnt the meat loaf in *The Odd Couple*.

And then there were the spectacles he wore. Marilyn Monroe was the one who said it – men don't make passes at girls who wear glasses. Well, what about a guy in glasses? It was unheard of – at least unheard of when the guy in question was the leading man. It had always been OK for an elder statesman on screen to wear a heavy pair of hornrims. The business executive sitting behind his desk could be made to look better in specs. Even Bogart wore them – playing the boring businessman in *Sabrina*. But Michael Caine has never been boring, never played a businessman or an elder statesman (at least until he played De Klerk of South Africa and then Josef Stalin, and neither of them wore glasses). But just imagine that voice controlling a business from one of those skyscrapers that Hollywood studios used to love to feature at the start of all those movies set in Manhattan. It would be a hell of a lot easier to imagine an East End barrow boy in charge of a real corporation than anyone ever doing it in a serious movie.

But Michael Caine taught the world that it was possible to have women on both sides of the Atlantic drooling over a tall, blond (another rule broken) star who spoke like the fish porters who worked with his old dad at Billingsgate market.

He has survived all the risks of type casting – or as he himself calls it 'being a fixed personality'. Never afraid to take what other actors of his stature might consider secondhand, he has a perfect reason for doing so: 'I often get scripts that have been turned down by major Hollywood stars. That's been my niche, which is to try to give a performance as someone else. I like to stretch myself, which sounds painful, but is not.' It is, I suppose, a matter of technique. As he has said: 'A lot of actors do actually hold up a picture of themselves and say: "This is me and this is what I do and can do and will do".'

'What *I* do and can do and what I like and which gives me pleasure is that I hold up a mirror and say: "This is what you are, what you do and this is how you will behave".'

People, he thinks, see themselves in the characters he plays on screen. That, too, was pretty revolutionary in a world where cinema-goers liked to have their stars on pedestals. 'It's the shock of recognition that people see in my work.'

The greatest compliment of all, he will tell you, is when they say: 'How does he know that about *me?'*

The really remarkable thing is that that Cockney voice could be understood and loved in New York as well as in New Cross, in Chicago as well as in Cheshire (which was probably more of a triumph than getting the Americans on side).

The real achievement, however, has been to show that he is a pretty good actor whichever way you understand that term. An even greater success was to show that while proving to be a nice guy. There had been talented actors before he came on the scene. Certainly, they've been good looking. But talented, good looking and nice?

Is that the Caine formula? Let's find out.

One

Peeper

They never wrote songs about South London. No 'New Cross, New Cross'. Nobody sang about being 'Deep In The Heart of Tooting'. No chart-topper was ever called 'Catford Here I Come'. As an area, it just didn't have the social cachet about it. The homes were miserable, some of them even as miserable as the weather. There were virtually no bathrooms and few indoor lavatories. The people living there didn't speak what used to be regarded as 'nicely'. Men went from infant school to forced retirement – if they were lucky enough to reach retirement – without ever learning to read or write. Women were skilled at giving birth, scrubbing floors and cooking a few scraps of whatever was left over on the shelves of the local butcher or fishmonger.

There were slums on the other side of the water too, but on the whole North Londoners seem to have hailed from a distant planet. People who know the two breeds of citizen living in that amorphous mass called London will say that they even have different accents – the Southerners have a lighter, more rhythmic lilt. Their houses looked different. The same London County Council ran the schools, but education results were better on the other side. It's not that the people there were richer, but the feeling always was that they were posher.

Yet it was the people from over the river who were the real Cockneys. Michael Caine would become the leader of what was unofficially and unfairly called the Cockney Mafia and he has always sounded like a Cockney. But is he a true Cockney? No. That was for the people who could genuinely hear the sound of Bow Bells and to do that you had to be an East Ender. The East End, slummy and unsanitary though it was, has always been away from the north bank of the Thames. That's a fact. That's geography.

But it says nothing about the pride. In 1967 – and the date is important – Caine told *Time* magazine: 'To be a Cockney is, well, like what the Negroes [*sic*; it *was* 1967] complain about in America. We're always sweeping the streets, washing the floors, operating lifts. The thing is that the Negro in America is militant about improving his position. But not the Cockney. I'm militant about improving *my* position, but I never had the backing of any of the others.'

Subconsciously, he knew that, all the time that he was living in South London, he was trying to get out of it.

It wasn't just the smells and the dirt and the poverty. Always there was the feeling of inferiority. It was bred, he would tell you, from the class system that was so endemic in the London of the 1930s and exists less but is still obvious in the society of the new millennium. East was east and west was west and the twain never met. (In all fairness, the north-south divide was less obvious.) The terrible thing was that the working classes knew their station as well as the middle and upper classes did and, as Caine seems to have observed, were content to allow that to be so. Not that there weren't disparaging things said by each about the other. As he himself once noted: 'I think if there was a Class Relations Act, like the Race Relations Act, a third of the British people would be in prison.'

Looking at histories of the South London area you might think it was the obvious place for the Micklewhite family. Certainly, they were not the only people with a background in the Billingsgate fish market who lived in Urlwin street, Camberwell.

It is not an address to send society editors into excited apoplexy. They will never have heard of Urlwin Street. The whole area, Caine would later say, was a place to stay away from, not to travel to. To Americans he would try to explain that his area of London was much like New York's Lower East Side – except that tourists poured into the East Side. Nobody in his right mind would want to visit the sort of place in which Michael Caine grew up. Most of those society editors would not have admitted to even hearing of Camberwell, although the chances are that there are people born in the area who are now editing those same publications – people as free with their 'darlings' and bottles of champagne as they are with sacking contributors and bitching about their subjects.

No, unless you are like the boy born Maurice Joseph Micklewhite on 14 March 1933, you don't talk about the days when you lived in that sort of environment. To him, however, it is like a trophy to be paraded whenever he feels in danger of escaping his roots. In truth, others have been in that sort of danger much more than he ever has himself. He remembers Camberwell, home of the famous Camberwell music hall and of the equally well known youth centre, Clubland, the way other people remember their first day at school, their first date or their first motor car. He remembers those, too, but it is the rough and tumble of South London that swims through his bloodstream all the time that he stands in front of a movie camera, accepts an award or welcomes celebrity customers to one of his restaurants.

The restaurants are important to him because he loves both good food and good wine. Put him in a psychiatrist's chair and the chances are, that he would go back to those early days of childhood when a good meal might be filling but not necessarily nutritious. He developed rickets, which meant that he had to wear special surgical boots. He always said that he quite liked those boots. They fitted perfectly – unlike all his other clothing which was always second-hand.

But Maurice Micklewhite senior had no thoughts about that on the day his son, Maurice junior, was born in a charity ward at St Olave's Hospital in Rotherhithe, an area that has become gentrified and much in demand by people working in the City of London or in the arts. Its river bank settings have become very attractive. In 1933, the area was dirty and unsanitary, the kind of place where stray cats were considered to be welcome visitors. They made a nice change from the rats which crawled up from the black disease-ridden waters.

In those days, before a National Health Service, which supposedly brought equality in medicine to all, the charity ward was always filled. Ellen – actually Ellen Frances Marie – Micklewhite was a rarity in the maternity section. She wasn't destitute. She wasn't a single mother. She didn't earn her living on the streets. But, certainly, she was poor. She would never have gained admittance to the ward if she had money.

The boy born in that ward never saw St Olave's again until, in the 1980s, he worked on a movie starring his friend Bob Hoskins, *Mona Lisa*. His scenes were filmed in a building with an eerie sense of *déjà vu* about it. An icy shock rattled through him when he was told that the building was called St Olave's and that it had been a mental hospital in the years since babies had last been brought into the world there – babies who by then benefited from a proper diet and many of whom were in better shape than young Master Mickelwhite had been. Even so, this baby tipped the scales at eight pounds, two ounces. It was an easy birth, he recorded in his own autobiography – 'the last easy thing I was going to do for the next 30 years.'

There were problems straight away. The family moved into Urlwin Street when their first home off the Old Kent Road, South London's main artery to the Thanet coast, was condemned and pulled down for slum clearance, an event which illustrated both the fact that the authorities were beginning to understand that human living conditions had to be improved and just how bad the conditions were under which the Micklewhites lived.

Maurice junior was born with an eye disease bearing the beautifully lyrical name of blefora. It was incurable, but we all know what it produced – the heavy eyelids of a star which, under his glasses, became the best trade mark of a British actor since the voice of Ronald Colman (to which as we know Michael Caine owed nothing).

If only for the numerous references he has made to it, he owed rather more to South London. If, thanks to some amazing time machine, the people of that deprived area of the capital had been able to forecast what the Micklewhites would bring to their home town, the chances are that the locals would have felt very proud. As it was, the citizens of the district went on with what the uncouth girl in *Singin' In The Rain* would call their 'humdrum little lives'.

It was a momentous time for the world, although the world hadn't yet realised it. After all, in the United States, Franklin Delano Roosevelt had that very month sworn to uphold the constitution of his country and serve it well as President for the first time. It was the start of a revolution. In Germany, Adolf Hitler was preparing himself for power and just ten days after Maurice Joseph Micklewhite's birth he would be granted full authority by the Reichstag. This would have an even more serious effect on the world – with a hundred lives sacrificed for every one given new hope by the latest occupant of the White House.

Meanwhile, in South London, the only real political event that seemed to have any resonance was the storming by 300 Communists of the British Union of Fascists' headquarters in the Walworth Road, just a few miles up in the Elephant and Castle, a district which would have plenty of associations for the Micklewhites before very long. For most of the women thereabouts, much more important was the opening of Hurlock's drapery store in the same street, a place that offered a free tea set with everything bought – including a corset for 4s 11p, slightly less than 25 pence in modern currency.

Politicians wanted people to be aware that the Government was spending £3,750,000 on 21 new warships. The politicians certainly were. The Tories and their 'National' Government were at last saying that they had become convinced of the need for some kind of rearmament. Labour's supporters tended to be much more pacifist and were appalled at such a huge figure. Meanwhile, a letter to the *South London Press* said that the Labour Party was busy exploiting workers.

Queen Mary, though, knew nothing about it. She opened a new 'lying-in' hospital at Lambeth – which presumably took some of the strain from St Olave's.

Within a week of Maurice's birth, while he was still innocence personified, a local clergyman declared that the youth of the day were 'pictures mad'. He wasn't referring to some burgeoning passion for art, a desire of the younger generation to know more about Matisse or Picasso. The pictures were what the movies, the cinema, were called in those days.

Of course they were pictures mad – when Raymon Navarro was in *The Impossible Love* at the Bermondsey Cinema and Marlene Deitrich was said to be responsible for the new 'vogue' in women's fashions, the trouser suit.

The influence of the cinema on the Micklewhites' child would be strong, as we shall see. But he would always say that his whole life has been guided not so much by what was up there on the screen but by 'family' – a term that seems to fit into his definition of all that is worthwhile, even when things in those early years of childhood seemed to be anything but that.

Being in 'vogue' was not for the likes of this family. Ellen, when she got back from St Olave's, would have known little of that and cared even less. Her life was the drudgery of looking after her baby, finding enough food for her family – her son would later say again and again that he never went hungry – and trying to make the little money brought in by her husband go a very long way.

Now, it has to be said that Mr Micklewhite was a good earner. He worked very hard indeed as a Billingsgate porter, lugging crate after crate of dripping fish from a cart or a lorry, newly arrived from the ports, to the floors of the market where they had to be opened with a lever much admired by murderers in those parts.

It was hard, back-breaking work. But generations of Micklewhites had done the job which in Urlwin Street was much sought after. A place at Billingsgate was like a seat in the House of Lords – give or take a bit of ermine or the stink of newly-caught haddock.

It was handed down from father to son. 'I can get you a job in the market,' he proudly used to tell his boy. He cherished that little evidence of influence in those scarred years. He knew that it wouldn't be difficult. His own father had worked there too. Maurice Micklewhite junior would shudder every time he heard what was intended to be a promise but which always sounded like a threat.

But in those days of restricted ambition, it was many a Billingsgate porter's earnest desire that his son should follow in his rubber-soled footsteps, don the big padded hat – to ease the weight of the fish crates and to catch the ice and water leaking through its slats – and launch himself on what was considered to be a good living. The adult successful Michael Caine, a man by then earning millions, once said that his father was earning £50 a week. It seems an unlikely figure. In prewar Britain, when the average wage was about £1 10 shillings a week, that was a fortune reserved for top businessmen. Members of Parliament earned a tenth of that figure. Even 50 shillings a week, £2 10 shillings, was good money in an age when a chain of men's shops could flourish under the name 'The Fifty Shilling Tailors' – the amount they would charge for a very good quality made-to-measure suit. Whatever the precise figure, the money that actually went into Micklewhite's pay packet was considerable.

It may seem strange, when you consider the fathers who want their children to follow their own professions – lawyers, doctors, clergymen, owners of big businesses who want them to grow bigger still – to think of a Billingsgate porter dreaming of welcoming his son into the market he knew so well, but he would only be doing what his own father and grandfather had done before him. He knew the youngster would be welcome. For like English public schools, the people who owned Billingsgate firms liked that sense of continuity. For years there had been Micklewhites working their guts out at Billingsgate and the merest suggestion that there could be one who would break the chain was unthinkable. As far as Maurice senior was concerned, his son would not just be throwing up the chance to go drinking with some very convivial mates from the same background as his own, there was that matter of the market providing a good living.

And it *was* a good living. Or rather it could be. Unlike those who laboured on the nearby docks – and lined up each day to see if there was a job for them or not – this was regular, assured work. And because it wasn't exactly the most tempting lifestyle imaginable, there were compensations – like a pay packet that to the average working man seemed like a small fortune. The trouble was that the fortune got smaller all the time.

Despite the degree of security that the job in the market seemed to offer, there was nothing to compete with the Depression. The porters in general, and Maurice senior in particular, were not allowed an escape from the dole queues. When eventually the market began hiring again, Maurice was one of the first to get back to work. He then insisted that his wife give up her charring, which was what they called cleaning for other people in those days. For a time, she did. She even gave up a second part-time job, sewing on buttons at a neighbourhood secondhand shop, which had probably given her some 'inside trading' opportunities when the need arose to replace the by then threadbare and hole-ridden clothes which were beyond even her skills.

It didn't necessarily mean that the family's problems were over. A wage packet in Maurice's hand was one thing, saving its contents was another.

Mr Micklewhite believed that he had a perfect right to slake his thirst at the end of a day that produced both muscles and melancholy in his workmates. He had the first of these qualities in abundance, but any tears he might have had were easily drowned in pints of amber liquid which, his son always maintained, had no visible effect on the man's ability to stand or have a coherent conversation.

What it did affect was his bank balance – had there ever been enough to put in a bank – which there wasn't. And then there was the little matter of what the Cockneys called the gee-gees – horses. He was as much a friend of the bookmakers as he was of Mr Tubby Isaacs, who kept the jellied-eels stall that he patronised with loyal regularity. Hardly surprising, considering the amount of money he spent with the gentlemen who liked to call themselves 'turf accountants' – except that Maurice senior's connections with the turf bore no resemblance whatever to those of the people who liked to call their activities the sport of kings.

There is nothing on the record to show that this propensity – to allow money to drip through his fingers as easily as the ice cold water that poured from the fish boxes – affected his marriage. The Micklewhites' son is intensely loyal. He speaks of his father being a highly intelligent man who knew what was what in the world, even if he couldn't actually read about it and whose writing skills were probably limited to what passed for a signature on his betting slips. He would say that his dad was the 'supreme example of the British class system wasting brains, minds, talent and intellect'.

There is no doubt that the child who would become Michael Caine loved and, indeed, respected the father whom he would describe as a man who taught him 'a lot about survival'. He was, he says, 'an extraordinarily strong man, very big and tough'.

But the trouble was he used that strength and toughness to bully his wife. No one has ever said that he hit her or that they didn't love each other, but it is clear that they had their spats, mostly over the money that was going into drink and gambling.

Michael Caine himself knows more about wine than most, and has drunk more than moderately in his time, but he knew when to stop. His father did not – which is why the actor has always had a contempt for gamblers. His father gambled practically everything he had away into the pockets of bookies not known for their love and concern for humanity.

He might have said it was due to his lifestyle. After all, Billingsgate porters didn't work the sort of hours 'normal' men put in. They started at four o'clock in the morning and packed up at one, lunchtime for most mortals and therefore a very convenient time to take care of all the things he thought his money was there to finance.

Ellen might have hoped he would come home to her at one o'clock. Perhaps to escape the sheer misery of living in Urlwin Street, he stayed away. But there were those mates who were always that much more matey and friendly and relaxed in the pubs after work. That was a good place to go when the last tray had been laid down, the drips of water rubbed down from their rubber boots. And what if he did smell more than was considered pleasant? So did the others. So did the pub. A hostelry so close to the fish market had to smell – of fish as well as of beer.

And the men spread that smell around. After the ever-lengthening sessions at the pub, it was time to pour the largesse still further – at the race track. Presumably Maurice won some of the time, but clearly the balance was not in his favour and Ellen saw neither him nor his money.

They had their rows, Ellen and Maurice, but they were faithful to each other and even when money was tight, the rent was eventually paid and no one went hungry, even when the bread on the table was spread less liberally than usual with dripping.

The older Maurice was plainly a man with a gift for words. He had all the prejudices of the age and society in which he grew up. It is not sure if he ever came into close contact with men now known as gay. In his day and to him, they were 'Nancy boys', a phrase not necessarily used with affection. His son, on the other hand, would grow up to be more tolerant. He said he always supported the legalisation of homosexual activity, 'just so long as they don't make it compulsory'.

It is also fairly easy to deduce that little Maurice grew up loving his mother that little bit more. From an early age, he knew how hard she worked, usually cleaning other people's houses.

Their own home benefited from her cleaning skills, too. Like the words of an old song, it was poor but it was clean, just as she was always clean as well as honest. Home was a tiny flat at the top of a three-storey house. The garden was two floors below the front door. It was an important consideration even though they might not have had too much enthusiasm for horticulture or the sight of grass. The garden was where the only lavatory was situated, shared by the five families who lived in the house.

North of the river, families like theirs might have lived in tenements. In South London, large houses, built long before the Micklewhites came to live there, were easily converted. A hundred years earlier, they might have been the homes of middle class families with the rooms below ground level reserved for servants. Later, when the well-to-do families moved on to something newer and more convenient, shop managers and clerks working in central and west London would find that these places suited most of their needs. But when these people too, moved – usually to the outer London suburbs – the houses fell into what was politely called disrepair. Even by 1933 standards, they were hopelessly out of date and all the scrubbing and the blacking of the lead grate until it positively shone couldn't alter the fact that this was the deprived home of a deprived family.

But you can almost believe that, like so many of her time, Ellen enjoyed her existence, as if giving birth was in itself such a reward there could be nothing else in life worth as much.

As her son described her in a television interview: 'My mother was the sort of mother every boy should have. A short, roly-poly woman who liked nothing better than being at a stove, cooking food and stuffing her kids with food all day long.'

It is all well and good saying that the Micklewhites lived in a warm, loving atmosphere. They did that. But they *were* always broke and always worried that the money would run out in the meter that controlled their gas supply. There was no electricity and gas fed the cooking stove and gave them all their lighting.

There was, however, another side to this story of poverty and deprivation. It proved to be good training for the actor who would become Michael Caine. At the age of two and a half Maurice Micklewhite learned his lines perfectly for a 'play' that more than once saved the family's bacon – a treat at the best of times. The words were 'Mummy's out' and they were recited with increasing confidence every time the 'tally man' came round to collect the weekly payments for whatever it was that was keeping the Micklewhites away from the cold world outside. Sometimes it was the rent man. As his mother hovered in the background, little Maurice – fortunately even then tall for his age – would go on tip-toe to answer the front door, and always had the same words to say to the visitor: 'Mummy's out'.

Whether he was believed or not, it is true to say that no one remembers the family being evicted or made to return some necessity of life. Whatever that necessity was, it certainly wasn't one of those trouser suits the *South London Press* said were becoming all the rage. Like Sophie Tucker's famous 'Yiddisher Mama' (as we shall see, not a totally irrelevant comparison) Ellen 'never cared for fashion's styles'. Indeed, her son would say that the first time she had a brand new coat was when he bought her one – when she was 56 years old.

There was nothing unusual in that. You didn't live in poverty and expect to be well clothed, and since no one around was any better dressed, it was just one of those facts of life that everyone took for granted.

As a young, successful actor, Michael Caine would reflect philosophically on what romantic stories like to suggest were the compensations of poverty: 'Sure people are friendlier in the slums, but they were friendly in the Blitz, too, and that didn't make it a good thing. I'd rather see a little more coolness and decent living.'

Maurice was two and a half years old when one of the great mysteries of the world confronted him. His mother gave birth to a new baby whom she called Stanley. Michael Caine is not sure today whether he accepted at the time that his mother's ever-expanding stomach had anything to do with the new arrival. He seems to have been more pacified with the explanation that he had been found under a gooseberry bush – a plant not frequently found in the vicinity of Urlwin Street or in Rotherhithe for that matter.

There were perks being an elder brother. At the age of three, he was given a real treat – visiting the market where his dad worked. It would be nice to think that that was the moment of revelation, the time when he initially disappointed his father and announced that the life of a porter would not be for him. The chances are that he enjoyed the experience enormously, revelling in the natural kindness and gentleness of the hard-worked porters who really were his father's close friends.

It was a simple life if you were three years old. It didn't seem any more complicated through those early years of childhood. The sense of deprivation was probably being stored up in their psyches but neither Maurice nor Stanley joined the other children in the area who sat, unwashed, on the doorsteps of their poor homes. They *were* washed. They *were* fed. The hatred of the district and all that it represented would come later.

For the moment, the only problems came at the Saturday morning matinée at the local cinema. As soon as he was able to appreciate it, the cinema was heaven – a place where little lights twinkled in the black, and where the images of real people were projected on to the huge screen in front. This was Magic. The use of the capital 'M' was the way he saw it himself in his mind. He was too young to think in terms of his future career, but he could imagine what it might have been like to be there riding a horse with the Lone Ranger.

Maurice was big for his age and the raucous atmosphere of the Saturday morning cinema sessions affected him as much as it did boys older and more aware than he was. Managers, ushers and usherettes went to work on those Saturday mornings rather the way lion tamers entered cages. For the youngster from Urlwin Street it was like taking part in a blood sport. The excitement of kids marauding a theatre didn't escape his attention. He shouted and screamed with the best of them.

As a five-year-old, he was in the maelstrom. And yet for him there was something more. Yes, for the first time he was with bigger boys who had bigger catapults than he had ever owned. Certainly, missiles flicked all around him and he enjoyed being part of this more grown-up world. And when he kicked out at a boy in front, the whole row of seats collapsed like a house of cards – an event as firmly planted on his memory as the time he kissed Christopher Reeve (about that, more later). Strange though it may have seemed to those usherettes, he was actually enjoying the films for their own sake. A new world was unfolding for him. Meanwhile, a new problem for the world was about to change everything.

Two

The Battle of Britain

Two things happened when Maurice Micklewhite junior was six years old. Firstly, he brought the house down playing in a pantomime – although it could have been more because his flies were undone than for his performance. Whatever the reason, he won the prize of five shillings – a fortune in those days for a lot of youngsters and for a few older ones too. It was to be the first inclination he had that he was going to be an actor. 'I realised,' he would say, 'that if I became an actor, I could be all of the people I was reading about.'

The other equally influential event in his life was that Adolf Hitler invaded Poland on 1 September 1939. Suddenly, the lives of ordinary people living in ordinary houses in very ordinary suburbs were affected more than they could possibly imagine. Young Maurice was totally mystified as to why a man called Hitler whom he had never met was threatening his very existence. Why was he so interested in Urlwin Street? Surely some deal could be worked out whereby if Mr Hitler would promise not to come and punch his dad his dad would promise not to go and punch Mr Hitler? When Maurice and Stanley Micklewhite talked that over, it seemed a perfectly equitable arrangement.

There were immediate results of Mr Chamberlain's announcement from the Cabinet room at Ten Downing Street on Sunday 3 September 1939, the one in which he said that the British ambassador in Berlin had delivered an ultimatum ... One was the terror of gasmasks. Children who started school at that time remember well enough the fright of being locked away in a mask whose purpose they could not fathom. The fact that the younger children had one shaped like Mickey Mouse didn't totally compensate for the horror of that air-tight rubber suffocation machine. Maurice Micklewhite had a better reason than most to remember the mask-training sessions his school – John Ruskin Infants – fitted into the curriculum along with reading, writing and arithmetic (known as the three 'r's) The children were ordered to run around the classroom wearing their masks – presumably to demonstrate just how enjoyable and normal life could be in the midst of a poison gas attack. Maurice Micklewhite, aged six, collapsed – his mask had a blockage in the one part of the apparatus that it was all supposed to be about, the bit that filtered the air and was supposed to allow him to breathe. It didn't and he couldn't.

An even more vital memory was of the time that he and Stanley were told to put on their coats while a brown card label was tied around their necks. They were told they were going to be 'evacuated'. In normal times, that was a word a young child would never know. To the Micklewhite boys' generation it was no less a part of their vocabulary than the names of their parents and siblings. But it was a lot more frightening. Even more frightening than those Mickey Mouse gasmasks.

Three

Victory

The boys might have felt that they resembled a couple of parcels – not the kind we're used to now, all nicely shrink-wrapped or tied up with ribbons, but a package, war-time austerity style, the equivalent of brown paper done up with string. The labels were tied to jerseys or worn flannel jackets, whatever the secondhand shops had provided.

It was done with most of the skill of a military operation – which wasn't exactly a recommendation. In those days, at the very beginning of World War II, military operations were not necessarily carried out with any particular skill at all. Ellen was at Waterloo Station to see the boys off and doubtless went home to Urlwin Street with more than a few tears in her eyes and a lump in her throat. Dad was probably worrying about it all more than he let on, as he hauled the ice-covered boxes of fish, brought to shore in the face of what was then still just the threat of U-boat action.

The train stopped in rural Berkshire, just the sort of place the authorities – and there were always 'authorities' in those days; it was another one of those words small boys about to be evacuated were expected to know, like 'London County Council' and 'air-raid precautions' – thought would escape the mass of German bombing. After all, given the choice of a nice juicy dock to bomb to smithereens or a few haystacks, there isn't much of a contest. On the other hand, the two little Micklewhites would very soon have reason to wonder whether Adolf Hitler could, after all, possibly be the worst human being in the world. As far as they were concerned, he had a great deal of competition. Not that it looked as though it was going to be that terrible when they first arrived at Walgrave, an hour's train journey from London, but a world away from Urlwin Street.

The boys had never seen anything like it, or been anywhere that resembled it. Streets were actually clean. There was no soot on the houses. The village had the kind of atmosphere you could breathe without coughing. You could actually walk in the street and not *see* what they thought was air. But there *were* smells there too. However, the boys didn't have much of a chance to breathe that air with its special smells – some, of which, it has to be admitted, did make people cough, but for different reasons than were apparent in South London.

They were bundled off – appropriate, you might think, for parcels – in line to the village hall, where they and their fellow evacuees were all assembled and told to sit on the floor. Children always had to sit on the floor in those days. (Why a nation that believed cleanliness was next to godliness and that ordered its children to scrub dirty faces as a matter of rote encouraged them to get filthy just by sitting down is an interesting question. But that was the way it was.)

At that age, Maurice was able to put to the test one of the first pieces of advice that his mother had given him: 'Be like a duck. Remain calm on the surface, and paddle like hell underneath.' The two youngsters knew the time had come to paddle. Their father was about to go into the Army and they couldn't be sure when they would see him again. Their mother, always the greatest of comforters, was at home where they should be too and here they were lost in what, to all intents and purposes, seemed like a foreign land. It was a situation underlined when the 'selection' process began. Now, Maurice and Stanley were given a reason to think that being left out was 'the way it was' too.

Villagers were encouraged to take evacuees – indeed, in some places, they were compelled to do so. They were paid allowances that were supposed to cover the expenses they would incur, which, as the boys found out before long, were perfect opportunities to fleece the state – take the money and run away from their responsibilities. They came to the hall in search of, well, none of the villagers knew what. Some were there just for the money. Others really thought they could be performing a humanitarian service to poor, little defenceless children. A few believed it was an opportunity to convert heathens to Christianity and save the world.

One by one, the children were sought out, singled out and ushered out of the hall, smiling – and snivelling, shuffling, shaking, too. There were as many reactions from the kids as there were from the prospective foster parents.

But the Micklewhites were not picked. The local vicar stood there, wondering what would happen. It was like a slave market (some writers have compared the experience to being in a cattle market; either was bad enough). But no matter how hard it was, being looked at and virtually measured like a corpse being surveyed by an undertaker, it was even worse being left behind.

Then, finally, came salvation – in the form of a nice, attractive women who smiled pleasantly and led them out of the door to her car. She even kissed them. The idea of riding in a car was but a dream for both boys. But the dream got better. This was no ordinary car. It was a Rolls Royce. 'Like the one the King has,' Maurice later reported.

The car purred its way to a large house, where the boys washed and were invited down for a supper, served – they couldn't believe this – by a butler. That night they slept on beds so soft they had never experienced anything like it. Alas, it was not to last. After breakfast the following day, they were told they had to leave. Those same 'authorities' had decreed that the kind lady and her butler lived too far away from the village school where they would be going. Not to worry, she knew there was someone else very happy to take them.

There was. But it was a very different kind of home that Maurice was going to. Even worse, he and Stanley were split up. The older brother was now housed in a place that made Dotheboys Hall resemble a holiday camp. He was fed nothing more than tinned fish once a day – when he was fed at all. The woman now 'looking after' him was the asthmatic wife of a local policeman, but any respect for the law the man in blue might have had was not passed on to his spouse. 'She was a real wicked witch,' Michael Caine has said on numerous occasions.

Maurice was made to spend three days locked up in a dark cupboard. He realised later why he was imprisoned in solitary in that way – not just for one stretch but every time she went shopping. 'She didn't want to take me with her because I was covered in bruises and sores and she couldn't afford to let anyone see.' A boy named Clarence was subjected to even worse treatment, and was beaten with a tennis racquet and ended up with an arm and leg broken. In reflective moods, Michael Caine would wonder what happened to Clarence. Clarence himself might still not realise that his former co-prisoner turned into an international film star.

The ill-treatment only went on for a couple of weeks, but it would be the subject of nightmares for years afterwards and he still shudders at the memory. He also hates being in confined spaces. It changed him. He was an easy-going child when he went into that cupboard. He came out tough and resentful. He was hard to handle 'and I am now'.

A teacher at the village school was the first to sound the alarm bells. She noticed the sores on Maurice's legs, which still bore the effects of his rickets. The NSPCC were called and earned the child's permanent gratitude and respect. The NSPCC remains to this day his favourite charity. He thinks how lucky he was to have parents who, on the whole, had a perfect marriage and he wonders about those children who didn't. He asks: 'What about children beaten up by their own parents? There's no one to rescue them.'

Ellen heard about it and rushed down to Berkshire to bring her boys home. She didn't just tell the woman what she thought of her, she demonstrated the fact. Fists were used and she beat up the alleged 'carer' and, according to her son, 'almost went to jail for it'. As it was, the 'foster mother' – the words would have stuck in Ellen's throat – was jailed for cruelty to children. The older Michael Caine would later describe it as 'child abuse'. He didn't refer to the details or to his mother's reaction to them in his own memoirs. Or to the fact that the woman was later convicted. All he has said is that he felt 'miserable'.

But there had always been hope. 'What saved my sanity in that dark cupboard was that I knew my mother would come and that she was going to punch the life out of that woman. The trains were bombed out, but I knew my mother would come to get me as soon as she could.' The effects of his ill treatment went beyond being the mere stuff of nightmares. 'Fortunately, I came away from there using my anger as a tool rather than a weapon. Although I didn't formulate it then,' he would tell Ovid Demaris in *Parade* magazine, 'I determined never to put myself in a position where anybody could ever use me again like that. In everything I do, I always have to be in charge of my own fate.'

They went back to London as the Blitz began its first onslaughts. But he had already spent the worst time of his life. Night after night the Luftwaffe rained high-explosives, landmines, and, worst of all, incendiary bombs on the docks in particular and the City and East End in general. But it couldn't have been as bad as that cupboard in Berkshire.

The excitement of the aerial warfare was now being tempered with an ever-increasing sense of fear. Nevertheless, the fact that there was a war on – a phrase that became the stock answer whenever anyone complained about anything – only began to hit home the day when his dad hung up his rubber boots, kissed Ellen and the boys and disappeared from Urlwin Street.

Where he had gone wasn't entirely clear to his children, but they knew something serious had happened. Maurice senior was away from home for months. When he did come back, it was to tell amazing stories about other soldiers being transported in little boats. He seemed to remember the name of the place where they had all been. It was called Dunkirk.

With the father of the family away – and with him, what had been, before necessary deductions like his drinking and racing bills, a substantial pay packet – Ellen had to think about her own future and that of her children. She was going to be evacuated, too. She decided to go to Norfolk, where it really seemed it would be quiet and safe.

For a time, the family were accommodated with others in a big, converted farmhouse where they shared sanitary and cooking facilities, not entirely a new experience for them. Altogether, ten families lived in two-bedroomed flats. But it all was starting to look like the happiest time in the young Micklewhites' lives. Children were spared the worries that adults had – of bombings that could rob them of their lives as well as their homes and of the constant and realistic fear of Nazi occupation.

They weren't at the farmhouse for long. Mrs Micklewhite proved that she had talents that some of the other evacuees had not. The Grange, the local 'big house' in North Runcton, needed a new cook. She went after the job and it was hers. Suddenly, she demonstrated skills that even she never knew she had. For their part, the family living in The Grange were to be given the best meals they had had for years. Ellen knew how to make the most of the rationed ingredients and her employers couldn't have been happier.

Young Maurice himself was as near to heaven as he could imagine. London wasn't entirely left behind. He led the best gang of young potential criminals – and bearing in mind the fruit they 'liberated' from the trees, the word 'potential' is being kind – imported from the capital. But it wasn't just the urban warfare to which he subjected the locals that appealed so much. He was also able to enjoy the sight of the first animals he had seen in their home setting – cows, a species of animal that had existed for him only on milk posters, as well as goats and sheep. 'That childhood,' he says, 'was one of running free in the country. I suppose that's where my ideas of freedom come from.'

As for The Grange, it was as though he had jumped into the screen in one of those Hollywood movies that still represented nothing less than the perfect life. Not only did he and Stanley have their own bedrooms – unheard of, indeed unthought of, in Urlwin Street – those rooms like the rest of the house were lit by electric light. Imagine, living in a house that had electricity. What was more, they ate the food their mother cooked – prepared for them with all the perfection she demonstrated for the family of the house.

'My preoccupation with things sophisticated,' he would say in middle age, 'comes from the fact that my mother was a cook in a rich man's house and I would eat the leftover bits.' Those leftover bits were not the kind of thing they knew much about in Urlwin Street, but they would prove to be a useful memory when he went into the restaurant business. 'I was eating leftover pheasant, woodcock and partridge, all washed down by vintage Bordeaux.'

It wasn't just a matter of the food. He wondered at the limousines in the garage – that first Rolls Royce drive apart, cars were things he occasionally remembered seeing chugging their way through the streets of South London. They didn't look much like those at The Grange. As for the furniture in the house, had he been told the tables and chairs had come direct from Buckingham Palace, he would have believed every word. He says he 'filed it away' – ready for the time when he would have a house like that of his own. Indeed, when it came to having his own mansion on the Thames, it turned out to be, he said, 'the incarnation' of The Grange. Plainly, anyone wanting confirmation of Freud's theory that childhood influences the adult has only to study the Michael Caine story.

His mother was no less intrigued by her surroundings than were her sons. 'She used to show me with great reverence, like [being in] a cathedral, how they lived. Their big rooms were lived in the back. So I knew what I wanted.'

The family liked him and he liked them. How could he not? Coming through the service entrance didn't demean him, perhaps because he knew of no better life or because he felt that that was his true station in it. Probably the former. Besides, when the employers went on holiday, he went in by the front door.

'Roger Moore and Sean Connery, my friends and I, share a sophistication based on a working-class background, a learned sophistication. We discard the boring. The working-class guys took the good bits and forgot about the bow ties and gaiters. We kept the good cigars and port wine.'

He also went to the village school, where it appears he thrived. His teacher liked him, encouraged him to learn and saw him through what in those days was called 'the scholarship', later dubbed the '11-plus', the exam which determined the possibility of his going to what were just being called grammar schools. Maurice passed the exam. In so doing, he was exposed to an education not necessarily covered by the 1944 Education Act. The school to which he was assigned was in King's Lynn, the big town nearby. It seemed like the obvious place for him to go – it was a school that had been evacuated *en bloc* from East London, full of boys who, like him, had never seen cows and sheep and goats before. It was now called, officially, the Hackney Downs Grammar School. But everyone called it the Grocers – a strange name for a school, except that it was sponsored by the Worshipful Company of Grocers, one of the ancient City of London guilds. (Other guilds, like the Haberdashers, had schools of their own in London.) It was a school with an international reputation. It boasted industrialists, chemists, diplomats – like this author's uncle, for one – politicians and artists among its old boys. (Harold Pinter was one of the many writers who went to Grocers). One of the older pupils of the school in King's Lynn at the time was Jerry Pam, who would become Michael Caine's American publicist.

The reputation of Grocers would only be sullied in the late 1990s. By then a comprehensive school in what had become a totally run-down area of London, it was placed in the ignominious position of being threatened with closure by a Department of Education appalled by its disastrous educational record. That could never have been imagined in the heyday of its pre-war attainment, in King's Lynn or during the first 40 years after World War II.

What really singled the school out from other educational establishments was that most of the boys – all but about ten of them – were Jewish. Maurice Micklewhite had never met Jewish boys before. He had been a member of a class who believed that these were exotic creatures who had horns sprouting from their heads like Michaelangelo's statue of Moses. When he went to Grocers, he was somewhat disappointed to discover that they did not. His mother wasn't so sure. To her, Jews were people with lots of money, who ate a great deal of fish – perhaps her husband thought he had much to be grateful to them for for that. But being educated among them was to have a profound effect.

Maurice not only did well at lessons, taught by some of the finest teachers in the country, but he learnt a lot about Jews and about Judaism. It was not a Jewish 'parochial' school as such but, as legend and numerous profiles of Caine have made out, simply one that accepted the reality of not teaching any other religion to a vast majority of children who could not be expected to keep it.

He joined in the prayers and learnt the 'Shemah' ('The Lord Our God, The Lord Is One') better than he knew the Lord's Prayer. He found out what kosher food was all about. He knew how to celebrate Passover and Hanukkah. He also learnt a great host of Jewish jokes, a fascination for which would never leave him.

Many of his fellow pupils were the sons of immigrants. Nearly all had grandparents who had come to Britain to escape the pogroms in Russia and Poland at the turn of the century. So the Grocers' boys sang Jewish songs – many of them trying to sound like Al Jolson, the epitome of the immigrant success story across the Atlantic – and filled their conversations with Yiddish expressions, all of which Maurice Micklewhite, son of a Billingsgate porter, learned himself and would never cease to use. They would turn out to be fairly useful when it came to dealing with Hollywood producers.

He loved his days at Grocers – although he says he was at first beaten up, 'as the sole representative of the *goyim*'. Older boys helped to straighten things out and it didn't happen again. Probably the intellectual stimulation of being with clever boys had something to do with it – although he says, modestly, that he naturally hung out with the low-achievers so as not to show himself up. That was not true. He also hung out with boys who, mysteriously, were called 'Maurice' or 'Morris'. Some were even 'Morrie'. Until then, he had been somewhat embarrassed by a name he thought was known only to himself.

One old boy of Grocers at that time – 'Don't quote me by name,' he said, 'I'd hate anyone to think I was trying to cash in on once knowing Michael Caine,' – told me: 'It must have been very difficult for him, suddenly thrust into what was very much a Jewish atmosphere. We never thought we were going to a Jewish school *per se*, but it was a Jewish atmosphere and I am sure that Michael felt very strange in it at first. It was so rare for Jews to feel in a majority that I am sure some of us took advantage of the fact that *there* we were one. But I remember Micklewhite very well. He was tough and could take care of himself and if he did feel he was bullied at first, it couldn't have lasted very long. I only remember him as being one of us – and, as far as I remember, very popular. He was never alone.'

It was a school that valued music. Other boys learned to play the violin. So he tried – and then decided that an instrument which had so successfully been picked up and run with from one pogrom to another, was the strict preserve of the Jews. When his mother offered the teacher something for his trouble, the man kindly said no.

The fact that Ellen wanted to support his musical ambitions was remarkable. It wasn't her usual way. She, too, had been influenced by the Grocers' ethic. 'What I liked about the Jewish families,' Michael Caine has said about the parents of the boys he knew at school, '[was] the support they gave their children. They used to try and make them stay on at school, be something. But mine.... I mean, they supported me emotionally, they were always there for me.'

Researching this book, people I met were convinced that the man they knew as Michael Caine was Jewish. 'He is, of course,' said Karl Malden, who was with him in two movies. 'You know his mother was Jewish,' said the delightful June Wyndham Davies, who, as we shall see, was one of his first influences in the theatre. She manifestly was not and wouldn't have thanked June for thinking so. But Michael himself has always been the first to accept that he has become something of a Jew *manqué*. 'Jewish in the head,' is how he puts it. Why anyone thought that Ellen was Jewish isn't clear, but Mrs Micklewhite was Protestant; her husband Catholic and of Irish descent – probably gypsy, which Michael Caine said accounted for the gypsy lifestyle of an actor that appealed to him so much. On the other hand, there can't be many gypsy caravans that resemble the sort of homes he has lived in for the past 35 years.

Grocers and its influence all came to an end in 1946. So did King's Lynn. The war was over and the Micklewhites moved back to South London.

Four

Gambit

It was a year after the war's end. His father was home and London had changed along with the Micklewhite lifestyle.

There had, however, been indications of the changes to come. Even while the war was still on, people had begun to get used to the idea of peace. The black-out was replaced by a 'dim-out' soon after D-Day. But then, when everyone thought that it was virtually all over, they discovered the grim reality that it wasn't. There were 'doodlebugs', the V-1 weapon that would fall to the ground the moment its engine stopped – an ominous silence Londoners came to dread. Then there were the even more evil V-2 rockets that would eat up whole blocks of flats after their virtually silent run across the Channel; death carriers that were unstoppable in an age when the Germans were the only ones who had any kind of guided missiles. Fortunately for humanity, the Allied troops were in the process of destroying the German war machine. Among them, Maurice Micklewhite senior, veteran of El Alamein and Dunkirk. When it was finally all over, Maurice went back to Billingsgate. He was a man of ambition. He wanted the younger Maurice to join him in a few years. His son had ambitions too – the main one, not to follow his father.

The family were not back in the Urlwin Street home. It had been severely damaged in a raid – blasted, not bombed, which sounds like James Bond's instructions to a barman, but which people who lived through those times will understand – and now the local authority rehoused them in the Elephant and Castle. The district was named after a local pub, an historic monument of an inn originally named after the Infanta of Castille, but corrupted as all good London names should be and then abbreviated into merely, 'The Elephant'.

Home was in what was another of those abbreviated words – a prefab, one of the thousands of prefabricated bungalows built all over

London on what had been bombsites. These were modest homes but, to people who had been used to living in places like Urlwin Street, veritable palaces. Propaganda films of the times made them seem like something out of the Ideal Homes Show put on every year at Olympia, London's principal exhibition hall, and indeed there did seem to be a lot to shout about. They all had built-in wardrobes and cupboards, indoor sanitation and electricity – still regarded by those who hadn't been lucky enough to ever live at The Grange, as an unimaginable luxury. There were modern stoves and plugs for things like vacuum cleaners, which the more affluent of the London County Council tenants were proud to show off. Above all, there were refrigerators. The idea of a fridge, even a little one, was left once again to those who had seen homes featured in the Hollywood films.

The Council said the prefabs would last for no more than ten years and then be pulled down – to make way for permanent accommodation into which most of the tenants would then be decanted. Twenty years later, they were still functioning all over the capital. What if they *were* made of asbestos? Nobody then knew it was a dangerous substance. On the contrary, everyone thought they were fireproof.

There was now a new school for Maurice – Wilson's Grammar. This time he wasn't in a minority, unless it was the one made up of boys who hated the school. The chances are that they were not a minority at all.

There was nothing about the place that appealed to him. There were battles in the street as well as in the building itself. One line in his film *Sleuth* said it all: 'We didn't fight to play games. We fought to survive.' At school it was trying to survive as a student and as a human being. He never thought that he had learnt anything there. He was absolutely convinced that his teachers knew no more about him than they did about teaching – and had no desire to know about either.

In an amazing example of ambitious prescience, he declared he was going to be an actor. 'Everybody took the piss out of me,' he later admitted. 'No working-class person ever said "Good luck" to me. They usually said the same thing. "What are you going to do? Sweep the stage?" ' His headmaster heard about his ambitions and declared that the only thing certain about the boy's coming career would be that he would be a labourer all his life. No, the 12-year-old declared, he was going to be an actor. 'You'll be a labourer,' said the teacher. 'Who do you think you are?' And then, as if to emphasise the point, gave him six of the best with his cane. (He was already a rebel; he refused to allow prefects to cane him.) A report from a subject teacher emphasised the point: 'This is the most lazy, conceited object it has ever been my misfortune to have to teach, but I am sure we will make a labourer of him.'

He would spend the rest of his life trying to show precisely who he was.

The memories of those reactions have never left him. It is the reason why he has always said he would never agree to being featured in a *This Is Your Life* programme. 'I don't want to meet all those people,' he has said. 'I didn't like any of them. What the hell would I want to see them for?'

The images may have become exaggerated, but he sees himself now as basically the typical self-taught man. After all, as a child, he haunted libraries almost as much as he did cinemas. It was not nearly as popular a thing to do at Wilson's as it had been at Grocers – among his fellow schoolboys, that is. They called him 'Know All' and 'The Professor', neither expression intended particularly kindly. He read avariciously, which was not likely to make his friends look kindly on him. He would often read two books in a day, and on occasion even more; the average of 14 a week demonstrating the immense thirst he had for reading. He loved American novels, particularly 'From Here To Eternity' and 'The Naked And The Dead'.

It was a time when the best jokes came in collections by Bennett Cerf, the eminent publisher. They weren't so much jokes as anthologies of anecdotes. Maurice lapped them all up. They were invitations to sophistication as he imagined himself sitting in a cocktail lounge in Manhattan and retelling the stories that Mr Cerf had put into his books, a long cigarette holder in his mouth as he leaned on one of the picture windows facing the other skyscrapers outside. It was a thirst that only made him less and less contented with his lot. And more and more ambitious.

He read one book from the Southwark public library that, had it got instant and successful results, would have made his eventual business no more difficult to pick up than hauling that tray of fish around. It was called *Teach Yourself Film Acting.*

He read another, more convincing work, by the Russian actor Puovkin. It instructed any prospective thespians never to blink. The teenage Maurice Micklewhite tried to take his advice. Minutes passed, not blinking once and as a result he was constantly having to remove all the grit that gathered in his eyes. Before long his non-blinking eyes – he managed it, he said, for 20 minutes at a time – watered, and his mother chastised him for staring at everybody around him.

What was really fascinating about this period in his life was that those books made him interested in things supposedly outside the purview of a kid from the Elephant. He took up anything, it seemed, between hard covers. One subject intrigued him in particular – wine. Now that was a fluid that was never poured into the glass his father lifted in the pub. If you asked the elder Maurice to have a glass of burgundy, he would have been convinced he was in the company of one of those 'Nancy boys' to whom he took such exception. But his son saw wine as an opening to the finer things of life, and not as a means of getting sloshed. After all, next door to their home was a Salvation Army hostel and he saw some of the effects of alcohol on its inmates. He also saw what it was already doing to some of the other boys at Wilson's or in the gangs to which he was still drawn.

Food interested him just as much – and again not simply as a way to assuage his hunger. Once a month, with the benefit of the results of odd jobs he did after school, he would treat himself to what then seemed the best meal in England and wash it down with a claret – one that he had read about. There were not many of his friends who did that.

He has never analysed it as such, but perhaps this boy, who was soaking up learning like blotting paper absorbed ink, was becoming something of a snob.

'I was much better educated than my parents,' he would recall in 1986. 'I was almost the most intelligent person around. So from the time I was 12, I was telling everybody how it was gonna be. And people listened because I was right. I saw through things, like how the working class was its own worst enemy.'

For a time, his intensity seemed to mean that he himself was his own worst enemy. He was never an ordinary kid. 'I was too wild. I had led a very strange life.' He was, he said, 'someone who had spent 14 years worrying about survival and being pushed around. And you see, you talk about higher education, but to me, and to my parents, going to grammar school *was* higher education.'

He himself would have liked to have had a different kind of higher education – the kind offered by the women round about. But he was shy – to say he was painfully so makes it sound like a toothache; for him this was the pain of acute arthritis – and a girl only had to speak his name for his face and neck to be covered in deep blushes. He knew that he wasn't God's gift to womankind. He had been more than six feet tall since he was 14 – and 'narrow like a milk bottle'. The one woman who was in his life, his mother, wanted to see some contribution to the household income, so reduced by Maurice senior's gambling and drinking. Both his parents wanted him to leave school almost as much as he wanted to do so himself. Except that they differed about what would happen after that. He has explained: 'There was this great big boy sitting around, eating like a bloody horse and not bringing any money in.'

Don't forget there was another big boy, growing like another bloody horse, in the same house. Any paypacket the junior Maurice might bring in would be a necessity, not a fringe benefit. Other people were following his headmaster and deciding that his thinking was above his own station. 'I said, "I've got no station".'

Maurice was already thinking seriously now of becoming an actor, but had he let on about that, the taunting would have been even tougher. It wasn't considered a decent trade south of the Thames. Actors, as his father would testify, were 'Nancy Boys', no matter what parts they played. 'It's difficult to believe now,' he says, 'but when I was a kid, there weren't any working class actors, not like Jimmy Cagney – people who spoke like real people.'

Ironically, no matter how much he already wanted to leave his surroundings behind, they imbued him with a sense of Cockney pride – an irony that has stumped people for years. It was a time when the class structure was still rooted in the British psyche. A new Labour Government liked to think that its basic philosophy in life was equality, a sense of everyone being the same. It was the mantra that came from the war years, that this had been a time when everyone mucked in together and all the troops loved each other to bits, sharing the good times as well as the dangerous and deprived times.

It wasn't like that at all. Service life intensified class differences – the officers and the men were as sharply divided as the cricketers who played at Lords as either 'Gentlemen' or 'Players'. As for those who lived near him at the Elephant... the chances of any of them ever being invited to dinner in Sloane Square just across the Chelsea Bridge were vanishingly slim.

'Cockneys,' said Michael Caine in 1968, 'used to be looked upon kindly, like Mickey Mouse or dwarfs. But we decided to be people instead.' There was a lot to be said for being in that social class, he has always been the first to admit. 'There's no way to go but up. Cockneys have the strongest sense of survival in the world, and an actor needs that. They also have a sense of humour – they have to, to be able to take the knocks. Have you ever met a pompous Cockney?' It was a question that had an answer he might not have liked, but the point was one to be taken in most circumstances. He was the first to say he couldn't get away from it all quickly enough. 'I hated the bloody environment of the Old Kent Road, the idea of staying where I was. All I ever wanted was out.'

His mother continued to work, scrubbing floors in the homes of better off people. It didn't worry him. 'All my female relatives were charladies and the men were fish porters. I didn't see anything wrong in that. I did see how I'd like to get her out of doing it.'

He was once asked what he did with all the anger that was building up inside of him. 'I became an actor,' he said. 'You can use all that in your life; those things in roles.'

Those visits to the cinema, going in early on a Saturday afternoon and staying till the lights came on late in the evening, were becoming more and more escapes from reality and the spur to follow the action on the screen in real life. Everyone of that age had been to movie musicals and danced their way out of a theatre on to a miserable street – for just a moment believing they were prancing down Hollywood Boulevard with Gene Kelly and Donald O'Connor. Maurice Micklewhite took it further. He would play with the accents he heard on screen, particularly the American twangs, the sounds emitted by cowboys in the West and gangsters in Hell's Kitchen.

He was, he agrees, 'besotted' by movies. His favourite actor was not Cagney, but that other staple of the Warner Brothers Studio, Humphrey Bogart. Bogart's 'f**k you' attitude struck more than a few responsive notes in the boy. 'Movies opened the world to me. They offered a way to a new life. America fascinated me. I thought of it as a great paradise, which it turned out to be. More important – much more important – the movies also told me that people of my own class with a funny accent could become great famous actors.'

But he already thought about other vowel intonations. He started experimenting with the 'posh' voices that were most familiar on the English screen. Had any of his mates heard him, he would have been laughed off the block. But he discovered a culvert close to a sewer, where he could go and not be followed, and where his voice echoed with vowels that were not familiar in the Elephant.

Subconsciously, he also thought there was a chance to do something for his own class. 'Until the late 1950s, the British working class was always represented by a stereotype, like what you might call an 'Uncle Tom' Black in America. We were the monosyllabic, kowtowing, forelocks-touching oafs. It was like being Black and watching Stepin Fetchit all your life. In American pictures, you had working-class heroes and your actors came from the working class. Even the ones from society families like Bogart looked and talked like they were from the working class. So you couldn't tell. In English films, you could tell immediately, because someone came on and said, "Hello, Bundy's having a party," and they were all floating through the French windows and playing tennis in flannels and the maid would come on just like in plays. We used to hoot with laughter at the way they spoke. Then when someone who was supposed to be Cockney came on, one of those from RADA doing an accent, we'd roll under the seats in hysterics.' When they heard an American try it, it was even worse – *'cor blimey, mite. It is somefin terrible when they come in lite.'*

Other actors were treated with respect. Laurence Olivier was a prince – which is perhaps strange. Boys from the slums didn't usually have a lot of time for princes. If he and his mates did appreciate Olivier, it showed a degree of maturity not usual among the truant-playing kids who thronged the cinemas. There was something else, of course, about those films – the education they represented about the opposite sex, a factor fast becoming an obsession. As a young teenager he dreamed of having a girl of his own as much as he fantasised about going to Hollywood. The idea of going to bed with one also crossed his mind, but for a 14- or 15-year-old in South London in the mid-1940s, that was usually pie in the sky if not love on the mattress. One youngster did, however, have more luck in that direction than most of the others. His name was Jimmy Buckley. He always seemed to be getting the girls, or at least he said he did.

Quite a few years later, Mr Buckley would prove to be something of an inspiration to Michael Caine, who at the time had to content himself with buying a pocket-sized sepia magazine called *Health and Efficiency*, a publication that played a part in the lives of most boys of his age at the time. It was the journal officially published to encourage people to consider the joys of nudism – or 'naturism' as they liked to call it. The publishers might also have guessed that adolescent youths who had no intention whatever of taking their own clothes off in public would take an interest in the naked women who adorned the magazine's pages. Strange women, they were – none of them appeared to have any sexual orifices, let alone pubic hair. Mr Buckley assured Maurice that the girls he knew looked slightly different. How much of what Buckley told was true had little bearing on the fact that Maurice wanted to do those things himself. There were always girls whom he thought would but wouldn't and those whom he thought probably would but about whom he hadn't the courage to find out. Someone told him that if he joined the Young Communist League, he would be able to partake of all the glories of the perfect society – not least of which was the belief in free love. He signed up and then agreed that if the kind of love they offered was free, it was still too much. Not one of the females he saw offered the slightest attraction.

He actually lost his virginity in a way that would never have occurred even in one of his fantasies. He went to a birthday party and was called out into the yard by one of the females there. Not one of the girls invited to the party, but the aunt of his host. She let him see that she was wearing no knickers and allowed him to advance his education. That's the story he tells in his autobiography. On the other hand, in a *Playboy* magazine interview, he says it happened when he was 15 in a park – with a nice, 'understanding' woman who satisfied him totally but there was no future in it; he couldn't satisfy her nearly as . . . well, satisfactorily. (There was one older female who was aware of his sexual appetite. The woman in the local cinema box office knew him well enough to suggest that he might like to give her the bar of chocolate he had just bought – if she lifted up her sweater and showed him her breasts. He agreed to the deal, but had to be satisfied with just one nipple. She then tucked the breast into her bra and he went in – annoyed to this day that he had been done. She promised to show him two breasts. What happened to the other one?)

That might or might not have happened on one of the afternoons when Maurice should have been playing football, rugby or cricket. He wouldn't now remember which of the sports he should have been playing, since great as was his love of the cinema so was his hatred of the playing field. The only thing he played with any enthusiasm was truant. Not that he would have turned down another opportunity to have full sex with a woman. But it would be another two years before it happened, and as he said: 'Two years is a long time, especially when you don't have any TV in the evening.' That was always Michael Caine's gift – getting down to the really important details in his life.

There were other ways in which this now very tall, blond young man with eyebrows so fair they could barely be seen, was maturing. There were those who considered his looks effeminate. He had to prove how wrong they were. It was a tough neighbourhood, dominated by young men who dressed like spivs – also known as the 'wide boys', a nickname that came from the extent of their shoulder pads. Michael Caine has said that spivs – taken from pronouncing VIPs (very important persons) backwards – were gangsters. Some were merely barrow boys and sharp businessmen who dressed in the long draped clothes and big hats that came into fashion in 1947 (at about the same time that Christian Dior introduced his women's 'New Look'). Others undoubtedly were tough, very tough indeed. They carried razors in their hats, Caine recalled, and would hit their targets with their oversized trilbys like Oddjob in *Goldfinger*. But he learnt to cope. 'If you grow up with a name like Maurice Joseph Micklewhite in that area, you have to be pretty tough. I was able to take care of myself.' The girls thereabouts liked that about him, which could be why some shared their favours.

He was a member of the Rev. Jimmy Butterworth's Clubland, an organisation that thrived in the slums of Camberwell and gained for itself an international reputation. Everyone knew Mr Butterworth and his club in the Walworth Road, perhaps the best-run youth organisation in Britain. It was so well known that when the man who later became Lord Grade went to Hollywood, to try to persuade Bob Hope to come to Britain and play the Palladium, he found Jimmy Butterworth waiting in the comic's dressing room. Yes, Hope told Lew Grade, he would do the Palladium, but his salary would have to go to Clubland. Now, Hope was not – and indeed is not – the man to part with a dollar without reciting some kind of memorial prayer, yet Butterworth had the power to change the habits of a lifetime. The effect he had on his members was equally powerful.

It was at the club that Maurice became seriously involved in amateur dramatics. It only served to make him yearn for the stage as a career more than ever – particularly when the parts were easier to get than were the girls. He used to go occasionally to the Old Vic, which was just down the road from his home, but a world away in ethos. If his father had got to hear about *that*, he most certainly would have been sure that his son was a 'Nancy'. His father couldn't have been more wrong. As the adult Michael Caine would say: 'I got this idea I wanted to kiss girls, which is why I joined in the club amateur dramatics.'

But Mr Micklewhite wasn't alone in his assumption of what the boy was doing in a drama group. 'All the guys thought I was a cissy. They would do all those macho things. I was downstairs kissing girls, while they were upstairs in the showers with a lot of other guys – and they called *me* cissy.'

It was also through the club that he appeared on film for the first time. A leader at the club named Alec Reed was a movie enthusiast who put his hobby to great use. He not only allowed members like Maurice to see his phenomenal collection of silent movies – all 16 mm – but made films of the annual club holiday to Guernsey. If any of these were to surface, they would be worth a fortune to a TV programme maker – with the earliest known appearance of Michael Caine, walking on a beach. He directed the film one year – a fact which he said made him convinced he had to change his name. Maurice Micklewhite on a film credit somehow didn't look right.

There were three reasons why he determined to take no notice of the old man (in reality a man in his early 50s) and become an actor. 'I thought I could do it. It interested me to do it.' And as he had said before, 'I was never very impressed by the way the working classes were portrayed in British films.' It was the old hobby horse.

At the age of 16, the time came for another of those changes that had figured so much in all that had happened to him so far. He left school.

Five

A Hill in Korea

Had the Grocers been Maurice Micklewhite's last school, the idea of leaving it might have been different. He wanted to learn and the atmosphere there had been stimulating. So had the companions in his lessons. At Wilson's, it was so different. The Grocers' boys would hope to stay on until 18 and then try for university. Nearly everyone at Wilson's wanted to leave the moment their School Certificate course had finished – and quite a few wanted to go at the earliest legal moment when they were 15.

The miracle was that the Micklewhites allowed their elder son to stay on until 16. A greater miracle would have been had they suggested that he go to the Royal Academy of Dramatic Art, or at least try for a job in a repertory company, then the nursery of so many young actors. They didn't. The junior Maurice would spend much of the next five years trying to convince his father that, no, it wouldn't be good enough to follow in his footsteps.

He had other ideas – the principal one of which seemed to be that he was not going to take a job that required him to get up at four o'clock or earlier in the morning. No one had yet told him that film stars have to do much the same thing – although sitting in a comfortable chair being smothered with make-up would then have seemed preferable to having melted ice run down his face and neck from a box of fish.

Various jobs offering a little money and absolutely no prospects seemed more appealing – like operating a pneumatic drill. He also worked as a dish-washer and was a night clerk in an hotel until the chance came about that he was sure was the first step to Hollywood – he became an assistant to a man who specialised in making movies of Jewish weddings. That came to an end when he fused all the electricity at the smart hall where a function was in progress, just as the trumpeter

Eddie Calvert was performing. But the film business still provided opportunities that he grabbed like a clapper board. The J. Arthur Rank organisation, then the biggest name in British films, wanted an office boy. And he wanted the job. He got it, but it didn't last long. Maurice was discovered smoking in a toilet and was instantly sacked.

It wasn't a time to worry too much about unemployment. Winston Churchill had plans for him. At the age of 18, Maurice was called up for National Service in the Army. The day that brown envelope thundered on to young men's doorsteps will for ever be etched on their memories. The instruction to report at a camp – accompanied by a travel warrant to take the train – sent an icy chill down their backs not unlike that which dribbled down from those Billingsgate fish boxes.

Maurice thought it might be something of a release. Certainly it offered him employment at a time when he might be faced with the dole. That would actually have been unlikely. In those early postwar years, full employment was the norm. But the kind of employment on offer was a different matter. The Army years would give him time to think.

Mothers all over the country said *au revoir* (not a term, it has to be said, much in use at the Elephant) to their sons in the knowledge that in peacetime they should not be in much danger. If Ellen thought that, she was in for a rude awakening. Her son was sent off to Korea.

He had been in Germany, living a quiet, nonsensical life, doing things vital to national security like painting coal white, when the invitation came from an officer. How would he like to stay in Germany? All things considered, it seemed a reasonable enough offer. It was safe and boring and that was how young National Servicemen wanted it to be. But the offer was conditional. If he stayed in Germany – officially, guarding trains – he would have to do it for an extra year – in other words extending his two years to three. That was not an offer that sounded at all attractive. Korea was an even less pleasant consideration. But by the time he was told he was off to the peninsular, it was too late. He was going, with no alternatives.

Korea wasn't really Britain's war at all – in fact, he would say 'I couldn't muster up much patriotism over Korea.' But try to tell that to the men who were called up to fight in the conflict. Officially, it was the United Nations' response to the invasion of South Korea by the North Koreans. The UN Security Council passed a resolution at the end of 1950 to send troops in to fight for the democratic South – who in reality were nothing of the kind – against the totalitarian invaders. It all seemed terribly simple since the Russians were having one of their frequent rows with the West and had walked out in protest. They were out when they could have been around to slap a veto on the proposal.

In effect, it was America's show, with men from the States doing some of the most vicious fighting in the history of warfare. There were contributions from Turkey, Greece, the Australians, various contingents from the Commonwealth and the British – a comparatively small number of soldiers who were all supposed to be regulars.

National Service was not intended as a means of increasing the country's cannon fodder, more as a training scheme for the troops of the future. But as the offer made to Maurice in Germany proved only too well, it was abused and, despite protests in parliament from MPs whose constituents didn't like the idea of 18-year-olds going out to be killed in an undeclared war, Maurice Micklewhite junior and a group of other youngsters went out to fight against what they were told was the Yellow Peril.

The little matter of the Chinese joining in the onslaught against the UN just happened to have occurred between his being called up and walking up the gangplank to the troop ship. The vainglorious General Douglas MacArthur, meanwhile, had been sacked by President Harry Truman for wanting to use the atom bomb on the nasty little men from across the Chinese border. The general went home. Maurice Micklewhite and his new pals didn't have that option.

They should never have been allowed into the war, but governments do not always think about the feelings of parents with 18-year-old sons, let alone the sons themselves. It brought more than a degree of resentment when people like Caine had to fight while others escaped. It was a thought that entered his mind when National Service was abolished in 1957. He agreed it had been a 'test, something you had to go through to become a man'. There was also 'an enormous gulf' between himself and those who had not gone through that test. 'At the age when I was in the Army, hating it like poison, but learning something about self control and discipline, those guys were at home, writing songs and forming rock groups. So I'm ambivalent. I feel as though I belong to a lost generation.'

In his autobiography Michael Caine tells about the hilarious events on this tour of duty as a private in His Majesty's Royal Fusiliers. On the troopship, they were ordered to sunbathe – in case the enemy by any remote chance thought they were pale, raw recruits from a city somewhere in the west, who didn't know anything about jungle warfare. Even more hilarious were his accounts of being called on as the camp doctor – he appeared to be the only one who could diagnose gonorrhoea by looking at the penises of his comrades. The man who has said he can't bear the sight of naked men hardly dared walk into the latrine because he knew someone was there ready to flash his willy.

Others were not so impressed with this well-educated youngster from the Elephant and Castle. They thought he was 'a Bolshie', a barrack-room lawyer and a know-it-all.

They were given the occasional leave in Seoul, the South Korean capital, times spent by most of the men in getting drunk and getting laid. Maurice himself considered more carefully the same sort of thing that worried his comrades and he decided that the local prostitutes were there to be avoided. Since then, he has said he would never pay for sex. What he saw in Korea gave him good reason for that decision.

There were also five-day rest periods in Tokyo. But 'they wore me out more than the bloody war.'

There was a great deal more, mostly centred around that word 'fear'. Facing a squad of North Korean soldiers and their Chinese allies who didn't seem to care very much which of them got killed was a whole lot more serious than a night dodging the spivs – and their hats – in the Elephant. On one reconnaissance exercise they thought they were surrounded by a Chinese squad. 'We realised that we were going to die,' he recalled, 'and our reaction was, "If you're going to get us, you're going to pay and you're going to pay the absolute maximum." ' Suddenly, the son of the fish porter was a general. He was the one who decided to lead a suicide mission against the Chinese, a 1950s version of the Charge of the Light Brigade. What happened after that, is a matter of interpretation. He has been quoted as saying that the Chinese left a clear path for them and they were able to run away. Another report had it that the Chinese he thought were there, weren't present at all. That doesn't alter the fact that he and his mates *thought* they were there, and it didn't make their fear any the less real.

There was one moment when he just *knew* he was going to be killed. His immediate reaction was, 'OK, but I'm going to take as many of them with me as I can.' He learned 'that if you can face a desperate situation like imminent death and not react with cowardice then you can knuckle down and face almost anything.' Including, no doubt a movie producer. He did also add: 'After that, as discouraged as I sometimes became with acting, I was never afraid enough to run from it.'

Another time, the Chinese let off fire crackers, intending – and greatly succeeding – in scaring the pants off these amateur soldiers who weren't very good at what they were there to do. 'I stood straight up through the earth like Godzilla. I'm afraid of heights too. When I was in the Army I realised I was ideally cut out to be a lounge lizard in the 1930s with lots of ladies, a Dusenberg and sunshine on the beach.'

It was not a collection of characteristics likely to make him particularly popular with his fellow soldiers. They thought he was too sophisticated for his own good – a snob? Perhaps – but a snob with a working-class accent which seemed to dictate that he was never going to get anywhere. The idea of his wearing one of those officer's caps in which he looked so dashing in so many films was quite laughable – to him and to the real officers who looked into his puffy eyes with their air of superiority. He was, in short, the best argument known to man for leaving soldiering to the soldiers and leaving young men who want to be actors to get on with the job. 'I began as a private,' he said at one time, 'and I had great difficulty in clinging on to even that rank.'

He left Korea intact, but after an attack of malaria that would have its results before very long. Others were not so lucky. Thousands were wounded, many killed and several suffered from self-inflicted wounds. As he was to say, 'A lot of heroic-looking guys shot their toes off while cleaning their rifles and a lot of crummy-looking bums turned out to be brave.'

He hated the Army 'and all that it stands for, especially the killing'. But he came to respect people he would describe as 'ordinary guys who just are doing the best they can'. Demobbed, he was given back his old clothes – he would have preferred to have something that more suited the Teddy Boy style then fashionable – while a military band played 'Colonel Bogey', made famous by *The Bridge On The River Kwai*. There was one determination in his mind: never to join the Army again. 'I am prepared to go to prison rather than serve,' he said. '[But] if somebody sets foot in England, then I'll be the first to join up. But I'm not prepared to fight wars in foreign lands any more.'

The question that faced him when he got back home to the Elephant was what was he going to do now? His father had the familiar answer. This time, he did not argue. Even 'schlepping' – as he put it – the trays of fish couldn't be as bad as anything he had seen in Korea. He stuck it out for a matter of weeks, and realised that the money he got wasn't bad, and he had succeeded in making his father happy, but all that stuck with him was the terrible smell of fish. It made him determined to go into acting. He took a few acting lessons in the evenings and, to everyone's surprise, his father agreed to pay for them. Now the older Maurice Micklewhite was finally earning between £45 and £50 a week, which in those days would have made him rich. But, as his son said, the money his father promised never materialised. 'The horses got it all.' The lessons would have cost two guineas (£2.40p) a time, but the money was never there for them.

Not that he had ever wanted to do anything else but act. He had considered the alternatives and didn't want any of them.

He did try something else – working in a butter factory. It really *was* work. He had to haul crates of the stuff that were even heavier than the fish boxes. But it was cleaner and he was able to benefit from some advice from one of his colleagues. The man had a daughter who was an actress. Through her, he knew about the trade paper, *The Stage*. 'Why don't you take it?' the man asked. It was to prove to be one of the most important pieces of advice he was ever given.

Six

Sweet Liberty

It took a long time for the man we now know as Michael Caine to be an 'overnight sensation'.

Certainly, the advertisement he read in *The Stage* didn't appear to offer instant stardom. But there was something tempting about it. Tempting isn't the word. He'd been out of the army for a matter of months – and for each of those months, there was apparently a new job. His distaste for 'schlepping' (the influence of the Grocers was never going to leave him) the fish around was clear to everyone. He wasn't displaying very much more excitement about lugging vats of butter the length and breadth of a factory floor.

That was why the conversation with a man who understood his sense of ambition meant so much. Trade papers are like the Bible in the theatre. You have to know what's going on, more important, who is doing what. If you were at the beginning of a professional career, you needed it for the jobs. The man, whose name has been lost like an item of theatrical memorabilia in a burnt-out attic, liked to talk about the ambitions of his daughter, a girl of whom he was justly proud and who he hoped would one day make it. Whether she ever did, is another one of those mysteries.

Surprisingly, *The Stage* had not been on Maurice Micklewhite's essential reading list. But he was off the following Saturday morning and, without telling anyone, got on a bus to the West End to buy a copy of the newspaper which he thought might hold the key to his future. He knew he could never find a copy of the journal in the Elephant. He also knew that buying it far away from home – the bus ride seemed far enough away, at least – would save him the embarrassment of being seen by any of those gentlemen in the wide hats and shoulders who might make awkward comments putting his manhood into question. And it was a reasonable consideration. Young men bought *The Stage* and buried it under copies of the evening paper, rather like they would if they were still reading *Health and Efficiency*. He didn't open the paper there and then in the shop in Charing Cross Road. (He still remembers the name of the store, Solosys.) That would have looked too unsophisticated and that much he did know: an actor who was going to make it just had to look sophisticated; he sat himself on a bench in Leicester Square. He may not have realised it at the time, but it was his first step in show business.

The year was 1952. Britain was still hit by post-war austerity, although things were beginning to look better. King George VI had died earlier that year and the country was brimful of artificial hope. There were still a few shortages in the shops, the best of British products were being exported, there were still bombsites in the centre of London, not a stone's throw from where the Micklewhites still lived in their prefab. The buildings that had survived the Blitz were grey and dirty. But a year before, there had been the Festival of Britain intended to make the country smile again and now, with a young Queen Elizabeth in her first months on the throne, people were talking of a new Elizabethan age.

In truth, there really was that spirit of optimism about. The reviews in *The Stage* – a paper that believed it should never be beastly to the profession and give a bad review to any production, were full of the show-must-go-on spirit. Intimate revue was in its heyday. The big West End theatres were packed out with people who thought the time had come to try to enjoy themselves and the American musical, not for the first or the last time, was king. *Carousel, South Pacific, Call Me Madam, Wish You Were Here* were all selling out.

Maurice Micklewhite wasn't looking for a job in any of those shows. He knew he wouldn't have got one. For one thing, he didn't belong to Equity, a union that epitomised the immortal phrase 'Catch 22'. You couldn't join the union unless you were working in the theatre. On the other hand, you couldn't work in the theatre unless you were a member of Equity. Fortunately, he didn't know that. He skimmed the jobs-available column and then studied it in more detail. Only one ad attracted him – although, it has to be said, not for the money on offer. The advertisement pulled no punches; it said simply: 'Wanted. Assistant stage manager for repertory company. To play small parts. Fifty shillings per week.' It is not certain now whether Maurice knew what an assistant stage manager was. But he did know what repertory was – that nursery of the theatre, a training ground which he surmised was probably more useful than a course at the Royal Academy of Dramatic Art – an opinion bolstered by the fact that he hadn't gone to RADA, was a little too old now to think of going to RADA and even if he could, would never have been able to afford to go there.

Repertory was certainly a much harder school. Companies took over theatres in provincial towns or in the London suburbs and they put on plays that were past their West End sell-by-date, plays that were now available and, most important, cheap enough to be played by outfits with more hope than money. They put on the same plays as amateur dramatic societies. What was more, they put them on every week. As June Wyndham-Davies said: 'When you think of it, it was silly. We never had a moment to ourselves.'

Each Monday night, a different show – just as the cinemas put on different films at the beginning of each week and just as in those dying days of what had been the music hall, variety houses changed their bills every Monday. For cinemas and variety theatres that was no problem. But actors had to learn new parts, new lines, new 'business' every week. While they were acting in one play in the evening, they were learning and rehearsing the next week's production during the day.

For obvious reasons, most young repertory casts wanted to get out of the companies almost as quickly as they had wanted to get into them. It wasn't that they didn't like acting. On the contrary, one week 'on the boards' fired their ambitions amazingly. A month in a repertory organisation and they talked as though they had been on the stage in Shaftesbury Avenue for ten years. A year and they were hardened pros. There were those who wanted to stay with the local rep. They had huge local followings and enjoyed being big fish in little ponds. But for most – although there were some who didn't enjoy the life as much as those big fish, but could get no other work – it was no more than a stepping stone, very much like the time on a local newspaper for a budding journalist.

As June Wyndham Davis said: 'After one-week rep, you'd try to get two-week rep and feel very posh. Then you wanted to go into three-week rep and, of course, the West End. You learnt an awful lot.'

The advert that caught Maurice's attention was for the repertory company at Horsham, in Sussex, a small town no more than a 40-minute train journey from London and, more important, a dormitory of Brighton, which liked to think of itself as London-on-Sea. Brighton was the home of Laurence Olivier and a clutch of lesser stars and the company always lived in the hope that one of them would stop by for a night of 'slumming', spot an incredible talent and then whizz them off to Hollywood or, at least, to their next West End show.

Whether that whizzing ever happened, no one could now say. It certainly didn't happen during the time that the Westminster Theatre Company was in charge of the Theatre Royal, Horsham (companies charged almost as regularly as the plays they put on).

The grandiosely-named Westminster Company was the brainchild of a man called Alwyn Fox, who had made his reputation – his stage reputation, that is (his off-stage reputation was a different thing entirely) – in pantomime where he excelled as a dame, and his live-in lover, an actor named Edgar Grey. There was also Ms Wyndham Davies, a stunningly attractive actress who had put £100 into the company to become a partner – a gesture that came more from a desire to be active in the theatre business than to make money. She was also the female lead in most of the Westminster productions. She it was who saw the reply that Maurice Micklewhite sent to Horsham in response to the advertisement. He didn't merely write a letter, he sent a photograph. He wasn't very pleased with the sepia-tinted picture that had been taken for him by Jerome, at the time as much a household name in the British high street as Woolworths or Boots, the chemists. It was the days before most people had cameras of their own and a visit to the local photographic studio was a regular activity for working-class families.

The picture, he was sure, didn't do him justice. It seemed to exaggerate his lips, giving an almost effeminate look to the macho features of the 12-stone, six-feet-something physique which had been strengthened by his time in Korea and all that 'schlepping' in Billingsgate and the butter factory. He didn't realise that it was that deceptive look which attracted Mr Alwyn, a man not much interested in the ladies except for what they could do for his company.

When Maurice Micklewhite's application arrived, he hadn't the slightest doubt that this was a youngster who had to be auditioned. He might also have had plans for auditions that went beyond the stage, but didn't reveal any such hopes when the youngster arrived, nervously, to be put under Alwyn D. Fox's scrutiny.

The meeting was held not at the Theatre Royal, but in London, where Fox went on his fishing expedition. The day it all happened seemed to bring as much salvation to the Westminster players as it did to Maurice Micklewhite.

June Wyndham Davies was partly responsible for his being taken on at Horsham. As June told me: 'Alwyn went to London and interviewed several people. He had been a wonderful dame in pantomime and was now branching out with his own ideas. He came back and said: "I have seen this very nice boy. Would you like to see him?".' She said that, of course, she wanted to see him. It was a decision that would resound through show business history. But you would have had to have been prophetic to have known that at the time. June welcomed Maurice warmly. 'I didn't audition people. The one thing I could do was to tell the others when I thought someone was terrible. I didn't think that about Michael. We were very glad when we found someone like him, one whom we discovered could act as well as be an a.s.m.'

Alwyn Fox was never happier. But Michael plainly didn't want to make him too happy. He was the first homosexual Maurice had met in a working environment – one where it soon became clear such proclivities were more the norm than the exception. The first meeting with Edgar confirmed those impressions. He allowed himself the thought that perhaps his father had been right. The theatre *was* full of 'Nancy boys'.

Alwyn might well have been disappointed when he realised that the man with bulging eyes and the long blond hair was not likely to provide him with any domestic solace, but he offered him the job just the same, told him he would smooth his way to his Equity card and informed him of all the great opportunities in store. Fame, stardom, wealth....

June pulled no punches about how difficult that fame, stardom and wealth was going to be to find – but only once they knew each other and had become the sort of friends people do become when they work together at such close quarters. She knew why they picked him. It was only partly because he was cheap and keen, not at all the sort who would demand more money than the Equity minimum. 'I was straight out of RADA and just a beginner, but for me, too, it was a chance to do something very interesting rather than make a lot of money. I am sure they thought that was the way Michael felt. The fact that he wouldn't have cost a great deal must have had some effect. But there was more to it. It was a vulnerable time. The Queen was about to be crowned and we all had hopes but wondered about the future. I remember the week very well because we couldn't do anything without an a.s.m., particularly one who could do a few parts.'

But his first rehearsals revealed a startling fault in his personality.

'He came,' she told me, 'as if it was straight from the Billingsgate fish market. I remember he wore a marvellous leather jacket. But it was obviously the one he had worn at Billingsgate. It stunk of fish – so bad that I remember my first meeting with him as the time I had to reel back. I had to kiss him.' Which, one supposes, would be a strong enough memory for any actress, with or without the smelly jacket – giving Michael Caine his first ever stage kiss. But it is the fish that really stays in her mind.

She had the answer to that little local difficulty, as such things were called in 1950s politics. 'My uncle lived nearby and Michael was the same size as he was. Michael was a fine strapping chap and my uncle's clothes fitted him – and the fish jacket didn't appear in any more rehearsals, I'm glad to say.'

Now, the significance of those days is not so much in the story of the fish but in the name she called the youngster who had signed on in the repertory company 'Maurice Micklewhite'. Alwyn D. Fox didn't like that name at all, and to be fair, Maurice Joseph Micklewhite junior hadn't liked it for a long time either. When Fox suggested he change it, Maurice raised no objection – particularly since the producer-director insisted on calling him 'Tickletight'. Years later, Michael Caine would justify the change of name by saying there was already a big star named Maurice Joseph Micklewhite. If you believed that, you would believe that his one real ambition in life was always thwarted – to work in Billingsgate. They pondered and wondered and thought and considered. Eventually Fox came up with the solution: Maurice would become Michael. Michael Scott. 'I think we had the idea that he had some sort of Scottish ancestry,' June Wyndham Davies now recalls.

So Michael Scott appeared at the foot of the programmes, usually as assistant stage manager, a title that really doesn't give any notion of his job. He wasn't a manager of anything. He was the props mover, he was the one who ran errands – like getting packets of Tampax for the actresses – and was the star maker of tea for everyone. He was at the bottom of a rickety ladder, a fact revealed by the money he was earning. June seemed to be making a fortune, at least a little more than the £2. 10s a week paid to Michael Scott, which even as 1952 was turning to 1953, was hardly enough for more than board and lodging.

But, it has to be said, Maurice was not looking for stardom. Incredible as it now seems, his ambitions were strictly limited. It was partly a question of civil rights. 'I didn't go on the stage to play Hamlet. I thought maybe I could do Cockney coppers and barrow boys better than the actors who usually played them. I wanted to play them with some dignity.'

And play them, if necessary every week, in a different play every seven days. Not that the locals knew how hard it all was. 'People would stop me in the street,' he later recalled, 'and ask what I did in the day time.' Early on, he had difficulty with his lines. 'I was bloody nervous,' he would recall. He played a detective who had to tell his quarry: 'Come along with me, sir.' The trouble was, he could never remember those words. June could – and she remembers them to this day. What Michael does remember is how difficult getting to grips with a theatrical career proved to be.

'I was very Cockney, so it rather limited anything I could be given. But I was much fitter and stronger then, when I was 20, so there I was up every morning doing the donkey work and everything – and then came a part with a few lines, then a few more lines and so on. That's how I actually started.'

He seemed to be happier than he had been at any time in his life. He enjoyed the work, enjoyed being with the company – in truth, with the female members in particular. The idea of being with so many men who were always known as 'queers' was uncomfortable. But it had its advantages. Since he was just about the only male who showed any interest in the women thereabouts, he was in great demand. His sex life had never been so active.

'I remember the girls in Horsham went crazy over him,' says Ms. Wyndham Davies. 'When they got to know him, they thronged into the theatre like groupies after a pop star. You'd hear them scream.' A suitably large number of them did not limit themselves to reacting from the audience. June Wyndham Davies told me about one in particular. 'This was Jane Beaney. Mike was very keen on her. What I remember is that she tried to keep it secret because her father had told her: "Don't you ever bring an actor home".'

He was fortunate in finding a sympathetic landlady who had no such prejudices. Horsham was not one of those theatrical towns with digs that specialised in taking theatre people, the kind who gathered around a large table for dinner in the evening, with the biggest star in town sitting at the top and having the first ladle of soup, the most succulent portions of the meat. He was well treated and the evening meal he received as part of the rent was always good and generous. That rent was £2.10s a week – precisely the wages he received. Fortunately, the company liked him and didn't seem to mind including him in the rounds they were buying. They enjoyed his company as much as he welcomed theirs. 'There was a wonderful pub in the centre of Horsham, called the Stout House, which was run by a wonderful couple, the Cagbys,' June Wyndham Davies told me.

'Mrs Cagby served the best meals we'd ever had – for 1s 6d (7.5p) a time, wonderful sausage and mash, which I just can't forget. They just loved us. It was a special rate for actors, I am sure. And they wanted to help us. We weren't starving, but we didn't have too much and they wanted to see we were well fed.'

There was never any doubt about what they were going to chat about over those sausages and mash. No one talks shop more avidly than actors and they were all full of the kind of ambition with which few other professions can compete. They were mostly young, nearly all at the start of their careers. 'And I think all we talked about was how hard we were going to work to get on and about the people who were coming to see us.'

They also talked about things that happened in the theatre, the idiosyncrasies of the customers who never seemed to stop coughing.

On a rainy night, they would laugh about the roof. It was made of tin and a mere shower would have a disturbing effect on the action below – especially when they were performing something like *Treasure Island*, set in a place not known for its rain. If the action required the fullest attention – one of those quiet moments when the coughs could really be disturbing – then the pounding of the rain was a near desecration of the playwright's work. The sight of Mr Alwyn D. Fox holding his head in despair was not easily forgotten.

The tin roof apart, the Theatre Royal was one of those treasures that local playhouses frequently were, the sort of small auditorium which gave a sense of excitement the moment you entered it. The seats were red plush. There was gilt around the balconies. But there were no boxes. It was as though that would have shut the best seats off from the rest of the theatre and repertory companies liked to think they were part of a community, with no barriers between them and their audience. Michael Scott realised that to his cost early on. He had to stand, doing very little, at the corner of the stage. A woman out front felt sorry that he looked so bored and stepped up to the apron and offered him a sweet. He reached over the footlights and took it. Alwyn D. Fox was not impressed.

But he survived that episode just as he survived his attack of nerves the first night he played a real part – as a suave, sophisticated lover, albeit one wearing his own too-big demob suit that hung around his shoulders like a gangster's overcoat. He had to get June Wyndham Davies drunk and constantly ply her with the fake whisky they used on stage. The difficulty was that he was nervous. And every time he poured the whisky it failed to come out of the bottle – because he had left the stopper on. (That sort of thing was always happening in rep.)

It took the leading lady's ingenuity to get the play back on course. The audience was laughing hysterically and Mr Scott had no idea why. He looked to his flies – which, in his previous stage appearance in pantomime, he had forgotten to do up. This time, the trousers were intact, but so was the bottle. June found an excuse to open it and poured the contents down her own throat – a gesture for which Michael Scott was eternally grateful. 'We taught him that, whatever happens, whatever you're playing, whatever goes wrong, even if the set falls down, you have to keep talking.'

It was not an easy lesson to learn, but it was an essential one. As he would say: 'When you make a mistake in front of a paying audience, and they laugh you down, there is no experience more humiliating. You will never make that mistake again.' He got better. And the set did fall down. As the leading lady recalled for me: 'We did a costume play called *The Case of Mrs Barry*. It was about a woman accused of murder and other terrible things and he played the sexton from the church next door. Of course, she had buried a few people around her house and he came in wearing his tricorn sexton's hat, all in black. He had never done that sort of part before and when he saw me, he raised his hat – and took the top off the door. It all fell around us.'

It was the real test. Everyone had said he had to keep talking if the set fell down. But they said it the way Broadway actors tell each other to break a leg. Now that the set did actually collapse, various parts of it crashing all over the place, it was a moment to separate the men from the boys – or at least the amateur hopefuls from the professionals. 'We were just transfixed,' she remembered. That was when he said: 'Mam, your house falls about our ears ...' As she told me: 'That transfixed us even more. And we just laughed. He did that himself. I mean from that moment on – and I really mean this – I knew he was going to be a great success.'

The local Press felt the same. When he appeared in *Love From A Stranger*, he was noted by the local critic 'A.S.D.F.' – sadly it was the time when journalists were told to be more modest than the people about whom they wrote. In this case, the initials were probably even more anonymous than those of some provincial scribe – just the ones in the central line of the typewriter keyboard. 'A.S.D.F.' thought he was the brightest part of the Agatha Christie story of an office girl who unexpectedly comes into money. June Wyndham Davies recalls this as the most important moment in Michael Scott's Horsham career. 'There was something indefinable about him. Like that line about the house falling about our ears. We were all impressed. I thought, "Yeh, you're going to do things." But I can't tell you why.'

He was learning and thinking. Some of those thoughts might now seem to be amazingly deep for an actor so young, but already he was working out what acting was all about.

It would take his film role with Laurence Olivier in *Sleuth* to put into practice one of the thoughts that came to him early on. 'You see actors on the screen about to be shot, and they don't do anything. I thought, someone who's going to have his brains blown out must be in abject, snivelling terror. He'd do anything to stop them pulling that trigger. It's a difficult, humiliating thing to do, to burst into tears, plead, beg, sob, especially for someone like me, who's not at all like that. But I thought, if you do it half-heartedly, you embarrass the audience. Better go right into it, and take the risk of overdoing it because actually there's no way of overdoing it. People in certain situations will scream themselves to death.'

If he had screamed himself to death at Horsham, it might have looked like overdoing it to an impossible extent, the sort of thing people would complain about in repertory. In those first days on the stage, he probably did overdo things, but it was there that the feel for what real acting was all about first took hold.

In *Love From A Stranger*, June recalled, he was 'made up to within an inch of his life. He was given a suntan. His eyelashes were blacked. His hair was made even more blond. And the girls came and screamed even more. The woman star screamed for different reasons when he entered the play and changed the life of her character. He was, said the critic, 'a tall, fair young man with the attractive drawl who was to sweep her off her feet and carry her off to an isolated cottage, there to reveal that his designs were on her fortune, rather than on her lasting affections'. And A.S.D.F. pointed out: 'This handsome stranger dominates the scene throughout. Blessed with the looks for the part, Michael Scott, nevertheless, turns in a performance that is astonishingly good to those who have only seen him in limited minor roles.

'The part is one, which could so easily drift into melodramatic interpretation, more funny than chilling, but Mr Scott switches alarmingly from quiet charm to maniacal frenzy in a manner which certainly promoted a succession of spinal shivers in the idolising bevy of high school beauty which surrounded your critic on Monday.' So June Wyndham Davies's assessment of his powers with the opposite sex had not been only her own musings.

Neither A.S.D.F. nor any of the other critics on the Brighton *Evening Argus* or any of the other local papers, seems to have picked Michael Scott out as the great star of the future. 'But,' said June, 'they always came on Monday nights and were amazed at what was going on. We, for our part, were all trying like mad to get on to other things.'

Other plays followed, each one as different from the other as they could be, as they tried – not altogether satisfactorily – to make the sets look different: *Rebecca of Sunnybrook Farm; Treasure Island* during Coronation Week in June 1953; *The Letter* by Somerset Maugham. June Wyndham Davies thought that this last was his most difficult role.

It was Michael's first appearance in a play that required him to lose his Cockney accent completely – which was no easier for him than it was for one of those RADA-trained 'anyone-for-tennis' types who had to try to pretend they came from the Elephant.

'He worked very hard at it,' his leading lady recalled. 'I mean he really worked at it, and he managed somehow. But when he had a Cockney part, he would let go. Then you saw the real Michael. He didn't exaggerate. He was very, very funny. Nothing was too much trouble. The thing about Michael is that then and now he has always remained the same.' Except that in those days he had a good singing voice. 'We used to love to hear him sing, although I think even then I thought he would be a better actor than singer.' When Michael Caine heard her say that, she remembered, he told her that 18 years of continuous smoking of Disque Bleue French cigarettes had put paid to any singing ambitions. Of course, he didn't need them.

His parents came down to see the shows. It may have been a spying mission, that first time they came. Michael Scott had sent home a photograph of himself in make-up and Maurice in particular caught fright. More than that; he had a fit, his son remembered. 'The company had taught me how to make up and were sending me out front looking like a raving tart.' The young actor himself had taken some convincing in that gay environment. But the presence of a homosexual element in the company did have its advantages. 'The first time I ever had to play a part I asked if someone could help with my make-up and they all said, "Yes, we can help you."'

For ages, he was to say he never met an actor in the provinces who wasn't gay. Each little rep company was a little gay society. 'Here I was – this big, tough, 20-year-old guy, six feet two inches tall and 180 pounds, just back from Korea and hard as nails – and I didn't know what gays did. I knew gays were strange in an amusing sort of feminine way. Even when someone finally told me what they did, I didn't believe it. When I talk about gays in the British theatre at that time, I mean real "whoops, dearie" types ... looking back on it, it's very funny. When you think of doing *The Corn Is Green*, with all those supposedly tough coal miners coming off stage with black faces and going, "Hello, dearie."'

Maurice senior was impressed, perhaps against his own better judgement. He still wanted to know if his son was a 'Nancy Boy'. If those in his company were not that, they were 'Queenies' to the senior Micklewhite. When he was assured that his son was not one of them, the fish porter relaxed and suggested the two of them went down to the nearest pub for a pint. It seemed a good omen. They made a good impression on the cast, even on those men Mr Micklewhite might not have wanted to include in his own circle. 'I remember his mother,' said June Wyndham Davies, 'she was a wonderful woman. Michael was so proud of how hard she worked.'

So, if she and the other members of the cast had already decided Michael Scott was exceptional, what was it that had led to that decision?

'He was fresh,' June now recalls. 'Just like Anthony Hopkins, who went to the pictures as a kid and wanted to be up there. Michael was a breath of fresh air. He was doing theatre, but we knew he wanted to do the movies. He applied himself properly. Things were so different then. If people had said then that we were drinking and drugging, we would have laughed. We didn't have time.'

What he did have time for was that burgeoning ambition. The youngster who had gone into the theatre to try to bring dignity to the Cockney, now had other thoughts. 'I saw the money film actors made and I said to myself, "That's for me." I never asked myself if I had any talent. I still don't know if I have any talent. If you ask me, talent is nothing but a little bit of luck and a lot of hard work.'

The hard work had begun in earnest. He was, as he would say, 'learning my trade'.

He even had to learn to try not to make the audience laugh during the most risible moments on stage – like the time he and the wimpish-looking Edgar Grey had to wrestle on stage in a scene from *Wuthering Heights*. Grey, the more senior actor, had the star part of Heathcliff – supposedly the macho hero of the piece. Michael was Hindley Earnshaw, the weakling. That may have been a fair recognition of local stardom or seniority, but it made no sense at all. Grey looked as if he had just about enough strength to open a packet of cigarettes. Michael Scott, the unknown, was twice his weight, had ten times his physique and had to play his part as though he were being beaten into a pile of tissue paper. Every performance it was like a champion boxer 'throwing' a fight and the audience enjoyed it immensely. It got the biggest laughs at the Theatre Royal since the last Christmas pantomime.

But that too was part of the learning process – to try to make the unlikely seem feasible. He didn't quite manage it.

It was during the run of *Wuthering Heights* that something happened which made it look as if all that learning and all the fun of repertory was going to be wasted. During the whole week, he had been feeling ill, but it was on the last day that the show-must-go-on mantra was tested to the full. Michael Scott collapsed during the Saturday matinée. 'I'll never forget the sight of him being carted away from the theatre on a stretcher,' June Wyndham Davies remembered for me.

Michael woke up in hospital, hearing doctors muttering something about infantile paralysis (later called polio). The big epidemic had been four years earlier, but, a decade before the vaccine became a standard prevention, it was still the most feared disease in Britain. Michael knew otherwise. 'I think,' he said, 'it's my malaria come back.' He was right. It was. He stayed in hospital for as long as it took to get him better – with dire warnings that there could be no final cure and that he would be lucky to survive into his forties. Then he went home to the Elephant and Castle before returning to Horsham.

He didn't stay there for long. A War Office letter informed him that there was a chance of curing his malaria. So he packed up and left for the last time. 'We were terribly sorry to see him go,' June Wyndham Davies says now. 'I can't even remember who took over from him. I know that he wasn't much good. Michael, on the other hand, was the only real star we produced. But we loved him long before there were any real signs of that happening.' The entire Westminster company packed their bags at the end of the year and all its members went their own way. 'Why Alwyn didn't want to continue, I have always wondered,' June Wyndham Davies says now.

There is, however, a poignant postscript to the story. Michael Caine, the brilliant Hollywood film actor, was sitting in his Beverly Hills garden when he read a letter from an official of the Department of Social Security in Hammersmith, West London. 'I was sitting with all the toys, the jacuzzi, the Rolls, the pool. I thought, "What the hell have they got on me?"' he recalled. Nothing more than that they had identified him and had a request.

A very sick, elderly man was telling everyone at the hospital where he was lying close to death that he had discovered Michael Caine. No one believed the story, but for the man's sake would it be too much to confirm whether that was true or not? And if it were a fact, could he possibly spare a little something to give the man? A certain Alwyn D. Jones, said the letter, was totally poverty stricken. Michael sent off a cheque for $5,000. It arrived just in time to give Alwyn a great deal of pleasure. His story had been confirmed. But the cheque was never cashed. Six weeks after the initial request, the official wrote again – to tell the star how much his letter and gesture had been appreciated. But Alwyn D. Fox died before he could spend the money.

Seven

A Shock to the System

The repertory bug had bitten just as deeply as the one that had caused his Korean malaria. The latter was solved after that letter from the War Office. An American Army medical officer believed he had found a cure for the strain from which Maurice Joseph Micklewhite junior suffered – no one in Whitehall knew that he was now Michael Scott.

He was in hospital for ten days, with a group of other soldiers who were now officially back in the army. The treatment, administered by a colonel named Solomons, a tropical diseases specialist, was highly experimental. It could be guaranteed to succeed in doing only one thing – making his blood so heavy that if Michael moved his arms without a great deal of care, he would knock himself out. He moved his arms and did knock himself out. But at the end of those ten days, the colonel was as happy as he hoped his patients were. They were all cured. Thus, Michael Caine played a part in one of the great medical advances of the century.

He was naturally pleased. He was also determined to go back to work. Horsham was out. But he was now a man of experience, a professional. Michael Scott still saw his immediate professional future in repertory. Once more, he bought *The Stage*. This time, he wasn't going for a job as an a.s.m., but as an actor. He saw a vacancy in East Anglia. It wasn't as close to London as Horsham, but the reputation of the Lowestoft repertory company was a good one; one in fact that made young actors feel proud to be among its members. The theatre group took him on and Michael Scott began dreaming for the first time of stardom. He wasn't going to be satisfied now with playing Cockneys as human beings who spoke the way Cockneys were supposed to speak. He was branching out – and he was learning elementary lessons.

He learnt how to play a drunk. It seemed the obvious and most easy part to play. Everyone knew what drunks did, they lolled around and slurred their words. The trouble was, he was told by the director, that was the way people *played* drunks. Real drunks did their best not to appear drunk at all. It was another vitally important detail. It was the difference between serious acting and doing the sort of thing people did in pantomime, or demonstrating what they thought was a real situation at parties. It helped make Michael Scott a real actor.

At Lowestoft Michael's learning took another step forward – he learnt what it was really like to play a man in love. He knew exactly what that felt like, because he was madly in love with the leading lady, Patricia Haines. To his amazement, she was also madly in love with him. In just two weeks, they were married.

Learning how to love and play it on stage was one thing. Learning how to be happy was another. It didn't take more than a few weeks for both of them to realise it had all been a terrible mistake. Their love may have been full of instant passion. It was not strong enough to make a successful marriage. But there was a problem about that realisation: Patricia was pregnant. When she gave birth to a girl they called Dominique it was obvious that the child was not going to grow up with a perfect set of parents. They weren't perfect in any regard. He looked for work. She looked for support. Neither happened. 'I wound up working in a laundry. She wound up with a baby.' If nothing else, it set at rest the mind of the old Billingsgate porter. Maurice senior never asked again if his elder son was a 'Nancy Boy'.

By then, the Scotts, as they were known, had left Lowestoft and tried to set up home in South London – not Camberwell, but Brixton, in a house owned by Michael's aunt. He describes it as one of 'many tragic decisions, the other one being getting married'.

They both tried to find work and neither of them could. 'I fell flat on my face,' he said. So did their joint careers and any idea they might have had of bonding together. There was no repertory company near Brixton and, with a little baby in the family, this was no time to go travelling in search of one that could offer them work. The days of repertory were rapidly dying and, as Fred Astaire once told me in another context, there was nowhere for a young actor to be bad any more. The parts were difficult to come by in a profession where 90 per cent of the members were unemployed. No one was queuing up to give either Mr or Mrs Michael Scott a role. That didn't make for happiness. She wanted him to give up all his acting ambitions. The young woman who had been so impressed with what he did in

Lowestoft – it wasn't just his body that attracted her – now wanted him to abandon it all.

'She gave me an ultimatum,' he later recalled. 'I wouldn't agree and we parted.' They were both responsible for the problem. He has never spoken badly about her. Sometimes, he has been extremely kind. 'Pat was very English,' he told Lyn Barber in *Vanity Fair* magazine. 'She was extremely nice. She wanted to be a success and everything, but I can see her being quite shocked at the depth of my ambition – or not so much ambition but determination ... I mean extremely determined. I mean it *will* happen.'

Not that it looked much like happening then. Patricia herself once said: 'He called himself a loner and he was. He wanted nothing to interfere with his career, even then. I didn't understand the depths of his ambition, and I could never quite forgive it afterwards.' She also said: 'I can't remember one single moment that was happy. There weren't any good times.'

This Michael Scott was not an easy man to live with and perhaps that has been the secret of his subsequent success. Easy men are contented. He was never going to be satisfied with his life. What he was doing was building up reasons to justify later triumphs, paying his dues and getting them all out of the way. He even believed that there was a lot to be said for suffering – almost as if he had been trained at one of those Method schools he was always reading about in the days when Marlon Brando was king. 'I quite enjoyed being pissed off for most of my life – because it drove me on. I was painfully shy as a boy, so I needed something else to make me go on and stand up in front of people and do things.' It was that anger again. 'I probably used the anger to overcome the shyness.'

Shyness wasn't what Pat had noticed at all. She went back to her own family in Sheffield and took Dominique with her. Michael was 23 years old, plainly not mature enough to be either a husband or a father faced with a crisis, and he went home to mother. Two years of marriage turned out to be another of those black periods in his life, the kind from which there seemed to be absolutely no escape.

He had little choice. He didn't have the money to live on his own, and his parents were ready to offer him back his old bed in his old home. He was also grateful for his mother's cooking. Now he was a chastened individual, not at all the cocky Cockney his friends thought he was the day he had packed his bags and gone to Horsham.

Once more, he was working in factories, taking odd jobs where they arose. The worst was working in a steel mill. In his autobiography, he described the job of greasing steel rods and then packing them as the hardest work he had ever done and, in freezing winter weather, the worst conditions he had been in since Korea.

For the first and only time in his life, he was almost beginning to envy his dad and the other porters at Billingsgate. As he said: 'At times, as I waited for jobs for months to get a one-liner I wondered if I should do something else, but I wanted to be an actor.'

But at least, in Billingsgate, there were some friendly faces. And there were always the fringe benefits – the older Maurice had a great line in fish that somehow didn't manage to get to any of the high street retailers. If, as he maintained, the fish had a habit of falling off the backs of lorries, he must have had direct contact with the transport department. If you believed the excuse – and it is the traditional explanation for having property which no one seems to have paid for and therefore not one to be taken too literally – the market needed to look closely at the state of their trucks as there seems to have been a huge problem with the tail boards of the vehicles.

As it was, the family were never short of fish to eat. Or, when they were children, to frighten Maurice and his brother. One night their father hung a selection of yellow smoked haddock in their bedroom. They didn't know about it – and thought that a ghost had suddenly materialised. Too late, their father told them it was the phosphorous used to dye the fish that glowed in the night.

If Billingsgate suddenly took on a charm that the actor Michael Scott had never appreciated before, things must have been pretty desperate. They were. It was the nadir of his life. He had never before felt so miserable, so depressed, so sure he was in the midst of a nervous breakdown.

He and Patricia both knew that their marriage had not been made in heaven. It had been infatuation and nothing more. They made a baby, but not a living. Not only were they no longer in love, they didn't even like each other. The only thing they had in common was Dominique, whom Michael called Niki. But, living with her maternal grandparents, her father was a virtual stranger to her. It wasn't enough to make him try to patch up the marriage. About this time and quite by chance, he bumped into Patricia in the street. She told him they had been divorced for three weeks – quite unusual at a time when divorces were frequently contested in bitter courtroom battles. Then, he discovered he had to pay her maintenance. With what?

Looking back, he would say that the marriage, such as it was, was 'doomed from the start'. 'My wife wanted security,' he said. 'What she didn't know was – so did I. But if I'd taken a job I hated just to live with her in security, what kind of security would it have been?' He failed, he admitted in an interview with *Playboy*. 'Any way you mention it, I failed the first time – as a breadwinner, as a husband and emotionally. You name it and I failed. Except as a lover. But that's not to say I wouldn't try again. That would be like an actor refusing to work with a director who has made a flop picture.'

Plenty of young men marry at his age, plenty of others father children. For them, it is the ultimate in life. If he wasn't too young to be a father, he was certainly too broke. If he wasn't on the verge of a nervous breakdown, he was in the midst of a deep depression. No more evidence there of the resilient Cockney, the wit who could outsmart the teddy boys who had taken over from the spivs in his part of London.

The profession called what he was doing now 'resting'. It was about the least appropriate word imaginable for what was happening to him between 1954 and 1955. If 'rest' is meant to indicate quietude and recreation, Michael Scott knew none of it. There were other jobs, mostly working at night, which would give him, he thought, an opportunity to use his mornings and afternoons for auditions. That was one advantage of being young, no matter how exhausted and frustrated he felt, there was still the energy to work as hard as he had to do. It was useful experience. He has since said: 'The talent I developed from that is being able to sleep absolutely any time of the day or night'.

But if life seemed hard then, it was as nothing compared to what was about to happen. Maurice Micklewhite, senior, that giant with the constitution of one of the horses on which he spent so much of his hard-earned money, was struck with acute back pains, so bad that he had to give up work. When his son heard that, he realised just how bad those pains must be.

The old man may have wasted what, when added up, would seem like a fortune to a family living in a prefab, but nobody had ever said he was a shirker. His illness – 'rheumatism', the family were told and everybody of a certain age had 'rheumatism' in those days – only got worse. But it wasn't long before it meant there was a crisis in the family. The diagnosis came – worse than anything they had previously imagined. He was dying of cancer. The big hulk of a man was a wafer-thin shadow of his former self. He was dying, bitter. As Michael said: 'He was a gambler – and he lost.' One day, his elder son lifted the father he had regarded as the personification of strength out of the house on the way to the hospital. He could have done it with one hand.

Maurice Mickelwhite junior had convinced his father that he was not a 'Nancy Boy'. He hadn't yet shown him he could make a living in the theatre, let alone be a star. It was perhaps the hardest fact of all that had to be faced. He had desperately wanted the old man to know that he had made the right choice of career and it hadn't happened. As his father lay dying, all the 23-year-old could think of was that he hadn't convinced his parent that he had made the right choice. There was none of the satisfaction that might have come from knowing that his son was a big hit. The older man, still in his fifties, died in hospital – with 3s 8d in his pyjama pocket.

For Michael Scott, there was a whole clutch of reasons for the terrible depression that then bit so deeply. At the funeral, his mother, who had worked so hard to compensate for Maurice's extravagances, was distraught enough to throw herself on the grave. A great wave of inferiority engulfed her son. He knew he could be good, but nobody else knew it and no one was giving him the chance. There was nothing less likely to boost a person's self-confidence than this continuous run of rejections. But his father's death had other more severe connotations. There was the continual feeling that, had the younger Maurice had enough money, he would have been able to spend it on making his dad feel better. 'I don't know for how long, but for quite a long time.' As it was, he always said that his father passed away 'knowing I was a bum'. Everything collapsed at the same time. 'I had no hope and that was the last he saw of me.'

His father's death was an event that would continue to haunt the future Michael Caine. 'The most amazing thing to me is, I always thought, "As my father gets old, if I make it, I'll give him twenty quid now and then to bet on the horses." He loved to bet on the horses and never had any money, because he always bet on the horses. I thought, "If I was rich, I'd say, 'Here, Dad, here's the fare'."' But it never happened.

Even so, the event did have a positive effect, too. It was yet another spur; he was determined to succeed although without knowing how to achieve that success. Nevertheless, the ambition was paramount. 'I determined to make money. I saw what [doing without] it did.'

As things were, he didn't even have enough to keep himself off the poverty line.

Not for the first time, it was his mother who came to his aid. Amazingly for the head of a family in their income bracket, particularly one who had been so profligate, Maurice had looked ahead to this day. There were insurance policies, usually thought of as the province of those dreadful middle-class people whom he disliked so much. One policy covered the cost of his funeral. The other provided the outrageous sum of £25 – a working man's wage, Michael Caine says in his autobiography. In the mid 1950s, it was only the most successful working man who came home with anything over £20 every Friday night.

Ellen knew how much he needed to make some kind of a success of his life, although now the target was getting lower and lower. He still wasn't thinking of stardom. One day, perhaps, he would be a noted actor, one who was never out of work. Ellen also knew that he had to get away, to try to refresh that mind of his, clear it of all the memories of his failed marriage, the terrible jobs he had been forced to take and the depression that came after the death of a man he had truly loved and whose aspirations for him were never met. 'Take the £25 and go away,' she told him. She allowed no arguments – and gave her son the cash. He took it reluctantly, but there was no other way in view to really get away from it all. The money was used to get to Paris – a ferry across the Channel, a train to the French capital and a search for digs.

Paris was close to home. Because of that, the fares were quite low. But few people of his class went abroad in those days, let alone to what still had a reputation as one of the most exciting and romantic places on earth. It was an opportunity to observe people, probably the most important kind of studying an actor needs to do.

He did it sitting at a table in a street café. That *really* was Paris. He tried out his schoolboy French – with disarming results, particularly when instead of asking for a glass of 'citron', he asked for a 'Citroen'. The eminent car manufacturer may have made one of the cheapest models on the road, but it cost rather more than a lemonade and you couldn't buy one sitting on a wicker chair with a tiny cup of coffee before you. The request caused a great deal of mirth to the waiter and much more embarrassment to the customer.

The money soon dwindled. He tried to compensate for his dire poverty by sleeping at night in an airport terminal. The police, the 'flics' who in their pillbox hats and black capes were as much a part of the local landscape as the Eiffel Tower, were not impressed with his ingenuity. He lived on sandwiches, given to him by an American. He would remember these days when he went into the restaurant business, a move that brought as much success as he later achieved in the movies. Things only started to improve when he asked the owner of another café if he wanted anyone to help with the washing up. He got the job and started to enjoy Paris. The satisfaction didn't last long. The future Michael Caine would forever be glad that it didn't. Before long, he realised that his life had hit an 'absolute, all-time, rock-bottom low'. Considering what he had been through, that was quite a statement. But the fact that he realised it, said a lot. 'My life would have been ruined for good if I hadn't awakened one morning and, instead of feeling like a coward, became possessed by furious determination that *nothing* was going to beat me. I had to go back to England and prove that I could be a success.'

There was no work from his agent and he took himself off to a casting outfit, usually regarded as the last resort among actors who still think that one day they may make it and it's going to be soon. He wasn't the only one in the office at the time, but he was the one whose measurements fitted a policeman's suit as perfectly as possible – at least as perfectly as any policeman's uniform fitted.

The trouble was that the uniform was sent off to the cleaners and came back shrunk. So another man, who happened to have a 38-inch chest was chosen instead. But there were be other days when they would need a 'skeleton' with a broad chest like Caine's. Then he would report to a small studio, say his lines and go home again – richer by a few pounds but with not enough to keep even a puppy from the door, let alone the wolf. It did, however, prepare him for another movie in which he would play an officer of the law.

The casting director's name was Ronnie Curtis, who presided over his office like a foreman selecting longshoremen for jobs lugging containers and crates on to a ship. Any day, his little empire resembled a scene from *On The Waterfront*, with Curtis selecting his 'meat' on much the same lines as the foreman's scale – size. If he wanted a man with a short haircut, he would direct his eye towards the one in the room who did have a short haircut.

If one accepted the cattle market approach, that was perfectly fine. Except for one thing. Curtis was cross-eyed, and every time those eyes pointed, three men stood up.

They waited all day for Curtis to choose his lucky victims. They took sandwiches for lunch as they sat in his waiting room, wondering always when the degrading operation would happen. They were even afraid to go to the toilet – in case they lost the chance of an 'audition'.

It is easy to understand the desperation of Michael and of most of the others waiting there.

And then came a call from the agent. He was to go into a movie about the Korean war. There was £100 a week for him for the eight weeks that *A Hill In Korea* would be before the cameras. But it wasn't simply that he was being chosen to play a soldier, a fellow just like the one he had been with the Chinese sniping around him – he was being retained as technical adviser.

That was not what he had expected of life. Washing up in a Paris dive one day, and then the next, offered a part and an important position in a film company that he had never sought out for himself. It was hard to believe.

But there would be at least a month before the work – and the money began. He had to give up his own bed-sitter and move back home with his mother and younger brother. Ellen was still scrubbing floors and Stanley was out at work, too. Until *A Hill In Korea* started filming, he was destitute.

There was not just the rent to find, a commitment of which he was now relieved as he took up residence in the prefab again. He still had to eat during the day. But there was a more pressing demand on his non-existent finances. He hadn't paid Patricia the maintenance he owed for her and the baby.

Now there were threats of imprisonment. One story has it that he actually went to jail – sharing a cell, he was quoted as saying in an interview with *The New York Times* (a newspaper that goes to inordinate lengths to check its facts), with a man who stabbed his girlfriend 28 times. In his autobiography, he merely says that he had to pay the money to avoid prison.

Whatever did or was about to happen, things were pretty dire. No court was willing to accept a promise to pay based on a job that was going to happen a month hence. Ellen realised that and took herself off to the Post Office savings bank. There, she withdrew £400, all the money she had saved during her years of charring, and gave it to her elder son.

It was the supreme act of maternal love. She may not have wanted young Maurice to go into Billingsgate, but she certainly thought that there were other, more respectable, solid ways of making a living in those unemployment-free post-war years, without risking all as an actor. But she wasn't going to argue with him over it.

'Her attitude,' he said, 'was, "I don't want you to become an actor, but I'll back you all the way, and when you fail, you can turn to something else."' Even she may not have realised that that would never be an option. The youngster who had happily made the tea and gone out to buy packets of Tampax would do it all again, if that was the way to secure a job in the acting profession and now it looked as though it might not be necessary. Ever again.

Ellen probably knew that. 'That was the wonderful thing about it. She was loyal enough to back me, even though she thought I was wrong. She wanted me to have my chance.'

Accepting the money wasn't an easy thing. In fact, it couldn't have been harder for the kid raised in Urlwin Street. 'The lowest of the low in the Cockney's world,' he recalled in the late '60s, 'is what we call a "ponce", a pimp – a man who takes money from a woman.'

That makes it sound as though he had just put his mother on the streets. But that was how bad he felt about taking her savings – even though there was a promise to return it the moment he got his first *Hill In Korea* cheque. (£100 a week in those days represented more money than anyone in his family or in his street had ever seen in a pay packet.)

But for now Michael worried about what he was doing and what that was, in turn, doing to his mother. 'No matter how poor they are, women are not really supposed to work,' he would say nearly 40 years ago, a statement which illustrates just how far away the 1960s really were.

It explains, too, a family tradition in the Micklewhite home – how either the younger Maurice or Stanley would, as children, pay the rent man, even when neither of them had the money. The child whose first role had been to tell the collector that his mother was out, now accepted the task of settling the weekly bill as his duty in life, even when it was actually Ellen's cash he was handing over. Now, though, it was a case of keeping up appearances. A woman who went out to work had to be desperate – and no matter how tough things were, she wouldn't want anyone else to know about it.

That notion that the woman's place was in the home was as firmly engraved on Ellen's psyche as on those of the men in the neighbourhood. The newly-successful Michael Caine was to say: 'My mother would never mention that she worked. She would never pay for anything – one of *us* had to make the gesture. She would give us the money and we would pay her rent. A man is always supposed to pay the woman's way.'

The fact that he now had work got him out of trouble and allowed him the chance to start thinking about a future which suddenly seemed to have a sun shining on it. For it now looked as if he might be able to hold his head up straight. 'You know,' he would say, 'there are two things that poor people have got. They've got pride. They've got honour. If you're strong, you can retain one or even both.'

His strength had been tested and was rediscovered, just before it was too late. 'Pride I don't care all that much for, but honour is another thing – and one of the greatest dishonours is losing a fight, or running away from a fight.' Perhaps without totally realising it, that fight which he had been waging and losing all the way, now looked as though it could be won.

If anyone had told the Michael Scott who pulled down the set at Horsham's Theatre Royal that he would be off to Portugal to feature in the cast of what everyone said was going to be an important film, he would doubtless have kissed their feet.

On the other hand, he knew how much he would enjoy the experience of being with a gang of actors who were among the most talented and promising of their generation. The *Korea* film starred George Baker and his namesake Stanley Baker (no relation). Harry Andrews, Stephen Boyd and Robert Shaw were in it, too. The name Michael Scott does not appear in the cast in most movie histories. Nevertheless, he seems to have enjoyed the social aspects of the movie, making friends who would remain his friends until their deaths. Stanley Baker, Boyd and Shaw in particular. He enjoyed the evenings in the bars and restaurants (where he was introduced to the delights of olive oil and garlic) even more than the dramatic possibilities – which turned out to be not too great for him.

He was not called on for much technical advising either; and even less acting. Most of his scenes, in the story of the struggle to keep control of the hill of the title were cut.

When Michael's agent, Jimmy Fraser, saw the film, he told him he would no longer be on the books. What is more, he didn't like the young man's blond eyelashes.

Eight

Beyond the Limit

He may have been sacked, but there was reason for optimism. There was a new agent ready to take him on, a lady named Josephine Burton – and she was full of plans. She found him a job in a Christmas production put on by the Theatre Workshop at the Theatre Royal, not in Horsham; but at Stratford. And not Stratford upon Avon, either. This was Stratford East, on the edge of London's East End. It was also one of the most adventurous theatrical institutions ever created in Britain.

The Workshop was the brainchild of Joan Littlewood, a woman who not only directed plays for their artistic possibilities, but who regarded each one as a personal vindication. She found it difficult to understand why other people didn't feel precisely the same way, why they didn't put their all into productions like this one, *Chimes*.

Ms Littlewood summed up her new find immediately: he was worth taking a risk on, but he was certainly not the sort of material she wanted for her number-one company. He was in the second unit.

In 1966 he told writer Ken Gouldthorpe: 'Joan taught us to work together for the good of the whole piece. But when the play came out – Joan was the star. She didn't want it that way, but that's how it was. And suddenly I understood the world as it really is.'

More recently, he has been less kind about her. But around that time he was singing her praises. 'Working-class actors like me owe a big debt to Joan Littlewood and to the Royal Court Theatre. We're here today because of them. Otherwise, we'd still be wearing cloth caps and tugging our forelock and saying, "Thanks, gov!" as stage Cockneys, because we were completely out of the teacup school.'

He has also said that Americans needed similar institutions, 'instead of plucking truck drivers from obscurity and making stars of them.'

But for all the nice things he said about Ms Littlewood at the time, the affection didn't last. Also, the idea of *her* being the star didn't appeal at all.

He admits that he was 'very tough' the moment he became a professional actor. 'I knew what I wanted to know and what I didn't want to know. No one could teach me anything, but I learned a lot. I had been in over 80 plays as an amateur actor. It was different from never having acted in your life. I always knew I'd make it, but I never knew how or for what. I mean, I could have become a director or something. But I knew I had to be in this business in some way.'

And then, he thought about that. No. 'Some way' would not do. He had reached that stage in his life when he decided to aim at the top. It was that matter of understanding the world as it really was.

'If you live in China, you're a Communist. If you live in a capitalist country, you're a capitalist. If you're in the theatre, you shoot your lot to become a star.' He was ready to shoot his lot.

Michael Scott was not Joan Littlewood's cup of tea any more than she was really his. But this woman, who ran what was the closest thing London ever had to an Actors Studio summed up her view of Michael and got closer to the truth than many: he wasn't going to be a great actor, he would be a star. And this essentially left-wing organisation didn't think much of stars. When both finally realised they weren't going to make sweet music together, he recalls in his memoirs, she offered these immortal final words, 'Piss off to Shaftesbury Avenue'.

It was no easier to 'piss off' to Shaftesbury Avenue, the West End's famed 'Theatreland', than it would have been to 'piss off' to Hollywood. There was no work – at least not enough for him. But nothing that happened – or failed to happen – made him feel that he ought to give up 'resting' and settle down to a sensible job.

There were occasional small parts in other films, in *How To Murder A Rich Uncle*, which was a foray into directing by a romantic staple of the British cinema at the time, Nigel Patrick. Then there was *Room 43* in 1958 and, the most important movie of the time, *Carve Her Name With Pride*, a quite distinguished film starring Virginia McKenna as a British agent sent to work with the French Resistance. 'I am so sorry,' the still lovely Ms McKenna told me, 'I am afraid I don't remember him in it at all.' The director of the picture, Lewis Gilbert, does, however. 'I only remember because Michael reminded me about it,' he says. 'It was a very small part indeed. He was one of a group of prisoners on a train. The camera panned on to this group and there was Michael saying, "Water, water, water." That was it. That was his part.' He got between £5 and £10 for the 'role'. 'If he got £10, that was bloody good pay,' said Gilbert who would later direct Michael in rather more significant parts.

With all those things going wrong, people wanted to know why he hadn't become a communist. He was poor and his family were poor. He had a sense of pride in his working-class upbringing and referred to it as such whenever he was asked. He was as class conscious as the editor of the *Daily Worker*. But he was the first to admit that his feelings about communism were not exactly in line with those of the party members.

'I'm not a right-wing fascist.' (Which many saw as the alternative for people like him from his background.) The experience of the countries in the communist bloc proved it for him. 'They don't work,' he would say. 'Believe me, if communism worked, I'd be a communist before all that other lot. I'd have been the first and the most avid communist, I'd have been one of the leaders of it, *if it worked*.'

Now, his agent had a new idea up her sleeve. She had a television role for him, a notable part, small, but important – as Boudousse in Jean Anouilh's play about Joan of Arc, *The Lark*. But there was also a problem. Michael Scott was the name of another actor and Equity wouldn't countenance two performers called the same. He could either change the Michael or lose the Scott. There had to be an answer in half an hour – when the BBC contract had to be signed and posted.

That was a tough one. All these efforts to lose Maurice Joseph Micklewhite and become Michael Scott were as nought. He was in a telephone box in Leicester Square, when this big, unexpected conundrum was thrust his way.

There were cinemas all over the square, the Odeon, the Leicester Square Theatre, the Empire, the Warner. At the Odeon, Humphrey Bogart was starring in a new movie. Michael adjusted his heavy glasses, looked closer and between the trees managed to pick out one word in the title. He peered even closer. Humphrey Bogart, his childhood hero, was always worth investigating further. By the looks of things, the film dealt with a mutiny and that had a relevance about it for him; he was always in one mutinous mood or another. But it was the other word in the title *The Caine Mutiny* that appealed. Caine. It was short, simple and went well, he thought, with that other name with which he had become comfortable, Michael.

He didn't bother to leave the phone box. 'You can call me,' he said, 'Michael Caine.'

Nine

Surrender

The name Michael Caine wasn't just going to be a new title, a name to be used one day on movie posters – if he was lucky. It would be his on and off the screen. He was going to reinvent himself.

It was as if he had found himself a new disguise. As Maurice Micklewhite, he had been painfully shy. As Michael Scott, he suffered desperately from stage fright, which might have explained why, now in his late twenties he hadn't done anything with his life. He had destroyed a marriage and fathered a daughter whom he only occasionally saw – he would take off for Sheffield as often as he could to be with Niki, but his career came first and his career meant he had to live in London – and the only roles he got in his chosen profession were the kind that most out-of-work actors got in between being out-of-work actors.

The Lark really gave him opportunities. It was directed by Julian Amyes, who had directed *A Hill In Korea.* Despite losing his agent – and seemingly any potential fans – with a role that emphasised how much this blond young actor needed to dye his eyebrows and eyelashes, Amyes liked him and, more important, *remembered* that he had liked him. He actually sent for him. It was only the second time in his life that a role had come to him instead of his chasing a part.

The play was well received. But not well enough to guarantee that the phone would keep ringing. Like other actors, he still needed to haunt his agent's office and almost every time he looked in her door, he saw Josephine Burton's head shake from side to side. Sometimes, however, she nodded that head. Which was how he appeared in what was one of the most successful TV series of the late 50s, *Dixon of Dock Green,* a Saturday evening favourite in which Jack Warner – the PC Dixon of the classic British movie *The Blue Lamp* – told everyone that our policemen were wonderful. In front of the old cardboard sets Dixon was the favourite uncle in uniform, who ticked off small boys for stealing apples, but reassured old ladies that they would be safe at home. For years – for far more years than it was logical that a man like Warner, in his seventies, would still be active as a police constable – he made British audiences feel safe at home too.

Michael Caine was an Indian in this series, an Indian speaking with a Welsh accent. It all seemed doomed, until the director was desperate enough to accept his explanation that voices sounded much the same in Calcutta as they did in Cardiff. In his memoirs, Michael says he got a fan letter from the eminent actor Dennis Price, who saw his *Dixon* performances. But as stars liked to put their names but not their addresses on their notepaper he was never able to reply to say thanks.

In the instantly forgettable *Solo For Sparrow* in 1962, he played an Irish gangster. His accent in one scene in the film – in which he told his victim to get down on the floor of the car in which they were travelling – was so appalling that the producer refused to allow him to say anything more for the rest of the movie. Maybe Irish hadn't been one of the accents he had practised in the culvert near the South London sewers. There were other parts in which he played psychopaths – a recurrent theme in his career – policemen, butlers and almost every role that every play needs but nobody particularly remembers. It didn't bode well for his future, particularly when he saw what his contemporaries were doing.

If there was nothing else notable about the career of Michael Caine as he got dangerously close to his thirtieth birthday, there *was* a factor that made him stand out from the other also-rans of his profession, one thing that he did do right. Thirty years later, it would be called 'networking' – meeting other actors in the same position, talking shop, discussing what was going to happen – a sort of senior common room of performers, a slightly more advanced form of the beer-and-sandwiches breaks they all used to take at the Horsham and Lowestoft reps. The only difference between those provincial gatherings and the sessions at the Arts Café, close to the Arts Theatre near Leicester Square, and the Salisbury pub, one of the actors' favourite watering holes, was that everyone was working in the old rep days. Now, they were all out of work.

'They' included John Osborne, Terence Stamp, Albert Finney, Peter O'Toole and a strapping youngster with a deep Scots brogue who was about to go into the chorus of *South Pacific*. His neighbours used to call him 'Tammy' and he had done pretty well in a Mister Universe contest. His name on the theatre programmes was Sean ... Sean Connery.

'We were all angry, post-war kids,' said Caine, 'and we all expressed our rebellion in separate ways. I expressed my rebellion by never getting rid of my Cockney accent. The thing to do would have been to get rid of it, which is how Roger Moore showed his anger, by burying it. Roger is a policeman's son and he talked the same way I do. I hate the class system, hate it very deeply... and the class system said, "You're never going to get out of it".'

So he declared war on that system. But it would take a long time to achieve victory.

Terence Stamp and Michael were as close as two men could be without giving rise to unfounded rumours about their sexuality. It was one of those relationships that many men experience, two people closer than brothers – until something happens. Caine hints today that there were disagreements and that the long-standing affection dissipated when the time came for him to leave the flat in London's Harley Street – where Stamp's girlfriend, the model Jean Shrimpton, was a regular fixture. (Michael went off to temporarily share composer John Barry's home.) Stamp says that when Caine got money, he didn't need him any more than he needed the flat. 'It was a question of economics,' he says. But in the early years of the 60s it was all Terry's economics. He was the one with the money....

As we have seen, Michael Caine's rise wasn't as spectacular as those of the other young men who were angry at the same time that he was. While *they* were on their way to stardom, he was taking a job as a hall porter in an hotel much used by ladies of the night. At least it gave him adequate opportunity to look for more work and, had he not been so depressed, it might have helped him reflect on the fact that he was still there, still able to contemplate being on the threshold of a great career – while seven other actors who at one time or another had been part of the Arts and Salisbury set had committed suicide. A hard life, show business.

He and his friends had a pact – they weren't going to be snobs. From their origins, that would have been a bit rich. But no one denied they were élitist. As Caine now remembers: 'The one thing the group would never do is speak to a bad actor. If they talked to you, then you knew you had to be a good actor. You would speak to someone who wasn't an actor before you'd speak to a bad one. We would always encourage each other because we seriously believed we would all make it big in time.'

But that didn't mean other people showed a similar regard. There was the indignity of at least one producer telling Michael to get out while he still had the chance and go into some more worthy profession. Anyone knowing the bolshie Michael Caine of the very early 60s would have realised that that was all he needed to make him keep going and try even harder. When his closest friends became stars he had either to sit back and cry or try to get in on the act himself.

In truth, opportunities did start to come now and he was getting close – almost. An exciting film that should have done much, much better than it actually did was being readied for production. *The Day The Earth Caught Fire,* starring Edward Judd and Leo McKern, had all the right ingredients – but didn't get a big enough audience. It was essentially a newspaper story. Arthur Christiansen, until a few months before the legendary editor of the *Daily Express,* then the finest newspaper in Fleet Street, played himself in a story about a nuclear explosion that had so upset the earth's tilt that it was moving inexorably towards the sun. The premise was that the world was about to fry.

The movie was beautifully made. Even the policeman, who directs Judd and his girlfriend (Janet Munro) away from the mass exodus of traffic, looked good. But then he was Michael Caine. His one line, however, wasn't enough to send casting agents knocking on his door. Indeed, it was only sufficient to have Val Guest, the director, warn him that he would never work in the cinema again.

So much for his abilities as a traffic cop. Wolf Mankowitz, who wrote the story, wondered about him, though. 'I didn't have any say in anything once the film was being shot,' he told me. 'But somehow I did notice Michael. Much more than I usually took note of bit players. Maybe Val Guest was right and he was terrible. Perhaps that was the reason. On the other hand, occasionally, very occasionally, you see a small-part player trying to get out of his strait-jacket. It would be nice to think I saw that then.' It is a fair comment but afterthoughts are always easy.

No, the casting agents hadn't started queuing for him yet. But he *was* now getting work.

There were small parts in bigger television plays like *Requiem for a Heavyweight,* which starred . . . Sean Connery. He also went on stage, performing in Liverpool in *One More River.* The company was run by

Sam Wannamaker, one of the greatest names of the theatre in the 50s and 60s and not praised enough for his own acting abilities. Just before his death he was best known for his single-handed efforts to have the Globe Theatre in London rebuilt. But before that he had been an imposing Hollywood presence, a star whose career was cut short by the McCarthy investigations.

He liked Michael Caine. 'If at that moment I could have had the power to make him an international star, I'd have done so,' he would tell me years later.

Back in London, there was more television. Caine was in the *No Hiding Place* series and then in the Edgar Wallace play, *The Frog*.

Then came the chance of a starring role in a new play. Willis Hall had written *The Long And The Short And The Tall* about the jungle war with the Japanese, with Robert Shaw and Terence Stamp in the all-male cast. Another actor was David Barron, who very soon afterwards decided he would fare better as a writer – if he changed his name back to its original, Harold Pinter.

It was to be Michael's big break – except that his stardom depended on the rude health of Peter O'Toole. He was his old friend's understudy. Michael Caine was all dressed up and ready to go on stage every night, but never did. The understudy never got a chance, while O'Toole got some of the greatest reviews of his life. They were so good that he was immediately snapped up for the *Lawrence of Arabia* role. It was all very frustrating. 'I had nothing to do,' he would say. So he'd go to the Salisbury and arrange parties, thanks to the out-of-work actors who thronged the place. 'A real load of bums they were. I'd pick up news there where the parties were going to be. If there weren't any, we'd have one in the dressing room after the show and I was in charge of getting the booze. I was always one of the smoothies. I was a lover, not a fighter. I used to be in the corner with a small drink, eyeing the room like a cobra while the others were quaffing it down.' And they called him 'Cobra Eyes'.

Meanwhile Michael Caine was being considered for other understudy jobs. But, no, once this play finished, he wasn't going to take any more work like that. Instead, he stuck with *The Long and the Short And The Tall* until O'Toole took his little ride in the desert. And finally he did play the lead role on stage – in the national tour that followed the London production. June Wyndham Davies saw it. 'I thought he was wonderful,' she told me with the pride of a schoolteacher at the success of a favourite pupil.

He earned £16 a week. 'But,' as he said, 'that's a lot of money when you're broke.'

And he was taking to heart some advice from Peter O'Toole: 'Don't play small parts in highly exposed places, because that'll make you a small-part actor. Play leading parts anywhere – in rubbish – but play leading parts.'

If this wasn't exactly show business greatness, it was a great time for his love life. There were always luscious young women who wanted to go to bed with stars – and if Michael Caine was only a star in certain provincial towns, he made a change from other theatrical gentlemen of the time. He was heterosexual in a business where the top touring show *The Dancing Years* was usually known as *The Dancing Queers*. That was show business talk. But, as he explains in his memoirs, the chance for any of the actresses around to go to bed with a man who not only looked like a man but also behaved like a man was too exciting for most of them to resist. For once, Michael Caine was happy. Would he be a star? Nobody else would have said so. But he would. His sense of ambition wouldn't allow anything else to happen to him.

Not that there were any indications of the future. He came off tour broke – and so impecunious that when he was arrested for non-payment of maintenance to Patricia, there was nothing to be done about it. He couldn't pay. He went to court, kicked his heels in a cell but was instantly recognised by one of the police warders – as someone who had helped to improve the image of the constabulary in *Dixon of Dock Green*, every copper's favourite soap. He made sure that Michael was well fed before he appeared in front of the magistrate – a man who took pity on him and ordered him to pay his ex-wife £3 10s a week, the precise sum he had in his pocket at the time. Pat appeared in court herself. It was the last time he saw her. She died of cancer 15 years later.

Meanwhile, at the very time he was trying to scrape together that £3 10s a week, Peter O'Toole was starring in *Lawrence of Arabia*, Albert Finney was going into *Tom Jones* and Terence Stamp was in *Term of Trial* with Laurence Olivier and Sarah Miles.

There was one part that might have made a difference, but he didn't get it. In fact, until a year or so ago, he didn't even know he had been in line for the role. And until now, the story has never been told.

The eminent actor Joss Ackland said it happened in about 1961 when he was working as artistic director of Bernard Miles's ground-breaking theatre on the Thames, the Mermaid. 'I found a play on the shelf written by Bill Naughton, who was a friend of Miles,' he told me. 'It was my job to choose plays, as well as both act and direct. We decided to do the play and there were three actors being considered. One was John Neville, the second was Bernard Cribbens. The third was Michael Caine.

'The play was called *Alfie.*'

But Michael didn't get the part. 'We had a conflab,' Ackland told me. 'And we thought that he wasn't experienced enough. I think that the people who were against him might have been right. He *wasn't* experienced for that sort of role, which needed a lot of technique.'

Bernard Cribbens wouldn't consider the part when the notion was put to him – because he didn't like the way an abortion was treated in *Alfie.* So John Neville got it. What might have happened to the Michael Caine career had he known he was being considered – let alone had he been selected for the role – remains one of those wonderful 'what if...' questions.

Michael would certainly have been offended by suggestions of his lack of experience. Eighty amateur roles as well as those years in rep, the lead in *The Long and The Short And The Tall,* the TV plays?

And then there was *The Dumb Waiter,* a Harold Pinter play at the Royal Court, about which he claims he 'hadn't the faintest idea what it was all about'. Then there was a play directed by Lionel Bart, *Why The Chicken?* Bart and he got on well. Or at least Caine thought they did. 'I never really understood Michael Caine,' Bart said to me just a few weeks before he died. 'I never really knew what he was after – was it just fame and money or was it artistic success? One day he said one thing, the next day it was something else.'

Caine would, of course, take exception to that. But then they saw their relationship in different ways. Yet the time came when Bart could almost, with some justification, have claimed responsibility for Michael's subsequent success. Had Caine passed a certain audition in which Lionel had some say, he would have escaped the doldrums of the very early 60s. But then, he would never have been a great star.

Michael auditioned for the part of Bill Sikes in *Oliver!* – and didn't get it. He likes to say how a few years later he would drive in his Rolls Royce past the New Theatre and see that the show was still running – with the same actor who passed the audition he himself failed, still in the Sikes role. Had Michael Caine got the part, there might never have been any reason to write this book.

But he didn't know that the day he failed the audition. It was a miserable time. 'To be 30 years old and absolutely nothing was terrifying,' he said.

There had now been 150 television plays. But they didn't mean much. It was all too ephemeral. '[There's] nothing to show for it. When the credits came on, the viewers would be out in the kitchen brewing up tea. Everybody knew my face, but I was still "Michael Who?" to most people.' He thought he had been doing it all wrong. It dawned on him that Peter O'Toole was being proved right all the time. 'Small parts get you other small parts and I decided to get selective.'

One play for which he *was* selective, was *The Compartment*, by Johnny Speight, later to be best known as the writer of the extraordinarily long-running television series, *Till Death Us Do Part*. Speight told me: 'Michael was the best actor for the part because he was the only real Cockney who wanted to be a Cockney on the screen, who wanted to represent Cockneys the way I did. His part wasn't of a normal person, but the way Michael played it you could understand his frustrations. I couldn't have played it better myself.'

The play lasted 45 minutes and for most of those 45 minutes Michael Caine was talking – to another character in a railway train, played by the eminent actor Frank Finlay who said very little. Finlay was supposed to be a well-spoken city type; Caine was the Cockney, trying to engage his fellow traveller in conversation and becoming so frustrated at the lack of communication that in the end he tried to kill him.

It made as big an impact as anything Michael had yet done. Roger Moore recalls seeing Caine walking down Piccadilly at the time that he was starring in *The Saint* TV series. He introduced himself, confirmed that it was indeed Caine who had been in *The Compartment*, told him how good he thought he had been and 'the very first words that this articulate, intelligent and sensitive Cockney said were: "Fuck me! Really!" '

His days in the backwater were over. There were to be half a dozen more major roles in TV plays. He wasn't a star, but he wasn't starving either. When producers heard his name, they were interested.

So were others in the business. Later in 1963, he looked as if he might be joining his friends in the big time – at least in London and at least in the West End. He had the lead role in a play called *Next Time I'll Sing To You*, by James Saunders. It made an impact not so much at the box office, but in the profession. Michael Winner, the film director and producer who came to appreciate Caine for his restaurants as well as for his performances, told me: 'That was when I first met Michael.

It was an absolute breath of fresh air. Here was this man behaving very naturalistically on the stage – but not in a posh accent. 'He was a total unknown. I went with an actor friend and after the show we went to a pub. I'll never forget this time in the pub. As a result of that evening, he became one of my closest friends.'

He says he told him: 'Michael, you have this immense charm and charisma and there is no question that one day you will be a star.'

'Well,' said Michael Caine, and according to Winner, 'he started moaning and groaning.' 'I'll never be a star,' he told the director. 'I'm too old. It's too late. My friend Terry Stamp became a star. There's no chance I will.'

Says Winner now: 'I'm so glad he was absolutely wrong.'

The critics would have told him the same thing – and did. Harold Hobson said that he played his Cockney part in what he called a 'surrealist extravaganza' 'with engaging nonchalance'.

But there could have been a reason for that 'nonchalance'. June Wyndham Davies told me that she bumped into him in the West End on the day of the opening night. 'He put his arms around me and said, "I don't understand a word of it. Not a word." ' As we've seen, he had said that before.

Once the reviews came in, he saw it as his chance to think about revenge. The reinvented Caine was reinventing himself again. 'That's how I came to mean whatever I do mean to anybody. That was based on a great deal of hard work, sacrifice, perseverance, some God-given talent and a lot of luck.'

The luck was beginning to go his way. He had a decent apartment, although he went back to the Elephant for his mother's Sunday dinners. And he was going all out to get that good luck that he believed he was due. 'I never gave up. But after years of rejection, something happens to you inside. If you get your success, you say, "All right, you rejected me that time. Now you're going to pay." '

The indication that people would pay – at the box office – came with an offer of a new and very big movie part. In a film called *Zulu*.

Ten

Zulu

How did his luck change? History, literature and folklore are replete with stories of people who go from the proverbial rags to riches. But this was much more remarkable: you didn't have to believe Michael Caine's own story about his origins to agree that everything that could go wrong *had* gone wrong and things had seemed as if they would never get better.

After all, in many walks of life, 30 is young, very young indeed. But when you have spent half your life trying to make some sort of future for yourself in your chosen career and haven't yet made it, it is very old indeed. Hoping for success after 30 is rather like being a runner who is constantly at the back of the race but still thinks, at 30, that he could be a champion. Professional footballers aged 30 are placed on the free transfer list.

Yet here was Michael Caine, finally recognised for his work in a stage play and offered a part in a movie, not quite the lead role but a very notable one. As for the film, it was BIG, not one of the great spectaculars, but big enough – wide screen, colour, made on location in South Africa and Michael Caine had a canvas chair with his name on the back.

That it happened at all could be included in a course called 'How To Succeed By Trying Very Hard Indeed'. There's never been a better example of sheer determination finally overcoming everything that stood in the way. What happened now proved something else: talent alone is not enough; you need the right vehicle to demonstrate it effectively. *Zulu* was right for him and for the age. It was a picture that enabled him to make an impact for the first time, but still without all the responsibilities of stardom.

It came about because once again he met Stanley Baker, who might well have thought Michael not really worth noting after their experience together in *A Hill In Korea*. Except that he had been one of the gang who used to meet in the Arts Club.

Baker, who in 1963 was about the biggest tough-guy actor in British movies – his nasty snarling expression made a whole generation of young women love to hate him, came to see the comic Cockney who was Caine in *Next Time I'll Sing To You*. He went round to the dressing room after the play, a time-honoured professional courtesy one actor likes to extend to another. When it comes from a serious star to a performer who hasn't quite made it to the same extent it can be taken in one of two ways – either as a flattering tribute or as a patronising gesture. Michael decided to accept the first explanation.

He was glad he did – because Baker told him he was going into production. He was now about to make his debut as a producer with a film about the Zulu wars at the end of the nineteenth century – the time when the noble savages, as they were so dreadfully described by people who thought they were being nice, were pitched against the great British empire's finest in their red coats and white pith helmets in the 1879 Battle of Rorke's Drift.

There was a part for a Cockney in the movie, said Baker, who was Welsh. Since Michael Caine was a Cockney he might do well in it. What did Caine think about that? Well, what would an amateur footballer think when he was invited to play for England? That's how big it seemed.

Right, said Baker. He was to go to the Prince of Wales theatre bar the following day and meet Mr Cy Endfield. Mr Endfield was an American director who didn't know very much about the Zulu wars and knew even less about Cockneys.

When he met Michael the next day, it wasn't exactly what he had been expecting. 'Sorry,' Endfield said almost before he had asked what the actor would like to drink. 'Can I be very personal? I don't think you're very good as a Cockney.'

That was astonishing to a man who had spent most of his life doing two things: hoping that people regarded him as an actor, and defending the status of Cockneys as though he were leader of their trade union.

'Well,' said Endfield, 'for a start you don't look like one.' And then, pouring a generous amount of salt into a bleeding wound, 'I'm an American,' [Michael knew that], 'and my idea of a Cockney is a little, down-trodden, working-class man.'

If Michael Caine had been a bull in the ring, he would have seen this as a scarlet cape. As it was, it was his face that was turning scarlet.

'Look,' he responded, knowing that it wasn't just his appearance that was being maligned but his whole being, 'I'm down-trodden and I'm still working-class. And anyway, I'm earning less money now than I have for a long time.'

There was more behind Endfield's decision. He had already seen another Cockney actor called James Booth – and he seemed to be much more Cockney than Caine was. It didn't have anything to do with the fact that Cockneys had to have been born within the sound of Bow Bells, more that the rugged Booth features seemed to fit in with his ideas of what an East End barrow-boy or a schlepper of fish boxes was really like.

Michael walked away, looking as dejected as he felt. He wasn't out of the bar when Endfield called him back. He had an idea; could this Cockney who spoke like a Cockney but didn't look like a Cockney talk with any other accent? Of course, said the actor who had spent so many hours sitting in cinema seats and had then practised all those voices he had heard near the sewers at the Elephant. What was all that training for?

Endfield had an idea that Michael would be OK as an officer. Which showed how little he knew about the class war in Britain, a conflict which at times was as furious as anything between the Zulus and Queen Victoria's heroes. He thought the actor looked 'aristocratic'. If that seemed like a compliment after everything else, there was another verbal jug of cold water to be thrown. Americans didn't have the same definition of aristocrats as did the British – any more than they thought the same about Cockneys. 'You've got a long face,' he told him, 'like a horse.' In later years, Michael Caine would have slammed the door on anyone who had the audacity to speak like that to him. But this was then.

They set up an appointment. Michael Caine would have a screen test the following Friday, playing opposite Stanley Baker. He would have to imagine himself as Gonville Bromhead, a junior British officer who looked and sounded like his name.

The screen test happened as planned – although the Caine performance was not exactly the way he himself had planned it. He was dreadful. As dreadful as Mr Endfield told him he thought he was – perhaps the worst test he had ever carried out. Michael was not surprised. But he was surprised at Endfield's decision. Yes, he said, he could have the part just the same. There was something there. He would have, as Michael later called it, 'the toffee-nosed part.' You didn't change your vocabulary just because you had been given your first big movie part.

The 'something' was what got Michael Caine his first serious reviews, the oh-so-blond, so-upper-class officer who constantly battled with Stanley Baker, the other officer in the plot who quite plainly hadn't had all Caine's advantages in life.

Caine enjoyed being in South Africa, although he couldn't tolerate the racist behaviour of some of the Afrikaaner members of the crew. For their part, the police didn't exactly take to the idea of one of the other members of the party creating a harem of Zulu women in his own little mud hut. The police took it seriously and the man was prosecuted under the apartheid regulations against mixed sexual relations.

The only trouble that Michael himself experienced was that he was expected to ride a horse, not something so far listed in his CV. Nor was falling off, which he did with such consummate ease that the company worried not so much about the damage it was doing to the Caine spine as about the effect it might have on their insurance policies.

The real problem came when the horse saw its own shadow for the first time, rose some 10 feet in the air and threw its rider hard on to the veldt.

It convinced him that there was no point in playing the hero for real. 'The first lesson I learnt in movies is, "Don't try anything dangerous."' He was lying on the ground, wondering whether he would ever get up, when he heard on the radio intercom nearby that it wasn't his own condition that really worried the director. What he picked up was: 'I think Mr Caine's hurt. Leave him. But get the cloak, get the hat and get on the horse.' A member of the crew who turned out to be a more experienced rider than the actor, took that as his cue to double for him. As Michael said, he never did anything dangerous in a film after that.

Had Michael Caine managed to carry off the riding as successfully as the acting, it would have been a considerable achievement. As it was, he had to content himself with giving a very determined performance as the foppish lieutenant who ends up winning the VC, the military equivalent of surviving in the theatre for as long as Michael Caine had done.

It was, however, what Caine did with the part that singled it out – and, indeed, allowed him to make an impact at last. As he would explain: 'The part was written as a complete ass. It could have been played with protruding teeth for comedy.' That was the way that Stanley Baker had told him to play the part.

But he had other ideas. 'I said, "You are in conflict with this man and you beat him. Wouldn't it look better for you, wouldn't it make you look stronger, if you had beaten a strong man, rather than that you beat a fop. If I come on as a weak, useless fop at the beginning of a picture, where's the conflict? They know you're going to win because you look and are so tough." ' He got his way. What is more, he called Stanley Baker 'Old boy'. Maybe that was what did it.

'I played it straight down the line as a man who was weak but at least *thought* he was strong and never went with the weakness. People were amazed that I took that attitude from around where I come from.'

If he could give that impression – accent and blond eyebrows notwithstanding – he must have had something. It all seemed to show in what *Time* magazine described as 'an African Western'.

There were a number of distinguishing features, little points that Caine himself added to Endfield's direction, ideas that no one else had thought of. They were his own ideas of what an aristocrat would do, but he spent time studying other aristos to try to find the authentic touch which he regarded as so important.

For two weeks, he was in the officers' mess at a series of Guards' barracks, officially researching background material. But watching the officers fire pistols and get on and off their horses wasn't his primary purpose. He was studying their accents. More than that, their 'movements, the way they treated each other, the timing of things.'

It wasn't, he reckoned, that different in Victoria's time.

He watched the Duke of Edinburgh in particular, and how he walked – years before Prince Charles walked that way too – with his hands behind his back. Later Caine would say: 'I walked the whole time like that. No one found out because they knew unconsciously who I was, because Prince Philip is so familiar. They'd seen him on the television news.' But there was something else that would be repeated a dozen or so times in later movies: 'I also realised that privileged people like him speak very slowly because they don't have to get your attention. You're already hanging on their words. They're not like some little Cockney salesman who's afraid you're going to shut the door in his face.'

It was the latest result of the people-watching he had found himself doing in Paris and everywhere else where there were people to watch.

But would anyone know anything about it? Any publicity for the picture, while it was in production, centred on the co-stars, Stanley Baker himself, Jack Hawkins and the amazing Cockney, James Booth.

But Caine thought he had done a good job. He had made a subsidiary part into a very important one. From the sort of feedback he was getting from both the director and the producer, he had done as well as he himself thought he had. Other things were on the up. His love life was blossoming. He is extraordinarily chivalrous about the women in his life. He has kissed plenty, but would never tell. Except that – and his friends noticed it – he would change girls the way he changed his clothes. There would be one for formal occasions, another for the more casual event, a third whom he thought suitable for intellectual evenings.

What he said was that he didn't believe in lasting relationships – until the time that he eventually got married again. Women would then think, 'I've got him' and 'start taking liberties'. He didn't want a woman to order him around.

There were other things that he *would* tell about, talking about some aspects of his life in a way that has always made him a gift to any interviewer. Like the story of his meetings with the real boss of the operation that made *Zulu*. This was Joseph Levine, who came to certain conclusions as a result of the Caine performance.

The film had shown Caine's talent as an actor. Mr Levine, for one, thought so. After all, how could he do otherwise? Even if he hadn't personally liked Michael Caine as the snooty hero, there was no arguing with the reports he was getting from the producer and the director. They told him all that they had told Michael himself – he was great. Except, except. Levine picked on something no one else had mentioned – Michael looked 'queer', a distinctly politically incorrect term now, but not back then in the swinging 60s. There was a letter from Hollywood that asked quite simply: 'Who was the limey fag in *Zulu?*'

Now, of all the things you could say about the 31-year-old Michael Caine, cocky, at times aggressive, with undeniable chips on his shoulder, 'queer' was not one of them. Mr Levine, a rotund gentleman who could have achieved his position as a latter day mogul as much by virtue of central casting as by his own talents, puffed his cigar and said that he knew perfectly well that Michael Caine was not a homosexual. The problem was that he looked like one – just as any number of homosexual men in Hollywood looked totally macho. So there it was.

Yes, he was a brilliant find. But no, Mr Levine did not want to give him a seven-year contract of the kind that Hollywood actors had for years been either complaining or dreaming of (depending on whether they were successful or not; the successful ones called it slavery; the failures were glad of the money they wouldn't otherwise get). Sorry, he said, he wouldn't even let him have a *five*-year agreement.

So Michael Caine was free. But to do what? For about a year, between his handing back his red uniform and the film's premiere, not much.

He was convinced that his day had finally come. Except that nothing really happened. Not in movies, anyway. He did have a notable TV part, playing Horatio in a small-screen version of *Hamlet* called *Hamlet In Elsinore*. Hamlet himself was played by Christopher Plummer and Robert Shaw was the king – all on location in Denmark. 'It was the finest Horatio I've ever seen,' said his new agent Dennis Selinger, the top show business representative in Britain who had spent most of his formative years working for Lew Grade and seeking out new trapeze artists for variety theatres. But it *was* good. Very good indeed.

Caine himself was sure he would never go on to a live stage again. The TV play – the only classical role in his career – was an interlude. He was now convinced that his future lay only in the movies. But there were no more offers.

He went to see *Alfie* starring John Neville, an actor who had made a considerable impact on stage and had played big parts on the screen without becoming a star. In the play he was sensational. When Michael heard that Neville was leaving the cast, he decided to audition for the role. He didn't get it. For the second time he was being turned down for the same part.

The stage producers just didn't think he was suitable and who could argue with them? Just imagine the foppish lieutenant now playing a Cockney by the name of *Alfie*? It just stretched the imagination too far. No, the play *Alfie*, so obviously associated with John Neville, was certainly not for Michael Caine. So Michael Medwin got the role.

But something was stirring. Word about his *Zulu* performance was getting around. Even before the opening, when the very first press previews were held, there was an indication that something big was afoot. Paramount, who distributed the picture, got a series of requests for interviews with the blond young man who played the lieutenant. 'What was his name? OK, him?'

It got better when the film opened. The tickets for the premiere were sent and with them all the fawning treatment for Michael that

Michael Caine, young star sometime in 1956 when he appeared in his first movie – *A Hill in Korea*. Overnight success took six years when in 1963 he made *Zulu*.

Money bought Caine a great deal – including a decent home for his mother. But Ellen Micklewhite never changed and, until he married, always expected Michael for Sunday lunch – here with younger brother Stanley, photographed on 3rd February 1964 following the release of *Zulu* the year before.

Harry Palmer's debut in *The Ipcress File*. In 1965 Caine was the first serious actor to wear glasses which, with the Cockney accent, set Palmer way apart from James Bond.

Alfie (1966) was the movie that did it for Michael Caine. Pulling in the birds as well as the customers – even 'the more mature' ones like Shelley Winters.

Caine in 1966, the year he made *Alfie*. Now, he contemplates his future – perhaps wondering if *The Wrong Box*, that same year, will be the wrong film for him.

Harry Palmer's second outing – Caine with Karl Malden in *Billion Dollar Brain* released in 1967.

'Michael Caine is a darling to work with, swift, efficient and with a comfortable sense of humour. It's incredible to think, listening to his light charming speaking voice that he started life as a Cockney barrow-boy in Whitechapel.' Noel Coward Diaries September 1st 1968, filming *The Italian Job*.

The status of a celebrity. It meant that other celebrities courted him – in this case Diana Ross, who with the Supremes, was given a party by the Duke of Bedford, the stars' favourite aristocrat in 1968.

On the set of *Battle of Britain* (1969) with Bianca de Macias who later became Bianca Jagger.

Too Late the Hero 1970.

Opposite above: In James Clavell's *The Last Valley* (1971), a film that deserved to be better remembered.

Opposite below: Florinda Bolkan and Omar Shariff with Caine at the party for the release of *The Last Valley*

From the start there was Caine the ladykiller and Caine the man with the gun (here as Jack Carter in Mike Hodges 1971 film *Get Carter*). *Get Carter* is now regarded as a classic of British cinema. Roy Budd's music and Mike Hodges' pungent screenplay, adapted from Ted Lewis's novel *Jack's Return Home*, allowed Caine to create a gangster with 'rare artistry and restraint'.

Paramount considered due to a star. He would, of course, bring guests. Yes, of course, a Rolls Royce would be provided for them all.

There was a beautiful girl ready to hang on his arm – although he says in his autobiography that he doesn't remember who she was – but the real woman in his life was his mother. She would have a place of honour. Ellen, however, decided otherwise. It would be too much of a strain for her. What she really thought was that she might embarrass him.

He says he got angry with her. He owed so much to the woman who had sacrificed almost everything for the sake of her sons. She was adamant that she wouldn't come and he was equally adamant that he was terribly upset. Never more so than when he saw her standing in the crowd as he walked along the red carpet. Despite all her protestations, she had come after all – by bus. And she was with all the other people who had taken buses to see the famous in Leicester Square.

Michael couldn't drag her out of the crowd, but he found her in time to take her to the after-movie party. 'She met all the Beatles, Barbra Streisand and all the Rolling Stones. She loved it.' But she wouldn't discuss why she had refused to go to the film as her son's guest yet went just the same in a way that Michael thought demeaned her. Every time he mentioned the fact to her, she changed the subject – usually to say, 'Have another cup of tea.' He was furious. But the critics were not. They had made a discovery.

As he said: 'Nobody had noticed me when we were making the film. Then the picture played. All hell broke loose.'

Leslie Halliwell, compiler of the famous *Film Guide*, singles out Caine's as the only notable performance in the movie. Frank Morris wrote in the *Toronto Globe* that he was convinced Michael Caine would have a 'brilliant film future'.

Fellow actors agreed. Joss Ackland still wasn't sure he had made a mistake in not offering him the *Alfie* part in the first place, but he was more than just impressed by the *Zulu* performance. 'The interesting thing for me about *Zulu* was how he zoomed in that part,' Joss told me. 'It was really totally false. You know, he wasn't playing himself. It wasn't a great part. But the star personality just zoomed ahead. It was his charisma.'

John Mills was at the premiere. 'At the party, Mary and I spotted him,' he remembered for me. 'I told him, "You know. I have to say that was a really lovely performance, thoroughly enjoyed it. It was absolutely spot on."'

These were the cultured tones of an actor who had played quite a number of officers and gentlemen in uniform in his time. 'Fanks,' said Caine in response. Sir John says he was overwhelmed by that. 'Dead Cockney. I couldn't believe it. I had never known anyone, who was a real Cockney, being able to play an upper-class accent.'

Caine had never had reactions like this before. Nobody had previously said that it was Michael Caine who had stolen a movie – other things perhaps in his early childhood, but never a movie – and it came at a time when he needed it and appreciated it most. After 200-odd television appearances by an actor people noticed but no one remembered, this was the end of the Anonymous Caine. More significantly, it closed the doors on what he himself had always regarded as the Dark Ages in his life.

Eleven

The Ipcress File

The puns came a-running. Writers spoke of the 'Caine Mutiny' against the way his career had previously been handled. The anger he still felt about his early life was, of course, the 'Mark of Caine'. On the other hand, they all had to accept that this Caine was 'able'.

And now things did start to happen. His performance in *Zulu* had been recognised in the way he wanted most – with offers of serious work. Producers began to notice the tall young man in horn-rimmed glasses who favoured suede coats.

The most serious offer came from Harry Saltzman, producer of the *Bond* films, whom he met at the Pickwick Club, a symbolic place, an institution haunted by those in show business who could afford to be there. It was one of the signs that he had now arrived. Saltzman sent over a bottle of champagne, with a word of congratulations for his performance in the African epic.

No one imagined then that the Bond idiom would still be around almost 40 years later, but it was already a phenomenal success. The only question was how long it would be before there would be a Bond counter-culture. Perhaps Saltzman had thought that one out – and decided that, rather than give anyone else the chance, he would run with it himself. That was how he came up with *The Ipcress File*. It was also how he came up with the idea of Michael Caine for the lead.

That it happened owed not a little to Dennis Selinger, now enjoying every minute as Michael Caine's agent. He told me just a few days before his death: 'Agents have to know what's going on and I knew that Saltzman was looking for someone for his new spy thriller. I desperately wanted to get Michael to play the part.'

Agents are also men of influence. When they can influence a top producer like Saltzman they have a very special part to play, one that can get results. So when he told Saltzman that he wanted to show a film for him, the producer was not going to say no. What he had on hand was *Zulu*, which was as far away from the *Ipcress* idea as South Africa was from Whitehall. 'But Harry saw the movie and was as impressed as I hoped he would be. That's how it happened.'

It turned out to be an inspired idea. But turning Caine into a superstar was not on the agenda. Yet there were distinct possibilities and promises. Saltzman invited him to lunch to prove it – at one of London's swankiest eateries, Les Ambassadeurs, where, Caine wrote in his autobiography, the only person who he had never heard of was himself. 'It was,' he said a couple of years later, 'the first time I'd been in a place as posh as that'. Saltzman asked him if he had ever read *The Ipcress File*. Stranger things have probably happened, but the coincidence that it was the book he currently had on his bedside table didn't do him any harm. It might well have been an omen.

'Like it?' Saltzman asked him. 'Yes,' he replied. 'Would you like to play the lead?' 'Yes,' Caine answered, no doubt without taking the time to relish the big change that the offer represented.

The Ipcress File was a spy story that was no more like James Bond than the Elephant and Castle resembled Park Lane. Bond, in his dinner jacket, frequented Mayfair residences and restaurants the way office workers queued up at a sandwich bar. The main character in *Ipcress* – he hadn't yet been given a name – lived in an apartment that even Michael's mother wouldn't have thought very nice. What was more, he cooked for himself. That last fact would have a certain significance later.

Mrs Micklewhite was having to change her attitude to life. Michael saw to that. 'She used to tell me proudly how she had sat next to a real fine lady. It would make me bloody furious and I'd ask her how she knew it was a fine lady. "Because the lady had a gold watch and a diamond ring."' That was perhaps strange coming from a woman who had taken her boys around the big house in Norfolk. Now, as the mother of a new kind of actor playing a new kind of spy, she was herself on the threshold of entirely novel experiences.

The thing that this spy had in common with Bond was that he was difficult and iconoclastic. He may have been apparently fighting against the Bolsheviks (as they were no longer called, but everyone knew who they were) in the movie, but he was totally 'bolshie' himself. He was difficult to work with, the kind who went his own way, and not at all the sort of chap his bowler-hatted bosses in Whitehall liked being with.

The film opens with a scientist disappearing and in the course of the action the spy is drugged and imprisoned on what looks suspiciously like the Eastern side of the Iron Curtain, although it turns out to be a lot closer to home – a home where he thinks he has met a beautiful girl with romantic intentions who actually has other things on her mind. But – and here is the difference – she is the one for whom he cooks. It is only an omelette but on film you can't make an omelette without breaking traditions. That had never happened in a movie before – a man who, despite what Joe Levine might have thought, was distinctly masculine, cracking eggs for a woman. He handled the whole operation with great dexterity, and he had no need to worry about people's assumptions as to his sexual proclivities. Certainly, the young woman, played by Sue Lloyd, didn't, which made the whole thing all right.

It was all his own idea. 'I invited a woman round to my home and cooked for her.' Yes, he was advised that people would think he was gay (or, rather, queer; gay at the time still meant happy). 'But I said, "If I am, what the hell am I doing with a girl? If I was cooking for a guy you could say I was gay, not cooking for a girl".'

So the world saw him not just make her an omelette – 'it's as easy to cook for two as for one' – but also wearing spectacles. When he kisses the girl, the glasses come off – and *Eine Kleine Nachtmusik* plays in the background.

But before anyone actually gets carried away contemplating that love-in-a-kitchen moment, the time has now come to reveal a little film history. He *wasn't* the one who cracked the eggs. While filming was in progress, the cameraman noticed he had fair hairs on his hands – which didn't look right. So the hands used in the omelette-making scene were those of the man who had dreamed up the whole thing – Len Deighton, a class cook in his own right. Nobody has so far complained about the subterfuge.

The picture was directed by Sidney Furie, a bright, up-and-coming Canadian-born director who was beginning to make a name for himself in Hollywood, where he would later direct – among others – Frank Sinatra. He found Michael Caine a lot easier to handle. Even Harry Palmer, the name they finally decided to give him as the British agent, couldn't be more difficult than Sinatra. Which is another piece of important movie information: the name Harry Palmer, now almost as famous as that of James Bond, was only dreamed up while filming was in progress. Len Deighton's book was written in the first person, a first person who saw no need to name himself. 'We had to give him a name,' Caine said at the time. 'You couldn't have a leading character walking all the way through a film with everybody just calling him "you" or "what's his name".'

Michael himself had been through that often enough and knew how it felt. But at first they did try to go down the anonymity route and found it didn't work. The name Palmer would fit him like a newly-made pair of horn-rims – 'the complete disregard for authority,' as he was to put it.

Saltzman gave permission for his own first name to be used by Caine – he made the point, Michael would say, of stressing that, anyway, he was really called Hershel – and he told Michael that he knew he was on his way to great stardom. There would be a seven-year contract to prove it.

The sort of figures he threw out when he had discussed salaries that first day at Les Ambassadeurs made Caine, the man who said he used to save a whole week to have enough to buy a plate of spaghetti Bolognese, take off into some kind of stratospheric never-never land. He had never seen numbers like that written down, let alone offered to him.

It was all wonderful. There was only one worry – and when an offer like that came his way, worry was putting it a bit strongly. He wasn't *worried* about anything – except that he might have been dreaming the whole thing. And the possibility of type-casting if the picture did well enough for a whole swathe of Bond-type sequels to follow. If he became so identified with Harry Palmer, how would any other producer want him for a totally different kind of role?

There was also the problem that Saltzman had him under contract for another ten films, over which he would have little control.

'I don't mind continuing as Harry,' he said, 'with some variations in between. They say Sean is typed as Bond, yet he has now done *The Hill*. Maybe I, too, can start a brand new image when the time comes.'

It may have seemed absurd to hear those concerns from a man in his early thirties who until a few months before was 'resting' more frequently than he was ever in gainful employment. But that's human nature and it can't be changed that easily. So he did have to address the problem and that's how he came to wear his glasses on screen.

He realised that his pal Sean Connery had countered his Bond triumph by growing a moustache for *The Hill* – at the same time as throwing off the wig he wore as 007. What 'disguise' could he himself now use? The answer was no disguise at all; just keep the glasses on. It really was quite a decision. As he says: 'No leading man had worn glasses in a film since Harold Lloyd. But I thought it would just mean I was an ordinary person.'

That was revolutionary in a business in which, as in his childhood memories, 'everybody had broad shoulders and wonderful suntans and wonderful teeth (even if you look at the extras in American films, you see that Arab beggars have $6,000 worth of bridge work.) This was before Dustin Hoffman and before Al Pacino. Before the little guys.'

It was a chance to rectify a situation in which 'nobody represented *me* up there, with all the things that are wrong with me. My acting was supposed to do that and that was my idea – that glasses would cut corners for me.'

His eyes and his heavy eyelids were already creating an image for him. But it was no trick. He couldn't recognise people without wearing those spectacles.

In his memoirs, Michael says it was Harry Saltzman's idea. In a television interview, he claimed the spectacles were his own idea. No matter. He would contradict himself a number of times on other matters over the years. But not on the question of who was actually responsible for his ultimate stardom. It was always untrue, he maintained, that Saltzman had 'made' him. 'Mr Saltzman put a very experienced actor in his movie. And I made that actor, nobody else. No academy, no teacher, no grants from the Government. So now I can sit here and say, "I owe nothing to anybody".'

But he wasn't quite as sure as that at first. He was very glad indeed to have met Harry Saltzman and it *was* clearly a good idea to create a trademark, a logo that, as things turned out, he would use and discard at will. They were thick, heavy specs, the kind that he wore at home and out in the street.

News of the upcoming movie was everywhere. Now people were intrigued by him before they had a chance to see anything on the screen. Even MI5 were interested. It seemed that the part of a British agent was going to get him into trouble with the real-life security boys. That was what he felt when secret agents knocked on the door of his West End flat, the one he was then sharing with Terence Stamp, and asked, ever so politely, about his activities with Russian spies.

The idea was plainly ludicrous. How could Whitehall be so stupid as to take a mere movie so seriously? But was it so stupid? The truth was that he *had* been meeting a Russian agent, but only because he thought the man might give him some tips of the trade, rather as the Guards officers had been helpful to his getting the *Zulu* part right.

What he didn't realise was that the Russian, a certain Comrade Ivanov, was being watched by the police and that the girl who introduced them, via Stamp, was being watched too, when all three were doing no more than drinking tea and talking shop. The girl's name was Christine Keeler. At the time, Michael Caine knew nothing of the Profumo scandal in which Ms Keeler was to be the above-the-title star. The secret servicemen seemed to accept that Mr Caine knew nothing more of real secrets than how to try to dodge Chinese fireworks in Korea and they left him alone to make believe he was an agent in *The Ipcress File*. They probably didn't think he could make an omelette either.

Roger Moore, who would play Bond after Sean Connery, has always said that Michael did the job well. He was much more real than James ever could be. 'How could you ever get a real spy whom everyone knew, one [about whom] everybody says: "Here comes 007 – vodka martini, shaken and not stirred".'

The fascinating thing is that people were equally shaken and stirred by Harry Palmer, although Michael Caine himself was the first to acknowledge how different they were.

'I think that James Bond, as he was written by Ian Fleming, would never have mixed with or come into contact with anybody like Harry Palmer. If they had, Palmer would have regarded Bond as a bit of a toffee-nosed twit. At least, that's the way I see it. Rather like a Cockney tearaway, who hasn't had any boxing training, coming up against the heavyweight champion from Cambridge. He would think of him as a bit of a twit, but, at the same time, he'd have been a bit worried. I think as Sean Connery played him he's a much bigger, tougher man than Fleming originally conceived. I've always imagined Bond played by a 35-year-old or 40-year-old Rex Harrison.'

Eventually, when the film came out, the inevitable comparisons were made with James Bond. It was up to Michael to defend himself and the role he had taken for his own. 'They [Bond] certainly started the thriller trend,' he would say, 'but I think our debt ends there. We're not cashing in on what made them successes: sadism and sex. To me, the two series are like steak and chops: they're both meat.' And both he and Sean Connery would now be able to afford to eat the very finest cuts.

Ipcress made a huge impression on the British public at the time, even more than Caine or anyone else connected with the picture could have imagined. It entered the folklore. It gave birth to spinoffs. There was even a Jewish West End stage parody that sold out week after week. Alf Fogel, who wrote the show, called it *The Teitelbaum File*. There were doubtless hundreds of Grocers old boys who enjoyed it and probably Michael would have done so had he seen it.

That Harry Palmer did seem real had a lot to do with Caine himself, taking advantage of what he called his 'psychologically shy' personality to work harder than ever to show that he could play an outlandish personality who was nevertheless himself.

Actually, the Cockney accent only sounded that way to the Americans. To the blokes down the Elephant, it seemed distinctly posh. It wasn't, but it wasn't his natural voice either. No American could possibly have understood that. It was the age of the regional accent, the kind that the Beatles used to show that there was life north of the London suburbs. So the accent in the film was a kind of compromise.

But the accent and the glasses and even the cooking, didn't make the part. And neither did the story. Nobody was at all pleased with the screenplay they were told they had to use. Sidney Furie told Michael 'What are we going to do? The script is bad, but it's an interesting character, an interesting story.' It was a moment for desperate measures.

The script was torn up – Michael says he actually set fire to it – and Furie rewrote it as the film progressed. He has always acknowledged Caine's help in that. 'Somewhere in our conversation, he came up with the word "ambience" and that was the key word in the picture – ambience; mood.' He did more than create that ambience. He – and most of the rest of the cast (Sue Lloyd, Nigel Green and Gordon Jackson among them) also provided their own dialogue to substitute for the lines that had gone up in flames.

Michael made much of the similarities between Palmer and himself. But he claimed not to like cooking – if that were really true then he made up for it in years to come – and he preferred pop music to the Mozart that was continually on Palmer's record player (actually, that music was itself a compromise; Deighton had made his spy a Bartok enthusiast but Caine said he couldn't bear to listen to that all the time he was on the set).

His mother wouldn't have liked either. The music she was used to was strictly of the 'knees-up' variety, but he wanted her to enjoy the finer things of life too. She was living now in Brixton, in the flat

Michael himself had used years before. He thought she could do better. But for the moment, she wasn't moving. Nor was she giving up charring – for the moment at least. She couldn't be sure yet that her elder son had made the right choice of career. No one had yet seen *Ipcress*, a movie that would earn him $250,000, plus a share of the profits, huge money for anyone in 1966. But what if it didn't last? Her scrubbing brush was his insurance policy, the umbrella should there be a rainy day ahead.

Mrs Micklewhite kept thinking that the film could fall on its face – and so could Michael. Actually, he didn't. *Time* magazine said that Caine was 'the stereotype we needed for the New Model Englishman'.

It was an expression that caught on. A producer trying to entice him into working for him said: 'Michael Caine has ... that lean, languid look ... that fairish, wavy hair, that sort of frontal understatement. Do you remember Leslie Howard? Caine is one of nature's gentlemen – Niven and Rex Harrison ... he is giving us [and here the man quoted *Time*] the stereotype that we needed – the New Model Englishman.'

Back home, *The Times*, still in the age when its critics were anonymous and when it called everyone 'Mister' or 'Miss', wondered: 'Whether this film will do for him what the James Bond films have done for Mr Sean Connery is doubtful: he is too good an actor for that. What he gives here is not bland, generalised star performance, but a real actor's interpretation of a particular man in a particular situation – and he does it superlatively well.'

And Judith Crist wrote in *The New York Herald Tribune* that he made spying seem like a beautifully exciting game.

The June 1965, *Movieland* magazine noted: 'Michael Caine is one of England's brightest new stars. His light is now shining as brilliantly as those of his friends, Peter, Al and Terry.' (O'Toole, Finney and Stamp.)

That was the moment Michael Caine realised he was a successful actor. He had made it. It is fashionable these days for big stars to say they never read reviews or things said about them. In recent years, Michael Caine has done his share of saying that, but he admits that the *Ipcress* reviews were the exception.

He was in a hotel room when the American papers came to him. The first ones he picked up were not any of those above. They weren't good at all, although he does not remember who said what. For, one by one, they got better.

'Once I got past any negative criticism,' he said 'I realised the reviews were better than I could have written myself.' That was always a fairly good yardstick to adopt – particularly if, like Michael Caine, you were almost as good at writing as you were at acting. He was also good at serving as his own publicity officer.

His reaction to those reviews was not to smile, pat himself as close to his back as he could comfortably reach and then cut out the pieces, ready for pasting into a brand-new, leather-bound scrapbook. Instead, he crumpled them all up – and threw them out of the window. 'Then,' he said, 'I burst into tears.'

It was the moment of *anti*-climax if you believed that life had been pretty much a failure until then. He had never truly believed that *Zulu* would be more than another of those occasional, better moments in his life. Instead of climaxing in the most gigantic failure of all, he suddenly found himself a success. It was more than he could take. 'It had been 12 years of extreme hardship. Reading the reviews, I was suddenly aware, that I had a future in films for the first time in my life.'

Again, the profession agreed. Anthony Newley introduced him to his former sister-in-law, Jackie Collins, sitting in the same Pickwick Club where he had had the vital meeting with Saltzman. 'I was so impressed with him,' she told me.

So was the film director, Lewis Gilbert, who managed to see an advance, uncut copy of the movie before release. He had two reasons for his interest, but at first he only talked about one of them. He had been offered *Ipcress* before Sidney Furie and wanted to see what had been made of it. 'Sidney did such a wonderful job with a film that was almost unrecognisable from the one I was offered – and Michael was so good . . . Well, we all make mistakes.'

Furie himself was equally pleased – and not just for the way Michael Caine interpreted his portrait of a spy. 'I'd say he had a sunny approach to sex,' he would say. 'He played it secure.'

The other reason Lewis Gilbert wanted to see the film was that he himself had an idea for Michael Caine. But no one knew that at the time. All Gilbert let on about, he told me, was that he was so impressed with what he had seen. 'Michael was so laid back. He was insouciant. So very different from Bond, which was the opposition at the moment. He was the one who got up and made his own breakfast – much more what a real spy is like.' A spy who was now earning about £2,000 a week, rather different from anything that had come his way before and a lot more than he could have brought home from Billingsgate. If only his Dad could have known that. The thought was rarely far from his mind.

In America, even more than in Britain, people went, as he put it, 'potty' over him. He did the American tour – 'schlepping the film' as his old Grocers' school pals might have put it – and was overwhelmed with offers of more work. He pretended to take it all in his stride. 'I've done nothing to be ashamed of,' he told *Movieland*. 'One day, I might do something I'm proud of.' As he said, the initial conversation with Harry Saltzman had given him 'in two ticks, the security I'd chased for years.'

It also gave him the part that Lewis Gilbert now had in mind. Now no one else was in line for the film he was about to direct, *Alfie*.

Twelve

Alfie

Alfie was a kind of revolution. Not just in the life of Michael Caine, but in that of the whole British film industry. To Caine it proved that he wasn't just a critical success, but that people wanted to line up to see him – and virtually for his own sake. To the film industry in general, it showed that a British movie could escape from what the Americans knew as the art house (and what some British producers called something rather less polite).

Above all, it was the Swinging Sixties on film. *Time* magazine was writing its famous cover story on Swinging London. Carnaby Street was telling the world that London was 'where it's at' as far as fashion was concerned (sexy young women changed in the windows of boutiques like Lady Jane to prove it, and more delicately, Mary Quant on the Kings Road launched the mini skirts, which were great for the men who enjoyed all they revealed, and tights which showed rather less and were distinctly less great). And if you didn't know exactly where it was at, you tried nevertheless to be 'with it' in some way or other.

Michael was benefiting tremendously from this new image. 'Americans used to be so frightened of the rain and the boiled cabbage and the asexual men in bowler hats, but the change has been going on for some time and at last the Americans have discovered it. They've discovered Turner, too. Friends used to come to London and say, "But where are your great English artists?" So I'd take them to the Tate to see the Turners. Now they've suddenly discovered him!'

Alfie was London's revenge on Liverpool – and Michael was the capital's standard bearer. The Beatles were Liverpool, the Mersey Beat. Michael Caine was the scene from the other side of the Thames. And if he wasn't strictly a Cockney, no one really knew that. His accent *was* Cockney and was turning out to be the nearest that Americans had ever got to the real London sound. It mystified them. Surely all Englishmen either spoke like James Bond (never mind that Sean Connery was a Scot) or like John, Paul, George and Ringo. Now they knew different. They also knew that the true Cockney didn't sound at all like Dick Van Dyke in the very recent *Mary Poppins*.

In a perhaps slightly perverse way, Caine was making up for all those cringing, toe-curling years in which he had listened to London voices on stage and screen that he didn't recognise as being from his own corner of the planet. But it was more than just a matter of accents. It was the cheeky Caine personality in which all that anger he had talked about before was given an outlet; it poured out in a performance which, dozens of movies later, still has to rank as among his best. It defined Michael Caine for years afterwards.

The film was a black comedy, all about a young man's conquest of the girls he persisted in calling 'birds' – from the delectable dolly birds like Jane Asher, Shirley Anne Field, Julia Foster and Millicent Martin, who had scored her own recent triumph in the BBC TV satire show *That Was The Week That Was*, to the (and the term is meant in the kindest way) veteran charms of Shelley Winters. He had his way with them all, not least the sad Vivien Merchant, at the time the wife of Harold Pinter, who played a seemingly more level-headed female, but the one who ends up having the abortion.

It's all there, romping, raving, drinking, along with an insight into a TB sanatorium, with Michael all the time commenting to camera on the way of this 60s world – speaking directly to the audience more effectively than anyone had done since Groucho Marx.

Caine is the naughty boy every girl thought she would like to take to bed and, for much of the picture, every mother wanted to forgive. The boys from Grocers would have called him a '*lobbus*', a devil you had to like. As he himself put it: 'He's a Cockney Casanova. Alfie is a kind of innocent sadist who inadvertently hurt others. There are people like that.' He tried to give him some redeeming feature, something that was part of his own character. As Michael had done from his mother, Alfie accepts money from a woman; and at Caine's own suggestion, he later gives it back. He knew a few like that down at the Elephant.

There were, however, problems for the picture in Europe. In Italy, the abortion scene was cut right down, although some of it remained – on the grounds that it was – 'anti-abortion', after all. At the Cannes film festival, it was whistled and booed. But it still won a prize. In France, the film died. Caine's own explanation was that the French 'could not accept that an Englishman could possibly make love to eight women. As far as the French are concerned, we're a nation of homosexuals, so my character to them was entirely false.'

The French critics objected to the abortion scene most of all. And for a long time, there had been doubt about it in Hollywood too. Paramount wanted to cut the abortion scene altogether. Five secretaries given a preview of the scene fainted – and so it was trimmed for general consumption. As things would turn out, general consumption was perfect.

It was, of course, third time lucky for Michael. He never knew that he had been suggested by Joss Ackland as a possibility for the original Mermaid theatrical production. He nursed his injuries and hurt pride long enough when he was rejected for the second run of the play in favour of Michael Medwin. Now he realised that had he got the part then, or passed the audition for Bill Sikes in *Oliver!* the big break might have passed him by.

Much of the credit must go to the friend of Bernard Miles, the man whose play had been put 'on the shelf', as people in the trade rather ungallantly put it. This wasn't an *Alfie* at all. In fact it was called *Alfie Elkins and His Little Life,* written for radio. Bill Owen, later one of the stars of the long-running TV show, *The Last of the Summer Wine*, played Alfie in that. On reflection, that might now seem a pretty humble origin – except that BBC radio has always broadcast plays that are not just of a high standard, they can dazzle with their brilliance. And, as Caine himself puts it in the autobiography, *What's It All About?* – from the theme song to the movie, 'What's it all about, Alfie?' – it had very good dialogue. It also shocked people listening to it in what was a much more simple – some would say moral – age.

That it then worked as well as it did on screen had more than a little to do with the rapport between Caine and Lewis Gilbert, who was to be both producer and director and who once said that he thought Paramount agreed to make the picture 'because it was going to be made for $500,000, normally the sort of money spent on executives' cigar bills'.

Gilbert, another veteran who began as a child actor in the 1920s – 'I've worked in every decade from then on,' he told me, 'so I've got to have something new to do in the 2000s', took to *Alfie* like a clapper boy to his first film set.

As we sat in his London house, he recalled for me how he and Michael first got together. It had been a long, long trail. It was also a risk from the very beginning. Gilbert owned the film rights to *Alfie* himself. Originally, he had bought it together with Leslie Grade – the agent brother of Lew Grade and Bernard Delfont and father of Michael Grade. But Grade changed his mind about its value and sold his share to James Woolf, the eminent film producer (with his brother John, he ran Romulus Films).

Having Woolf there didn't help Lewis Gilbert get his own ideas across. The producer was a close friend of Laurence Harvey and he wanted Harvey for the *Alfie* role. That stopped being a problem when Harvey got the lead in the West End production of *Camelot*. 'Laurence said he still wanted to do the film. He wanted to do it if the play flopped, but I said "No" and so he backed out.' But not happily, according to the director.

'There was a whole kerfuffle,' he remembered. A kerfuffle not helped by the entry of Terence Stamp, about to star in the Broadway stage version of *Alfie*.

'Stamp was the red hot guy at the time and he came to see me when he was in Hollywood to do a film. He said, "I know you're going to do *Alfie* and are looking for someone to do the part. I will do it for nothing." '

That was the word that got his juices going, 'nothing'. Paramount were quite pleased too. As Lewis Gilbert told me: ' "Nothing" impresses a Hollywood studio which is financing a film more than anything.'

They then came to an agreement more complicated than anything since Faust. Stamp was told that the part was his once the play had finished – providing it was a success. It wasn't. 'It was a disaster,' Gilbert recalled. 'Two days and it was off.' Stamp then rang Lewis with a request, 'I've done the play and it was a flop. Would you release me from the film?'

Gilbert said, 'Of course.' Strangely, perhaps, the director wasn't too chastened by the news of the Broadway disaster. He wasn't thinking of Broadway. It was only British audiences who were going to get back Paramount's cigar bill for them. Or so he thought. The play had done well enough in London to go for its second run after John Neville had left and nobody in Britain cared much about Broadway, even if they did know what had happened.

According to Caine himself, 'the role was turned down by every actor in England. Tony Newley turned it down. James Booth . . . and several other people. When I say every actor in England, Laurence Olivier wasn't asked to play it.' Christopher Plummer, at one time, was likely to take the role – which would have required an incredible stretch of the imagination for the suave Canadian actor. But then Plummer accepted the male lead in *The Sound Of Music* instead.

On the surface, it wasn't an attractive role. 'They were bouncing in and out of bed with the birds and first you have to set it up, that this is how life is for a lot of guys and the girl marrying the other fellow.'

But at that point, after everyone else had turned it down, said the director, 'came the problem of who the hell we *will* have?' It was then that John Gilbert, Lewis's son and a friend of Caine's, said: 'Why don't we get Michael? He's a real Cockney. I've seen him act on television and he's very good.'

That was when Gilbert suggested that he and his son, who was to be the associate producer of the movie, should see *The Ipcress File*. As he told me: 'From then on, I knew that he would be right for the film. I got on to Paramount. They were a bit unhappy about it.'

That was an understatement – even in an industry where velvet gloves are frequently used to break news that deals are off. 'They didn't know him, couldn't understand why I wanted a complete unknown.' And that was despite Joseph Levine's risk-taking in *Zulu* (maybe they agreed with his judgement about Michael's manliness) and Saltzman's evident pleasure with *The Ipcress File*. But *Ipcress* hadn't been released yet.

So, there were the usual nerves – and doubts. 'The interesting thing is what happened when he was all signed up and ready to go. He came here for lunch. To this house. We were in the sitting room and he was very quiet. It was the first time I had spoken to him about the film. Because he was very quiet, I thought I'd made the most terrible mistake here. "My God!" I thought. "This is terrible." He wasn't the Michael Caine of today ... Remember, he was still waiting to see what was going to happen to *The Ipcress File*. He didn't come with a great deal of confidence – certainly not the sort that Alfie himself had.'

But he was already signed. He couldn't now be rejected on the basis of the impression he made at a lunch party – although it is pretty easy to imagine what would have happened had the lunch taken place *before* the contracts were signed. For the moment at least, they had to press ahead. But Gilbert worried. 'I thought this was really going to be impossible. He's never going to play this personality, this Cockney Lothario. To say my heart sank, doesn't say enough.'

The first step had to be to take Michael to a tailor. 'We wanted to get him his clothes and go to a tailor who made the sort of suits for that era in the 1960s. We went to this place in the Elephant and Castle which Michael knew.' Even if Caine thought he was headed for great things, he was in no mood to leave his roots totally behind.

That's when it happened. 'He started to walk around the shop like Alfie would walk around. He had the sort of walk that Cockneys had, a sort of arrogance. And it was wonderful. As I saw him swagger, my worries left me and I thought, "My God! You're going to be fantastic." Suddenly, it jelled. Suddenly, I saw how it would all be.'

That's life, isn't it? You can never tell what's round the corner. Know what I mean? Down one minute, up the next. Drop a tenner, look around and what do you find? Ruby. – Michael Caine in Alfie (Ruby was Shelley Winters)

He would say that he based his performance on that old friend who never worried about chatting up the birds, Jimmy Buckley. 'Jimmy, better looking than I am and an extraordinary girl puller. I got the leftovers.'

Not after *Alfie* he didn't. But there would always be a difference between his approach to women and that of Jimmy. 'I know exactly what it was. He always looked as if he didn't need them. I, of course, was standing there with my tongue hanging out all the time, looking like a potential rapist. But Jimmy was always very casual and charming. If the girl said, "I can't see you tonight", he said, "Oh, that's wonderful. When *can* I see you?" He didn't mind waiting. But if she said the same to me, I was immediately uptight because I had nothing else to do.'

He said it was through Mr Buckley that he learned that 'the way to a woman's heart is to talk to her, which is something men never used to do. Jimmy would talk and be sincerely interested in what they were saying – or, if the girl wasn't particularly bright, but had a good body, he'd pretend to be interested. So I became, like Jimmy Buckley, a talker.'

And from that moment on, his producer/director friend remembered, he was not without his women. 'He always had girlfriends, some of them quite famous, some not so famous. He seemed to have them one at a time. Not like most young men who seemed to be rampant.' But he knew the kind of women that he wanted and even tried to make it sound philosophical. 'The sex scene in London? Forget it. I don't want birds coming up to me . . . I am the gov'nor. I don't want these girls, who one moment are telling you they want you and the next are raving on the parquet with LSD. Not for me. A one-night stand means two months.'

Gilbert says now that Michael was not just talented, but also lucky. 'He was in his thirties, actually 33, very handsome, a very good-looking boy, but also a very good actor – which is almost unique. Those factors would help him in the near future – there were all those Hollywood girls, film star ladies, who needed someone to play opposite and there weren't that many who were good looking and English and young and had everything going for them. Michael didn't stop working from that moment on.'

The surprise about the film was the reaction it received in America. Despite all those protestations about only seeking a British audience, everyone was worried about it. The biggest anxiety of all for Paramount was that accent. Yet, according to Lewis Gilbert, it was the big salvation. 'It was *because* he didn't have the posh professional actor voice with every vowel and consonant pronounced properly that he did so well. That turned out to be a big plus for him.'

The studio went to great lengths to try to assuage their concerns. 'Don't you think we ought to dub him?' one executive asked. 'We could get Tony Curtis.'

Gilbert told them: 'That would be ridiculous. Michael is just the kind of man the Americans *could* understand.' They let him have his way. After all, Paramount only had to cut their cigar bill if things went wrong. But Caine did have to do some dubbing himself. 'They asked me to do 120 loops of the lines with a clearer voice so Americans could understand what I was talking about.'

There were the usual panics during filming and they all got resolved – even when Shelley Winter's face disappeared in front of Michael's eyes. The 'invisible' tape melted under the heat of the lights and a smooth, lineless visage suddenly vanished while he was supposedly making love to her. Then there was the problem of her corset – a whalebone pinged in the middle of another scene and projected itself right up Caine's nose.

There was one other incident that has since passed into film industry folklore. This is how Lewis Gilbert explained it to me: 'Shirley always wanted to do the love scenes. She insisted, however, that she have three glasses of water around the set. She would do a scene and take a glass of water from behind a picture or somewhere. They had this scene in which they were all but wrestling together in their love-making. Michael said, "She's practically killing me!" At which point, he reached out for the water. But it wasn't water. It was pure vodka. It wasn't that she was an alcoholic. I don't think she was. She just needed it before she could do a scene.'

She liked Caine. But she was aware of the competition. 'There were always these young girls on the set,' she said. 'Very cool little numbers, none of them talking much. They just stood around sending out waves to Michael. I think the basis of his appeal is a certain narcissism, an attitude that suggests, "You will have the best time of your life with me, even if it's only for one hour." I think it's – oh, I don't know *what* it is. If I did, I'd bottle it and make a lot of money.'

Michael was probably getting to worry, as a lot of suddenly successful people did, about the idea of others taking a piece of what he considered to be *his* action. 'I think possibly,' he said at the time, 'what I project is a quality of loneliness. No, that's not right. Loneliness – privacy. And that is what a woman seeks, isn't it? To enter a man's private world. Yes, perhaps that's it. I'm not really sure.'

But of course, *Alfie*, the one on screen and the one people thought was represented by Michael Caine, manifestly was not unsure; not unsure about anything. And, contrary to what he said, that was what women liked about him. They wanted a man to be handsome and funny – and very sure about himself. In the days when he demonstrated he was *un*sure and insecure, he couldn't get a 'bird' near his bedroom. Now nubile young women with breasts and hips and faces and hair and voices that made him go crazy were begging to be taken. It was a Swinging Sixties thing and he was born for it.

Shelley Winters knew it. They became good friends – although she used some unconventional means to achieve the goal. In *What's It All About?* he says that on their first meeting she suggested going to bed with him – just to test him, he makes clear. And then there was the incident on their first morning filming at Twickenham studios.

'She'd only been in a few minutes before she came rushing into my dressing room,' he said soon after the film was finished. 'She stopped and said, "Good morning." I said, "Hello, Shelley how are you?" "Fine." Then I sort of waited to see what she wanted. Finally, I asked, "Well, what do you want?" "Nothing," she replied, "I just thought someone had put me into one of the extras' rooms out of some sort of disrespect or they were trying to insult me. So I thought the best thing to do is to check up and see what the leading man, somebody who would obviously know, has got." By now, she'd looked around my room;

"Yours isn't as good as mine, is it?" I said, "No, you've got the best one because you're the lady."' She was happy after that and their relationship went swimmingly.

Michael Caine has gained a reputation over the years for cracking up the crews – not, as some stars do, because the other artists and technicians think they *have* to laugh; in his case, he is genuinely funny. On the set of *Alfie*, he wasn't the one who made the outfit smile.

'We were shooting a scene at the Tower of London,' said Lewis Gilbert. 'They had given us a room for make-up and wardrobe and so on. Suddenly, a beefeater came in and looked at Michael and said: "Getting made up! Caw, what an idiot you look!" And there he was, this man standing there in his outfit straight out of the Elizabethan age and couldn't see the joke.'

That the film worked as Lewis Gilbert hoped it might had a great deal to do with the way Michael portrayed the leading character. 'After all, Alfie is a man you should have hated. The way he treated women was kind of despicable. But Michael did it with such charm, that you understood.'

There has long been a debate about whether Alfie really was more Michael than Michael admitted. He sympathised with some of the things that Alfie did – like hating having a girl's powder on his shoulder – but he wouldn't put a handkerchief down where the young lady was resting her cheek the way Alfie did. Not only that, he could never make love to a woman in a car like Alfie did – his legs were too long. The great thing is that audiences did understand. Britain, and not just London, loved it. British critics voted the movie the best home-grown film of 1966.

But when *Alfie* opened in New York, no one had any high expectations – and they were therefore prepared not to worry too much. It was another one of those experiments. They knew that as far as Manhattan audiences were concerned, South London could have been South Georgia (the one near the Falklands Islands, that is) and there was always a tiny market for such exotic locations.

It opened in two small cinemas – art houses, of course; no British film apart from the Bonds (which since they were financed in America were never regarded as British anyway) had ever had a respectable run in a 'normal' theatre.

The film was a smash. The reviews were exciting – exciting enough for *Alfie* to move into the suburbs. Pauline Kael wrote: 'Michael Caine gives us Alfie, the swaggering Cockney Don Juan as he sees himself.

Alfie doesn't know his own limitation.... Caine brings out the gusto in Naughton's dialogue and, despite the obvious weaknesses in the film, he keeps the view absorbed in Alfie, the cold-hearted sexual hotshot.'

Vincent Canby, the eminent critic of *The New York Times*, had seen *Zulu, Ipcress* and *Alfie*. 'It is impossible for Michael Caine to give an uninteresting performance,' he noted in one of those historic statements quoted for years afterwards. Archer Winston wrote in the *New York Post* that the picture showed 'an inside skill that defies adequate description'.

There were others, however, who took the initial Paramount line. Another *Times* writer hated *Alfie*. He couldn't play a Cockney if he tried, said Renata Adler. She had seen Julie Andrews in *My Fair Lady* and knew the accent well.

Still, Paramount weren't expecting anything. As if worried about pushing their luck, they played it all down. 'It's different out of town,' they told Gilbert. 'Get out of the art house circuit and into the ten theatres where it's going now, you'll see that it won't go.' But go it did.

'It went to other cities and this man was still saying to me, "Well; it won't go in Philadelphia." But everywhere he mentioned, it was a terrific hit. And even when he got down to Chattanooga and really little places, it was always a great success. But he kept saying, "It won't go down there you know!" '

But it always did. And so did Michael Caine. He had broken two barriers – his own and the British cinema's.

Thirteen

Bullseye!

Everybody wanted to cash in on *Alfie* – which is why the former Mrs Scott, Patricia Haines, allowed an article that appeared in Britain to be headed, 'My Life With Alfie'. Michael was furious. 'I don't understand how she could do it,' he said. 'What really gets me is that she let a photographer take pictures of Niki. She's *my* daughter and I don't want her to have another father. It's confusing enough for the kid as it is.'

He has said how pleased he was that Niki was being looked after by her grandparents, who were 'not doddery old people,' but a couple in their fifties – which probably still seemed old to the child. And, he said, contrary to all the music hall jokes, he loved his mother-in-law.

'I want to see to it that she has no problems. I want her brought up in a proper manner. A child can't have a proper up-bringing living with a working actor or an actress and her mum and I are both working. Now she's got a solid, middle-class, safe home. You see, having been one, I figure it's like this: a child doesn't need love from anyone special. What she needs is continuity. Now she's got that and she's also got her own mum and dad who pop in on her when they can and when they do it's like a party.'

It wasn't quite the party he expected when Pat started spilling the beans. But most of the results of *Alfie* were more positive than he could possibly have predicted.

Inevitably, the two images of Alfie and Michael Caine became completely mingled. As he himself said: 'People identified with me as Alfie. They always thought of me as being Alfie, whereas in actual fact I never was.' That might have been wishful thinking on his part – or another of those contradictions. There was an awful lot of Alfie and Jimmy Buckley in Michael Caine.

People especially made connections between Alfie and the dolly birds and the Michael Caine who always had a different woman on his arm, like Bianca de Macias (who became Bianca Jagger) and Edina Ronay. Shirley Anne Field noted it and said a few years later, 'Michael seemed to prefer foreign girls, maybe because they don't understand him. He may have the feeling that English girls might find him out. I think he was actually insecure. I don't think he's all that sexy. He's a quiet, rather sweet man.'

He had to defend those suggestions – perhaps most of all the idea that he was a sweet man. Yes, he'd heard that he only wanted to go out with foreign ladies. There was the reporter who asked him what English birds were really like. 'How do they compare with French birds, Danish birds, American birds?' 'So I told him – and now I am considered an expert. I have taken out one French girl, one Danish girl and one American girl. Really, I don't know very much about women.'

And, there were those who were attracted to him because of his fame and his reputation; but there were others for whom Michael as Alfie became a distinct turn-off factor. 'One night,' he said then, 'I called a girl for a dinner date and she turned me down flat, saying "Oh, no, I saw you in *Alfie*, and you're not going to add me to your collection." '

Clearly, however, there were plenty of young females who did think he was sexy. And that was another reason that they made the connection between the real Michael Caine and Alfie. 'People do say,' he commented, ' "well, you do go out with a lot of women . . ." and I say, "Well, I'm a young man. What do you expect me to do? Sit indoors?" I say there's a very subtle difference between me and Alfie. Alfie will go out with anybody. I only go out with the ones *you* can't go out with.' A fellow actor once asked him about his secret with 'the birds'. 'It's my cobra eyes,' he answered.

But there were still the responsibilities of parenthood. Once filming was over, he was back up north to see his Niki. One American writer asked him what sort of wife he would want if he ever remarried. 'A mistress,' he replied, 'who is also a mother to my children.' The drift was easy to get. One thing he was sure of was that he would never marry an actress who had done a nude scene.

But he was beginning to tire of the girls who seemed so wonderful as well as sexy. Perhaps he was ready to move on somewhere else. He had a solution to the problem, he told Gloria Steinem, before she became known as the feminist guru. He didn't want either famous or successful women in his life, he would tell them – flattering the ladies at the same time as giving them their marching orders. Only unsuccessful, unambitious females would be free to be with him whenever he was not working.

But while the reputation of *Alfie* was being blasted across the media, people continued to believe that he and his character were inseparable. 'I guess the *Alfie* image stuck because there was a grain of truth in it when I was single,' he has said. 'What you have to remember,' he explained ten years afterwards, 'is that I was for quite a while the only unmarried, more or less eligible, well-known British movie actor. Some of the married ones fooled around quite a bit – but the press never printed a word about them. I was doing it for everyone, so to speak. Anytime the papers wanted an Errol Flynn type of story, I was their boy. They'd just get together the clippings and a bunch of pictures of me escorting different girls to premieres. Usually, they didn't even bother to interview me.' Such was the price of the fame he had courted so assiduously.

He also made the point – not very convincingly – that the only woman who was really important in his life was his mother. Ellen Micklewhite, meanwhile, was carrying on with her job, scrubbing floors.

Michael was furious. But apparently there was nothing he could do. She wasn't going to allow anything to alter her own lifestyle. She had always worked and was not going to stop now. Just because her son was a star.... After all, he had paid back all the money he had borrowed.

He admitted he loved money. 'Money means power to me. And power means to be free from the telephone bill, the gas bill, the electricity bill – and no fear for the cold, for the dark, for the silence, for the future.'

He wanted his mother to have that, too, but he didn't want her to scupper either of their chances. Then he hit on the answer: 'What if the papers found out? The mother of the star Michael Caine who was making hundreds of thousands of pounds still went out charring.' That was when she handed in her knee pad and scrubbing brush for the last time. She didn't want to risk bringing disgrace upon her son – who was looking for the better things in life.

He had a new West End apartment and he thought the time had come to buy a car – not that he could drive, or had any intention of doing so, but he could afford a chauffeur.

But she was saving all the money he was now regularly giving her – still waiting for that rainy day; *his* rainy day. If things got hard for him and the movie offers dried up, he could be sure that once again she would raid her Post Office savings account and let him have it all, just as she did after Korea. He was certain that when the time came, she would will to him every penny she had ever saved.

As if to demonstrate to her that he needed none of that cash, Michael set about buying his car. He went into Jack Barclay's Rolls Royce showroom and unwittingly provided a great deal of amusement to the black-suited assistant.

There is a wonderful story of the Rolls Royce salesman who escorts to the very seat a man who came in, asking to use the toilet – 'because it is the only genuine inquiry I've had all day'. It was almost like that when Michael Caine called at Britain's most famous Rolls dealer in the heart of Mayfair – but in reverse. He looked at a black convertible and said, 'I want one.' The man thought that the Cockney wearing the *Alfie* suit made in the Elephant was having him on, gave him some pamphlets and directed him to the nearest door. He repeated he wanted to buy one. 'Just one?' chortled the man.

Shortly afterwards, Michael had his revenge. His newly installed chauffeur drove him up to the showroom – in a Rolls he had just bought from another dealer.

But it wasn't the car that brought him respect. It was his whole 'fuck you' attitude to those who had previously tilted their noses at him. What was more, he gave a new image to his profession. As he said: 'Until *Alfie*, film stars were unapproachable. When they saw the film, they started to say, "He's just like me."' And, he maintained, so were most of the young men in the Swinging City. 'It was what the majority of the men in the audiences were doing.

And when it got to the girls who were being done down and treated badly and loved and left, unwined, undined and undone, one realised that practically every girl in the audience was in sympathy with the girls in that position in the film.' What was more, he said, 'Many of the ladies in the audience identified with the lady having the abortion.'

The Cockneys loved it all. 'Michael opened the doors for all of us,' said Bob Hoskins. 'He's got away with things that you would have thought would have held him down, like his accent – and wearing glasses.'

Julie Walters, who worked with him years later in *Educating Rita*, said: 'He broke the mould. He was the first working-class actor to play a working-class person.'

There were two things that convinced Michael about *Alfie*. The first was that it really would help his crusade for justice. 'The working class perpetuates the class system in a sort of masochistic way. I fight it constantly. The reason I speak this way is *because* I am a success. The English don't encourage their children. When they want to do something with their lives, the parents say, "Who do you think you are?"'

He had been through that too often. Now he knew who he was – and that was the other lesson. He was now a film star and it was in films that he was going to stay. There would be no return to the live stage. 'To me, theatre was a woman I loved dearly but treated me like dirt. The movies are a woman who I adored who showered me with gifts.'

The first of the post-*Alfie* gifts were Oscar nominations – one for him and others for Bill Naughton, Vivien Merchant and for the title song.

Fourteen

Woman Times Seven

What Michael Caine was now was bankable. The studios really were queuing up for his services and he was revelling in the mere notion that, after all those years, he was no longer in financial trouble.

The question was, what now? His answer was to establish, even that early on, that when an offer came for a film in which he did not star, it was still worth considering, even though there would be others who would get all the credit. A psychiatrist would no doubt have had an explanation: the old insecurity was still difficult to shake off. Others would say that Michael Caine was already demonstrating a characteristic that would always be his: he was a workaholic.

In 1999 Joss Ackland summed up the Michael Caine career for me in words that would have been no less relevant 35 years earlier: 'Michael has done some wonderful work. He has also done a lot of crap.'

No one would describe his part in *The Wrong Box* so indelicately. He did very nicely in this film, based on a Robert Louis Stevenson story, playing a medical student. But it wasn't work that would have justified stardom even if Ralph Richardson, John Mills and Wilfrid Lawson – a marvellous actor who died soon afterwards from the results of his heavy drinking – had given away their top billing to him.

The film, directed by Bryan Forbes, with a script written with *Mash* writer Larry Gelbart, also featured Forbes's wife, Nanette Newman. Forbes told me that both of them were exceedingly grateful that Michael was in it too – although not for strictly professional reasons. 'He saved Nanette's life,' he explained.

The film with its Victorian setting was about two elderly brothers who try to murder each other – for the inheritance they have had to share. It involved horses and carriages – one of which looked as if it were going to crash with dire results when the horses suddenly reared.

If *Zulu* had not convinced Caine to stay away from the equestrian life, *The Wrong Box* certainly did.

It happened when he and Nanette were riding atop a hearse being drawn by six horses. 'I was shooting Sir Ralph Richardson somewhere else,' Bryan Forbes told me, 'and a second unit were shooting this scene. It wasn't an easy one. On Victorian hearses, you sit about 12 feet above the ground and Nanette was in full Victorian dress – the long skirt and, of course, a corset.' So, dressed like that, and in that position, you hope everything will go well. Unfortunately, it did not. 'The second unit cameraman got too close,' said the director, 'and the horses bolted. Six horses bolting, pulling a Victorian hearse was quite frightening. I heard Nanette scream and everyone was shouting to her to jump.' Everybody, that is, except Michael. 'Michael was saying, "Don't jump!" Somehow, after about two miles, he got those horses to stop. He needed a very large brandy, but I've always been grateful to him. There is no doubt that he saved my wife's life.'

Sir John Mills remembers him in the film with great affection, too. 'I was trying to kill Ralph Richardson in all the most ghastly ways you can think of,' he told me. 'And there in the midst of it all, was Michael Caine, a superb actor in front of the camera – one of the best that we have. I think he is so good because of his theatrical training.' So, all those days in rep and struggling to find parts in the West End, roles that he would never get, were paying off in the eyes of one of the great theatrical knights.

'Yes,' recalled Bryan Forbes, 'Michael proved that he is an extraordinary actor – a chameleon in many ways. He came to *The Wrong Box* after *Alfie*, *Zulu* and *The Ipcress File*. He always showed up, no side, no temperament, no bullshit. Just does it. He's a very down-to-earth Cockney. But then I'm a Cockney too. He's like Tony Hopkins. No bullshit. There's too much preciousness surrounding acting. We're very lucky being actors. I love being an actor too. Most actors I've found, the greater the talent, the less the temperament. That's true with Michael, as with John Mills, Katharine Hepburn, Ralph Richardson and Dame Edith Evans.'

The American *Family Weekly*'s writer Peer J. Oppenheimer saw *The Wrong Box* and said he was concerned at what all that success would do to Mr Caine. 'Everybody seems to worry about that,' Michael replied testily. 'Nobody tells me how good I was in *Ipcress* but only, "Don't let it change you". I really don't think it will – precisely because of what I have gone through.' And then came the modesty that the writer had been hoping to hear at the start of their chat. 'I am not out of the acting woods yet. I feel I need all the professional help I can get. That's also why I don't want to get married again right now. Someday when I am really secure, I want a wife and children because if I have success I want to share it with a woman. But if I'm a failure, I want no witnesses.' He was proving that not only was he aware of the problems – and of his insecurity – but was wonderfully articulate in expressing them, too.

He was giving more interviews now than at any time in his life, which was logical considering that he had never been so much in the public eye. But there was another reason too: he was in America for the first time in his life. The Big Apple was the Big Paradise he had always imagined it would be.

But this was no holiday. It was work – with the main task on the agenda being to convince the Americans that he was no one-day wonder. He said the big problem would be to convince them that he wasn't a 'fag'. His father would have appreciated the difficulty, although he would never know as much as his son on that score. 'The Americans,' he explained 'think that British actors have no balls . . . on screen, anyway. One trouble is that the British accent is just like the American fag accent.' These were politically very incorrect days.

To actually walk the streets of New York, those wide avenues that had been featured in so many of the movies he had seen since he first saw a Saturday morning film, was like dying and arriving in front of the archangels. How could it be otherwise when he had a room at the Plaza Hotel? The place where the flags flew over the canopy sheltering the front door and steps was all that he thought it would be. He was but a few yards from the golden statue, the site of all those black and white sophisticated pictures that he had gladly substituted for maths and physics lessons. Outside his window, there were views of Central Park to one side and the horses and carriages to the other. He maintained that he was so filled with wonder that he didn't sleep for five nights. 'I just lay in bed for a couple of hours once in a while with my eyes open. Excited.'

Tired, too. But apparently he had been even more tired when he first arrived. So much so, in fact, that when he had first set foot on this near sacred ground, he hadn't been sure which hotel he was actually visiting. The Plaza was a dream come true, but as in most dreams, he wasn't sure what was real and what was not.

Neither did he understand why he was woken up at 6.30 in the morning to appear on the 7.30 *Today* show. For most Britons, the idea of morning television was almost an affront. The mornings were times to wake up, read the paper over bacon and eggs and if you were really adventurous, turn on the radio. Britain had three TV stations at the time, BBC 1, BBC 2 and ITV. Apart from the test card, you didn't see much on the small screen during the day time. But he did the interview and did it well.

And then he went to Los Angeles and gave more interviews – and tried to satisfy more people that he wasn't .... that word again .... a 'fag'. 'Most Englishmen who arrive in LA, well, they don't whoop it up in clubs at all. Either they take a girl with them, or they start taking one out, just one, in a nice quiet way. Well, I didn't give a fuck. I'm not trying to project any image.'

To prove the point, Jane Russell asked him to have lunch – her date had failed to turn up for a Christian Science charity do – and he found himself sitting with the owner of those breasts of his childhood dreams. The regular conversation of young boys who drooled over *Health and Efficiency* had been how amazing it would be to see Jane Russell in one of those poses. Her bust had stared out of a hundred thousand posters for the Howard Hughes picture *The Outlaw* with the word 'Banned' screaming from the direction of the cleavage. She was an icon like no other and the experience of being with her more memorable than could have been imagined. If only the other boys from Wilson's could see him now.

The other major experience was meeting John Wayne – who gave him some sound advice: don't wear suede shoes; the last time that 'Duke' had worn them, he was in a men's toilet – the man next to him was so amazed at seeing him that he urinated over his shoes. That was an experience that he was happy to pass on – oh yes, that and the recommendation that Michael speak more slowly. There weren't too many natives of the Elephant and Castle at the Alamo or in the squad of Green Berets that Mr Wayne led, and he couldn't understand them.

But that sort of thing didn't happen all at once.

The visit to the States was partly to give interviews for *Alfie* and partly to make his first American film, to be called *Gambit*, which contained a lot of action, enough comedy not to be affected by the subtle approach and a great deal of sex appeal, without either of the stars taking their clothes off. This was, after all, the mid-60s and real film nudity was a couple of years away. Caine's part had been originally earmarked for Cary Grant, which gave some idea of what it would all amount to. His co-star would be Shirley MacLaine, for once not playing the kooky innocent with the heart of gold. She would be the one to make him feel comfortable in America. But she took her time – even though it had been she who had asked for him as her co-star after seeing *Ipcress*.

He said he sat alone in his room at the Beverly Hills Hotel, one of the smartest of all Hollywood hostelries with its distinctive banana-plant wallpaper famous throughout California. It was where Marilyn Monroe had a series of love affairs, where Errol Flynn took his lovers to one of the bungalows surrounding the swimming pool and subjected them to his 'wicked, wicked ways'.

Michael maintains that the phone didn't ring for two weeks. He spent that time studying those banana plants on the walls, glancing out at the swimming pool and watching television. He hoped his agent would call, but he never did. Nobody had spoken to him, and he hadn't had the chance to take a girl out to dinner. 'I thought, "Well, Jesus, I don't mean very much over here."'

Yet he was frightened to leave the room because he didn't want to miss a phone call. It was like waiting outside Mr Curtis's office again, except that this was a lot more comfortable and the room service was better. But nobody was ready for him to go into a studio yet.

Someone asked him why he didn't go out and take a look around. After all, California had been as much his dream as had New York. Even the hotel was amazed that he never left. Why not rent a car? Not easy when you can't drive.

Then it all changed. Shirley MacLaine phoned to invite him to a party – at which he would be guest of honour. It was a sort of 'Welcome to LA' do. Five hundred people were invited. But he kept saying to himself, 'Nobody will ever come'. It became an obsession, a recurring nightmare. But come they did. (He later said he was sure that 3,000 were there, but that could be an exaggeration.)

The first person he saw was Gloria Swanson. That might not have been a wonderful omen. Ms Swanson, heroine of dozens of silent movies who had made the most spectacular comeback in *Sunset Boulevard*, hadn't done much for 15 or 16 years and a lot of people thought she'd now come to *anything*. But then the second person to pump his hand was Frank Sinatra. That made him feel rather more optimistic.

Optimism from someone who suddenly realised that 'it was like watching all my heroes at the Saturday morning cinema come to life.'

The fact that Frank Sinatra never made the sort of films he saw on Saturday mornings had nothing to do with it.

'I took Shirley MacLaine out on to the floor and we went mad. Swung.... You could see the looks on their faces that they didn't expect me to frug. They thought I was going to do a foxtrot or something.' But then he was faced with sudden reality. He overheard another guest pronounce the devastating words, 'Who the fuck is the guest of honour?'

But after that little experience, the phone did start ringing – and didn't stop. From that moment on, he was never without a dinner invitation.

Shirley MacLaine was one of those callers. In the movie, she played a Eurasian beauty, who looked suspiciously like the empress whose statue she and the Caine character were out to steal. The cheongsam with its slit skirt suited her magnificently. So did the upswept hairstyle. Even the eyes looked more realistic than studio make-up departments are usually able to achieve (as Sean Connery's did too in *You Only Live Twice*).

'Will she co-operate?'
'A girl making 50 cents a dance ... of course, she'll co-operate.'

The Americans failed to see the difference between the real Michael Caine and the one on the screen. He had had that problem before, of course. But he didn't dispute the similarities at the time. It could be argued that it was just good publicity business. But then he always invited trouble. When he first met American girls he said, somewhat indelicately: 'Oh the birds! They're like unbroken horses – very independent. They've never been controlled by anybody. If you do break them, they're grateful, as all women are.'

He never said he regretted saying that, but he doubtless did. Perhaps even his mother did too. She was very much part of his life still. It wasn't a question of the Caine image. He wanted his mother to enjoy a better life for her sake, not his. Yet in some ways she changed no more than he did. His image was questioned. But he was convinced he needed no help in that direction – which was why he refused the offer to take on a press agent in the United States.

Jerry Pam, his fellow pupil of Grocers in King's Lynn, told me how he wrote to Dennis Selinger suggesting that he should represent Michael, looking after his press arrangements.

Michael wasn't interested. He could deal with interviews himself and when he was working on a movie, there were always publicists on hand to cope with such things. 'So many young British actors think it's a bit vulgar to get publicity. Once I saw I had a possibility of being a movie star, I worked harder at publicity than most people do.' So he didn't need anyone to do it for him? Someone suggested he ought to be in the advertising business. Ever since his first radio interview, when he was told not to be content with saying 'yes' or 'no' to a question, he said, 'I've always had sumpin' to say.'

Caine and Jerry Pam met at a party while Michael was filming *Gambit*. He invited him to the studio the next day. He went, but still nothing happened. After all, he believed he was in full control. And if he wasn't, it really didn't matter to him. 'When I get back home, they'll ask how I liked Hollywood and I'll tell them. Then they'll go ahead and print what they feel like printing. Least, I'll have had the satisfaction of telling them the truth – which is, "It's better in Hollywood. The weather, the dressing rooms, the filming."' And, as far as he was concerned, the American reporters. He always believed that the American Press treated him better than the Press at home. In his memoirs, he infers that he and Pam struck a deal straight away; but initially it was more important to the publicist that it was to Michael himself.

There was a great deal about this trip that he loved. Danny Kaye invited him to his house for dinner as Shirley MacLaine's escort. 'It'll be in the kitchen,' he said, which took Caine back a bit, back to South London and back from where he was standing at the time. He didn't realise that he had jumped two steps in American terms. To working families, like the one he came from, eating among the stove and pots and pans was the best they could hope for. For the middle class, it would be something to avoid, something that showed they didn't know what was right. When you had reached the higher echelons of society, you could get away with anything – like proving that you had nothing to prove.

What Michael may not have realised at the time was that Danny Kaye, once considered to be the greatest comedian in the world, was a man with a certain reputation – that he *was* Walter Mitty, the character he had played in one of the great comedy films of the late 40s personified. He conducted symphony orchestras (OK, using a fly swatter instead of a baton sometimes) as well as did many professional conductors; he had learnt to fly and instead of being satisfied with that, obtained a licence to pilot jumbo jets; he was a frustrated surgeon and once tended a woman dying of a heart attack on a flight, so well that she lasted much longer than might have been expected; he was the table tennis champion of Beverly Hills. Above all, he had a reputation as California's best Chinese cook. He never ate any of the food he cooked himself, but to be invited to sample his achievements sitting in his long Chinese kitchen, surrounded by Chinese woks and pans was the epitome of having arrived. All the big stars in the movie capital had done it. So had dozens who were stars in different fields.

It was the same on this evening. He arrived to find other guests sitting around the table, Cary Grant among them. And a couple of gentlemen in Royal Navy uniforms. Then, after him, another Englishman arrived – by the name of Philip, Prince Philip, Duke of Edinburgh, that is. They were introduced. Caine knew who the royal figure was. Philip called him 'Ipcress'. It was probably one of the only places where the consort of the Queen of Great Britain and the Commonwealth would be invited to eat in a kitchen. It is quite possible he had never even been in a kitchen before. As for Michael, 'We were seated at a table for eight. It was an incredible thing for me. I enjoyed every minute of it.'

From the Prince to the President. Michael let it be known that he would like to meet Lyndon B. Johnson – and then Bobby Kennedy, brother of the assassinated JFK. He was still Attorney General, but was making no secret of the fact that he, too, would one day like to reside in the White House. To Michael Caine, he was another star. So was LBJ and he wanted to meet them both. That was arranged too. It was another one of those things that could have happened only in America. He loved everything about the place. He said it was like watching the whole of *Richard III*.

He even became more tolerant. Caine learned just to smile when visitors to the set of *Gambit* were heard to say, 'Michael who?' Or, worse, 'The What File?' He was having the time of his life. There were dates with Shirley MacLaine, Nancy Sinatra, Carol Lynley, Natalie Wood, Liza Minnelli and the 'hot ticket' from America's most-watched current soap *Peyton Place*, Barbara Parkins. One friend asked him to define the kind of girl he liked most. 'A tall, slim bird,' he replied. It was his birthday the following week and the friend sent him a stuffed flamingo.

But it was the girl he was dating most frequently of all, Camilla

Sparv, a Swedish actress, who gave him the present he treasured most – a £500 gold watch. He said he went into the bathroom, locked the door and cried. He couldn't believe that anyone would care that much about him. They were to be together for a year. But it wasn't to last. 'I adored her,' he said. 'The best so far, I think. But the trouble is I've never been able to think in terms of "for ever" with any girl – for ever with her, for ever without her. I'm too much of a romantic, I suppose. I love how it is at the beginning. You know, the holding hands, the looks across the table. Adolescent, maybe, but it's enough if you happen to be a busy fellow.' And that was it. He was asked if he loved her. 'Sure I do,' he said. 'Will you marry her?' 'I wouldn't be surprised,' he said. But, he got busier and busier and soon, there would be other women in his life.

He met Brigitte Bardot, who, he said, made him fall over the chairs in front of him when she said, 'I've always wanted to meet you.'

He liked being seen with these stars who at the time never left the pages of America's newspapers, but he was taken down a peg or two when he realised that Natalie Wood had been on two dates with him before she realised who he was. He might have been satisfied that she wanted him for himself, for his looks, for his personality, but that wasn't the name of the game at all. All in all, he was thoroughly enjoying being so much in demand, although at times he wished life were more simple. 'We men,' he said, 'are stuck with the courtship ritual.' He denied that he lied to women. 'But I don't tell them the truth either.' Alfie couldn't have put it better.

There were bonuses in dating Nancy Sinatra. Her father entertained him royally – even flew him in his private jet, although it seemed as if he were keeping a rather close look on their progress together. Mr Sinatra was nothing if not protective.

He did seem to trust Michael, however. He and a friend, Harry Kurnitz, were deputed by Ol' Blue Eyes to look after the young woman who was shortly to be the singer's wife, Mia Farrow. That was quite a responsibility, knowing the Sinatra reputation. Caine didn't worry about it – until a picture appeared in a newspaper showing Mia on his arm with a caption that suggested she was his latest girl. That was not good news, but no men in long overcoats or with broken noses came to call, so either Frank didn't mind or he hadn't kept up with his reading.

Without that to worry about, the kid from the Elephant couldn't believe just how his dreams had come true. But it got better. It was

Christmas. Nancy Sinatra senior, Nancy's mother and Frank's first wife, rang Michael and invited him to spend the holidays with the family. 'Christmas Eve is just fine for bachelors with the sort of parties you can have,' she said. 'But you've got no family here, so why not spend Christmas with us?'

The night before he left to take the plane home, some Hollywood types threw a party for him, one of those tongue-in-cheek affairs where, like the famous Friars Club 'Roasts', the guests are not so much praised as insulted. Mike Nichols, at the time Hollywood's most in-demand director, wore a badge that proclaimed, 'Limey Go Home'. Praise and honour didn't come much higher.

In the story of *Gambit*, written by Jack Davies and Alvin Sargen from a short story by Sidney Carroll, he played a Cockney thief – if he wasn't careful, he was about to be type-cast, but he wasn't going to give up that accent – who conspires with the girl to steal a priceless statue. The most memorable scene in the movie is when they try to beat the electronic beam that will set off the alarm. Hollywood had discovered the laser and was enjoying it. (Bond had also faced the beam when, in *Goldfinger*, he was about to be sliced in two the painful way: between his legs.)

He was getting very close to being made a star in the States. Back home, he was already that, but there's a quality about the British which supposedly goes with the stiff upper lip – you don't make any more fuss of anybody else than you would like made of yourself. That's a nice way of putting it. Not so nice would be to say that there's an element of jealousy about. Another might be that celebrities need to be taken down a peg or two.

That's what happened when Caine, already back in Britain, decided to take a bus ride. It wasn't that he didn't still have the car and the chauffeur. It was just more convenient. 'Look who we've got here,' called the conductor when his august passenger was reasonably comfortably settled in his seat on the top deck and had paid his fare. Michael smiled – until the ticket man asked, 'Now, what's your name?' The star didn't appreciate the joke and slunk off the bus at the next stop, while the other passengers stared. It was going to be his last trip on the bus. Now he'd walk to Harrods, which was where he liked to do his shopping. He had luxury tastes and, at last, could more than afford to indulge them.

He was having to get used to the idea that people might want his autograph. He said he didn't mind that at all – how could he, it was a wonderful sense of recognition after the dark ages. 'What I don't like are the ones who hang about trying to decide if you're you. I may wear specs but I can always see them out of the corner of my eye. I walk fast and I'm off before they can make up their minds.' He agreed that he had become less tolerant of people, suffering fools less gladly than at one time. 'If you're working hard you can't be bothered with layabouts.'

When he was asked about the degree to which success had spoiled Michael Caine, he said, 'In many ways I think success has improved me. I have more confidence. I worry less. Becoming a success is something you can do something about, work at it. Failure is what you can't do anything about. In an actor's case, it just means fewer people want to pay to see you – and what can you do about that?' Nothing.

At this stage in his career, *more* people wanted to see him than ever before.

They mobbed him when he went to West End stores, looking for furniture for the new flat, which was big enough to entertain the birds in, that he had just bought off Grosvenor Square; a nice touch that – in London, but almost in America, too. The square is the site of the American embassy and a dozen or more US enterprises. Maybe he felt that by being there he would be in easy reach of the next call from Hollywood. There is an eagle hoisted above the embassy – a great big gold-coloured one that had worried planners for some time before they got the all-clear for it to be placed on what is, legally, foreign territory. As he said, 'I'm thinking of putting the Cockney sparrow over my flat.' But it was comfortable – more luxurious, in fact, than he imagined a home of his could ever be. He even had one of the luxuries of which he had dreamed from the time he first stayed in a good hotel – clean sheets on his bed every day.

It was a time when Grosvenor Square wasn't the most peaceful place to live. The Vietnam War was in its most controversial phase. All over America, youngsters were burning draft cards. Americans in London did the same thing outside the embassy, joined by worthies like Vanessa Redgrave who demonstrated each Sunday in support of them. They were among the most violent demos London had ever seen – or would see until the anti-Thatcher riots some 13 years later. 'There's nothing to do on a Sunday but look out the window and watch them,' Michael said. 'Then you can go out and pick up the cigarette butts and earn the rent.' He was not saying anything about politics himself unless he had no choice. Then he would let it out.

The Labour Government was soaking the rich – not that he knew how much money he himself had; about £15 in his wallet was all that he could report. 'The moment Labour came in, millions of pounds got transferred out of British banks. Fascinating how those rich old bastards did it.' As for Vietnam itself. 'My sympathies are with the fellows in Vietnam,' he said, recalling his own experiences in Korea.

'Nobody wants you to be there. It's like "even your best friends won't tell you". Vietnam is worse than Korea. There was a time when, if one was at war, everybody went when called up. Now we have these "police actions". It's a question of whether you want to go around being a policeman. I find that patriotism is usually strongest when people are too old to be called up. The best thing, I suppose, is to be born Swedish.'

That was why he had never gone in for the demonstrating business himself. 'I can remember the marches to ban the A-bomb and [then] we got the H-bomb. That's progress! The marches to stop Korea and we got Vietnam. The marches to stop Vietnam and we got Cambodia. The marches to stop Biafra and we got Belfast. What did all that marching achieve except a lot of sore feet?'

It wasn't a case of not caring or not being patriotic. Michael Caine was now approaching 35 years old. Old enough to decide if he was patriotic or not. He was – as far as his family were concerned.

Until he moved to Grosvenor Square, he had been sharing a mews flat with his brother Stanley – the younger Micklewhite had suddenly returned, following an absence of six months. Now he gave Stanley the flat for himself. His mother, however, wouldn't accept a new home from her son. Brixton wasn't smart, but it was a step up from the Elephant. A block of flats was an improvement on the prefab – the 'temporary accommodation' was still in use – he hadn't liked the idea of it any more than he had the idea of her scrubbing other people's floors.

It was enough, Ellen thought, just to know her son was doing well and be able to praise him when she felt like it. He was getting that praise in all sorts of forms now. The fact that he had a listing in 1967's *Current Biography* said something. 'I see myself as a bit nutty but nice and kind,' was how they quoted him summing up his personality. 'Just ask my mother.' Ellen was still a vital part of his life.

And so was Harry Palmer. There was now a sequel to *The Ipcress File*. Harry Salzman was determined to carry out his intention of making a cult out of the second-division James Bond. There were going to be more and more Harry Palmer movies and Michael saw no reason to disappoint him. After all, this was merely the beginning of his career. The fact was that he was also beginning to establish his philosophy for the next 30 years – take whatever work that comes, or at least a great deal of it.

Funeral in Berlin turned out to be a worthy successor to *Ipcress*. But it would never achieve the cult status of the first film. The critic Tom Milne partly explained why. It had, he said, 'so many twists that even Sherlock Holmes might have been baffled. Before long, it becomes difficult to remember who is watching whom and why or indeed whether anybody *was* watching anybody at any given moment.'

It was unkind. Most of all, it was unkind about a highly polished performance by an actor who was making a career of playing a very unpolished, very rough diamond. In many ways it stands out as a highly sophisticated impression of the unconventional agent.

The problem was that the better he got, the more patronising people became about him. He told one writer: 'I wasn't just standing outside some East End youth club with a razor in my hand and Harry Saltzman came riding up in a Cadillac and discovered me.'

Everyone wanted to know how much he resembled Harry Palmer, just as they had wanted to know if he really were Alfie. That was when he got philosophical. He didn't deny that people had a legitimate reason for wanting to make the comparisons. 'What I try to do in acting is to create what I call the shock of recognition – to make the gesture so much a part of the observer's experience that he recognises the truth of it instantly. It's what Brando did in that scene when he was trying to talk to the girl in *Waterfront*... it's not a competitive thing. I watch other actors in case I'll be able to learn something, or steal something.'

As it was, he thought he could best be described as 'a winner – who comes on like a loser'. And that, he thought, was Harry Palmer too. That was the trouble with this kind of success. Just like Alfie, Harry Palmer was being identified with Michael Caine, and Michael himself couldn't escape from the comparisons.

Comparing himself with Brando was easier – particularly since he didn't have to apologise for it. He was happier doing that than talking over and over again about the clichés of being a Cockney. As he said, 'All that Cockney boy-made-good bit! Just forget it.'

People begged him not to change. 'Change? What they really mean is please don't get big-headed. Well, I don't know about that. All I know is that I am never going to have to take that stuff they handed me. Not any more. As I see it, I was rich from the day I was born. I just didn't have the money.' He acknowledged: 'I'm a big success, aren't I? Let's forget all that modest stuff.' Foreign journalists keep asking me about the pearly kings and queens. I get embarrassed by the pearlies. They're from the old days when Cockneys were kissing the ass of the upper class.'

That was what *Funeral In Berlin* was all about, or rather wasn't. Harry Palmer was his own man and never kissed the ass (or arse) of anyone. You could assume, however, that he kissed most parts of the anatomy of the girls in his films – in this case Samantha Steel, who played an Israeli agent. (And in that regard you have to sympathise with Mr Milne; it *was* very difficult to work out how that fitted into the story.)

The movie was shot on location in the Tiergarten and elsewhere in the western half of Berlin. The city was making great strides in showing that it was a lot more prosperous than most of the countries who had spent a fortune to put it back on its feet.

Harry Saltzman banned the company from even trying to work in East Berlin. There had been trouble there recently – a Russian MIG came down in the British sector. So areas of West Berlin were meant to double for the East. To provide the atmosphere, there were a lot of scenes of Checkpoint Charlie.

Palmer was as bolshie and as determined as ever. Michael was also as good as ever. In fact, he was better. Unlike many sequels, this film was as good as the first. But Caine had noticeably benefited from the experience he had gained in the couple of years since making the first picture. The definitive character of *Alfie* hadn't imposed itself on his old characterisation. The fact that the thief he played in *Gambit* was a Cockney called Harry might have helped him build up the momentum.

The movie, directed by Bond veteran, Guy Hamilton, was set in Cold War Berlin; it involved the funeral in the title and had a lot to do with crossing over the border between East and West. Michael liked Berlin, but was a little bit shaken by some of the Iron Curtain shenanigans – like the East Berlin *politzei* shining lights from their side of the Wall so that they glinted in the camera lens. He seemed to have established himself as Harry Palmer, which might have threatened him with typecasting if he hadn't had so much else to do as well.

Look magazine got it all wrong when they published an interview with him, but the sentiment was good and you understood what they meant. Palmer, the magazine reported, represented 'the death by consumption of a superman named James Bond. We don't speak any more of Sean Connery. We now speak of Michael Caine.'

The interviewers all wanted to know about Michael's love life and about his movies. Even *Playboy* interviewed him in one of those multi-page spreads that they hoped gave the impression of gravitas to someone who knew a decent pair of breasts when he saw them. *Playboy* said they chose him as a subject because 'if any single symbol could be said to epitomise the breadth and bizazz of Britain's renaissance in the lively arts – and the age-old disintegration of its age-old class system' – he did.

David Lewin, one of the most respected British show business writers of his generation, asked him how he accounted for his great success, phenomenal for someone from his background. He said it was simply because he was an 'ordinary man' and people recognised themselves in him.

He spoke so freely that you now felt he could probably make a film without any dialogue written for him in advance. 'God, I talk,' he admitted. 'Shy people usually talk more than the others. I'm shy and so I talk, talk, talk.'

They always wanted to know about his background. He said he came from a loving family and hoped to have one of his own – a new wife with new children – one day. Inevitably, David Lewin wanted to know about the women in Caine's life and about his attitude to women in general.

He said they had to have self-respect and a good sense of humour. As he said in another interview, he would never go out with the kind of beautiful girl who went to restaurants with 75-year-old, fat multi-millionaires. 'If ever I do find myself out with girls like that, it means they are taking advantage of me.'

Would he be faithful? He hoped he would, but he said that marriage as a concept came into being when life expectancy was about 37, so it wouldn't have been difficult not to cheat in a marriage that would last for perhaps ten years. But then he did emphasise: 'When I marry, I stay faithful.'

'There are several different kinds of sex,' he told another writer. 'If you contemplate marriage, you must also at the same time contemplate fidelity. It's no good in getting married if you're going to be running around all over the place, so you must contemplate the type of woman who's going to keep you happy for a long time I don't know how you contemplate that, but you get a feeling, don't you? I only intend to be married twice – it will occur to me at the time. It's the same way I do about acting. It occurs to me at the time. What I particularly look for in a woman – femininity. There are certain women who look like they'd be good mothers – and that's essential. I want a family and loyalty.'

For the best part of the next decade, that would be the subject all interviewers would want to deal with – and with subtle variations his answer would always be the same. He also expected his daughter to remain a virgin until she married. 'There'll be bloody hell to pay if she doesn't.' Inevitably, that was the sort of thing people wanted to know. The more cerebral publications would concentrate on his attitude to the world, his philosophy and what he told his psychiatrist on the black leather couch. If he had denied that he had a psychiatrist, nobody would have believed him. That went with stardom. Didn't it?

McCall's magazine in March 1967 didn't find out enough. 'What Caine has is a colossal cool,' Martha Weinman Lear reported. 'Detachment. No Trespassing signs and the subtle suggestion – always, in any role – that he may succumb to many a game and many a folly and many a pretty face, but never to a broken heart. Bright, but not intellectual, amused but not excitable, aware but not intense, he is able to convey that special existential bat of his peculiar time, his place, his circumstance better than anyone else around.'

He was a 1960s male. 'Perhaps, too, I project the sense that a woman can lean on me. I quite deliberately do everything that needs to be done. It is a quality of maleness, I think, rather than masculinity.'

Michael Caine was being fawned on everywhere he went. Although there was plenty of evidence to the contrary, he insisted that he wasn't a star yet, but, as he said in the *Playboy* interview, 'I'm a hell of a rocket'.

But then he also said: 'If I work fast enough and pack enough bleedin' pictures in, I'll be a star before anyone realises I am not star material.'

Fifteen

Billion Dollar Brain

It was when he got Jane Fonda on to a bed and tore her clothes off down to her bra and pants that he realised he was not only going places, he had already arrived – places that weren't entirely bad.

This wasn't one of his romantic trysts. It would have been entirely out of character for him, given the degree of violence. It was all in the line of work, in the course of furthering his art.

He and Ms Fonda, swiftly establishing herself as one of the leading Hollywood girls, were starring in a film being directed by Otto Preminger, affectionately dubbed the Himmler of Beverly Hills by the kinder citizens of Hollywood. He was known to make strong men cry and to make weak women run home clutching handkerchiefs – once, that is, they had recovered from their fainting fits. The Teutonic tyrant was not exactly a pussy cat – no more so when sitting in the director's chair than when, as an actor, he wore the SS uniform to which he seemed so suited. It was one of the great ironies of his life for he had actually fled Vienna when the Nazis came to power.

'Otto goes stark, raving mad,' Michael said, fresh (although nobody felt particularly fresh after a Preminger film) from finishing the film he made, *Hurry Sundown*. 'Rather than sacrificing the actors, he tries to prove he *is* one.'

There had to be some redeeming features in the man and the fact that he had chosen Michael himself after seeing *Ipcress* was one. 'I was simply bowled over by it,' said the director. 'I decided then and there to get him for my film. I called him. The price was right. He agreed.' It was all helped by the additional assurance that he would try not to shout at him. Mr (or Herr or Führer) Preminger gave Michael some very specific instructions that appeared to faze him more than they did Ms Fonda. They amounted to: Come in the door, go over to the bed and rape her. Such was the movie business.

It was also because of the movie business that the man born with the southern accent – from South London that is – had to adapt it to the tones of America's deep South. For the first time since *Zulu*, he was giving up his principal trademark, all in the cause of his art and to within perfume-sniffing distance of Jane Fonda and the very young Faye Dunaway. Learning the accent was more difficult than coping with the sex and a lot less fun. The film was set in Louisiana and so a genuine Southerner (American version) was deputed to record his Louisiana lilt for him. Caine played Henry Warren, an unscrupulous farm manager who was very adept at taking farm land from people who needed the money. He said about that: 'With any other director, he would be the villain. He's a Southern bigot, but I play him trying to show what he does to himself with his own hatreds. I don't play villains. I can't. I can just play people. You know what I think? I think being villainous is just a cop-out for some people. It's why Hitler dressed his men in Gestapo uniforms, to make idiots look great.'

That was a kind way of looking at what was, to anyone else, a distinctly villainous part. Except that perhaps the most villainous thing of all was the picture itself. His thoughts about Mr Preminger would not remain kind. But he would admit that there was something of that director in his own psyche – 'because of what I consider one of the worst things in my own character, a complete hatred of inefficiency.'

As the years have gone by, he has gradually changed his verdict on Preminger, becoming more and more bitter every time he spits out his name. He told *Time Out* magazine in 1992: 'He was nice to me but I didn't know how nasty he was to everyone else. He was particularly nasty to Faye Dunaway and I pulled him on it. My attitude was if he says anything to me I'll fucking deck him.'

Hurry Sundown was set in 1945 and was about racial unrest – filmed in 1967 at a time of such racial unrest that in the course of one night, all the stars' trailers were riddled with bullets. That was nothing compared to what the critics were about to do to this film – dubbed 'the Nigger Picture' by the people who were so generous with their gunfire. It proved that you can have too much of a bad thing.

Even Michael himself admitted that 'it didn't turn out to be such a good idea'. And he wasn't just talking about working in Louisiana, but it was that too. 'I can't say I'll miss that part of the country too much,' he said. He hated all the racial tension. 'The whites there can't give in and they can't succeed,' he said just months before the new civil rights legislation introduced by Lyndon Johnson.

Then he made one of those comments that would not have endeared him to the black population. 'The Negro [it was still a politically correct term] has created his own fascists. The white man has been wrong for the past 300 years and it looks like the Negro will be wrong for the next 300 years. At one moment, the Negro will say, "Treat me like an individual" and the next minute he'll say he has inherited the white man's hatreds.'

Of course, it was the scene in Jane Fonda's bed that excited attention. He said he found it 'very difficult' – as he did all 'lovemaking' scenes. 'If you get the reality you are supposed to get in a love scene you'll always get a bollocking when you get home from a premiere from your wife or girlfriend. [They'll say] "You must have sort of loved her a little bit or you couldn't have done that. I saw the way you looked at her." All my life, it's been like that.' So he said he had found a way to deal with it all. 'I always insert a little artificiality into it, so that I can point it out when I get home.' Most of the critics pointed out quite a lot of artificiality in *Hurry Sundown*.

Rex Reed, the critic who believed that the only thing worse than a poor film was one starring Michael Caine, quoted a fellow critic Wilfrid Sheed who had written that 'no film is ever so bad that you can't find some virtue in it.' Said Mr Reed: 'He must not have seen *Hurry Sundown*.'

Caine and Reed didn't like each other very much – dating back to the time when Michael failed to turn up for a Reed TV programme. 'There had been a mix up,' a friend told me. 'Michael didn't know anything about it, didn't show up and Rex Reed got miffed.' The critic had said that Michael was 'like a bowl of oatmeal'. 'Reed,' Caine responded, 'is a silver-frosted flake.' That wasn't nice.

Mr Sheed himself was more ambivalent, but I think I caught his meaning: 'To criticise it would be like tripping a dwarf,' he said. And *Cue* magazine said: 'Preminger's taste is atrocious. His idea of erotic symbolism is Jane Fonda caressing Michael Caine's saxophone.'

Current Biography said of the movie: 'Critics generally agreed that the film was a bathetic exercise in pulp fictional sex perpetrated under the guise of a holier-than-thou cardboard sermon about social and racial injustice.' In other words, it wasn't a very good picture.

Actually, it was Caine's first bad move in the picture business, but most of the vitriol was reserved for Preminger and he himself would live to fail another day. Michael didn't worry about it. Dennis Selinger told me that he had advised him – as he had instructed his other top client, Sean Connery – to do as much as he could. 'If one out of three was good, you were still ahead.'

Over the years, Lewis Gilbert would occasionally meet his *Alfie* star and discuss his attitude to work. 'He knows he has done some terrible things in his time, but he'll say, "I'll do ten films and in that ten, there's bound to be one gold one. One will be good, two will be passable and the rest will be terrible. But the terrible ones don't matter because nobody ever sees them." There's a certain amount of truth in that. People don't go to see them if they're bad.'

No, but they do see them on television.

It certainly did look as if Joss Ackland's contrast of the marvellous Michael Caine films with the 'crap' he often made was proving remarkably apposite early on. It was like Laurence Olivier who once told me that he made terrible movies like *The Betsy* and *The Jazz Singer* because people would only remember his *Hamlet, Richard III* or *Rebecca*. He 'needed to put something in the larder'. Michael Caine felt the same way, but then, as Joss Ackland noted: 'Your stuff can also grow stale in the larder.'

The *Los Angeles Times* critic Sheila Benson commented: 'At times, he's gone through films the way sharks go through the water, because they must always be in motion or die.'

The truth was, that no matter how much promise he was now showing, Michael had moments when he was still insecure, although he would joke that his daughter Niki was responsible. 'Next time you see a horse, look at him. He's eating. When my daughter was growing up, one picture in four was made by me just to feed her horse.'

But he could get serious about it too – a kind of seriousness you could conveniently shoot holes all the way through. 'People only remember your hits. Gable was in 100 films. Can you name more than 10?' But studios and producers had longer memories. An actor was only as good as his *last* movie. He had to hope that they understood why he felt it necessary to keep going, waiting for the quality.

When he said: 'I plan to make so many bloody movies that I'll be a star before they realise I'm not star material' it indicated that he didn't consider himself to be a star. But he did. One of those big glittery ones that had their handprint on Hollywood Boulevard. Nevertheless, he would feign modesty about the star thing. 'I tried several times to do film star things, meaning utilising personality and familiarity and every time I did, I fell flat on my face. I wanted to do Cary Grant-type things, but I realised I'm not a film star, so I have to give acting performances, which is a lot harder.'

Nevertheless, he was still telling people that he was afraid that 'it will all be over in the morning.' As he said: 'Once you get to the top is when the real climb begins – because you're a target. Everyone can see you. You're a full-length target standing on a hill. Before that, you're just a big head that shows for a moment and ducks down before it gets shot off. But once you're a star, they're waiting for you. The Press, subconsciously, takes on the thing of, "We made you; now we can break you." '

It was a question of breaking what David Lean had called 'The Envy Barrier'.

Perhaps for that reason, he was always remembering lessons, analysing what it was that he and others in his profession did for a living. 'Movie acting for me is much more a matter of holding up mirrors than pictures. I worked for the moment of recognition when some part of the audience will wonder, "How does he know that I would do exactly the same thing in that situation?" '

And he had respect for the instrument that brought him to his public. 'I'm aware of what the camera is seeing. You play the camera. I mean you ignore it, but you're aware of it because you use it,' he said. 'It's a bit like a romance. The trick on the stage is physical presence, the way you hold yourself. They teach you to put your weight here – the waist. But in the cinema, they tell you not to blink. That concentrates people's minds and you hypnotise people and they wait for you to blink.'

He still had that thing about blinking but there was a good reason for it. As he once said on BBC television: 'Blinking makes your character seem weak. Try it yourself – say the same line twice; first blinking and then not blinking . . . by not blinking you will appear strong on the screen.' To prove the point, he went around one day blinking all the time. People on the set thought he had either developed an eye problem or had gone out of his mind. Which is why when he had the opportunity to wear his glasses, it was all so much easier.

He had to think of all this in the film in which he didn't wear those glasses, *Hurry Sundown*, a picture from which, soon after it opened, he realised he should have hurried away. The book on which this latest Caine epic had been based was a bestseller. The movie itself was not.

Michael Caine, however, patently, was. When he was in America, matchmakers tried to fix him up with suitable unmatched females, as if he needed them. The problem now was keeping them away, or having got them, getting rid of them when a new one was waiting at his front door. He had spent a lot of time working out the technique which would always allow the ladies to recite the exit line. He would bore them into submission, like taking them to films in Albanian, which appeared to be an obsession, but one that they did not share. When they could stand it no longer, there was usually a mutual agreement that, without similar tastes, there could be little future for them together.

He still wanted a woman with whom he could settle down. 'Marriage is tremendously important to me. I would like to have a large family and for me to stay with a woman regularly means that I could get married to her, giving up my present life. But this would be an enormous sacrifice.' So there you had it, Mr Caine was laying out his cards on the table. They were all aces, which meant that if he made that enormous sacrifice, the girl would have to have as many good cards as he had.

The only female who didn't have to worry too much about his fickle love life continued to be his mother. He said that his family relationships with Ellen and Stanley were better than they had ever been. At the end of 1966 he had taken his mother to Paris. He was there to make a guest appearance in a Shirley MacLaine film, *Woman Times Seven*, directed by Vittorio De Sica; the director was one of the reasons he agreed to do it.

That was another demonstration of his success. In the old days, he would jump at a tiny part and accept that he was a bit-part actor. Now, he did no more and said no more but was in the credits as giving a 'guest appearance'. In terms of time, it amounted to no more than in the worst of the old times, about three minutes in which he played a private detective. In prestige – and money – it was something very different.

The movie consisted of seven sketches in which Shirley MacLaine, Anita Ekberg and Adrienne Corri had to deal with men making guest appearances, like Peter Sellers, Lex Barker and Alan Arkin. He was involved in a very different collection of star appearances in a film called *Tonight, Let's All Make Love in London*. Along with Vanessa Redgrave, Edna O'Brien and Lee Marvin – to say nothing of Mick Jagger, Pink Floyd and The Animals – Michael was one of a group interviewed in a feature film on swinging London, produced and directed by Peter Whitehead.

Sellers and he became fairly close friends. Or, as he said, as close as one could ever get to Sellers. It was he who supposedly put the words, 'Not a lotta people know that' into Michael Caine's mouth, words that he swears to this day he never said, any more than Cagney called anyone a 'Dirty rat' or Bogart told the piano player to 'play it again Sam'. Peter was known to change his cars the way other men changed their socks. He refreshed his collection of gadgets equally frequently. When answerphones first came on the market, Sellers had one. He probably had one before they came on the market. Michael phoned him one day to be greeted by the genuine Peter Sellers answerphone – speaking in the kind of voice that had made him a fortune. 'Peter Sellers is not in at the moment,' he said, 'Not a lotta people know that.' Michael was unimpressed. 'What a bloody awful voice,' he said to the person with him. 'Which's that supposed to be?' 'It's you, Michael,' said his companion. 'It's you.'

In his way, Vittorio De Sica was equally enigmatic. Why else would he make some of the greatest films in the history of the cinema *and* this one? But he turned out to be all that Michael expected, even though the film probably ranks as the great Italian actor-director's worst effort, as different from *Bicycle Thieves* as a Rolls was from the average two-wheeler. 'He acted out my part for me before we started shooting and I was amazed. I'm not sure my performance on camera was anywhere as good as his was off camera.'

Nevertheless, he liked the part, not just because it wasn't time-consuming and gave him a chance to be with Shirley – he said he picked up a great many tips from her – but because he was able to enjoy Paris, which he hadn't really managed to do after Korea. This time, there were no dives where a proprietor felt sorry enough to give him a sandwich. If he saw the airport terminal, it was simply to walk through while a chauffeur collected his bags. Now it was to be the premier suite at the Hotel Georges V.

He took Ellen along for the ride and she had a wonderful time. But it was at a certain cost to Michael himself. He hadn't realised that she expected to be with him on New Year's Eve – and when he found out, he didn't want to disappoint her. So he cancelled the idea of joining friends at the *Folies Bergère*. His mother had just had an expensive hairdo and Michael had bought her a mink coat and she had no idea it wasn't for the New Year celebrations. He wasn't going to let her down. Many years later, he confessed to having 'feminine qualities'. He was, he said 'overly sensitive for a man. Nobody ever sees this side of me. My sensitivity manifests itself in that I know what effect everything around me is having on other people. It's a good talent for an actor to have. I'm not afraid of people questioning my masculinity by crying or expressing my emotions in public.'

As we have seen, Ellen was always a welcome guest at his house. If old Maurice Micklewhite had seen her, he would probably have thought she had robbed a bank – and then run off to the race course. When Niki came to London to stay, Ellen came too – and so did the little girl's grandparents, who were still her guardians and who still liked the young man who had once been their son-in-law. Pat was nowhere to be seen.

He didn't worry about his ex-wife wanting a piece of his action any more. Maintenance agreements had been drawn up and there was now no risk of his ending up spending a night or more in jail. He was investing in as many insurance policies as he could take out – just in case he found himself no longer anyone's flavour of the month.

A couple of years before there wouldn't have been money for those policies and he wouldn't have thought in those terms. Life had never been going to get better than the £16 a week he earned on the stage and he had been beginning to feel grateful for it. But now....

'Success gives me a great deal of satisfaction,' he told an American journalist in one of his few understatements. 'Everyone assured me I'd never make it. I saw all the others arriving without me. And now it's my turn. However, I can't completely believe it. This last year has been absolutely extraordinary for me. I've passed, without a moment to reflect, from zero to a hundred. I may be able to go even higher in my career, but a shock such as that will never happen to me again.' That was no mere understatement. No, whatever might happen in the future – and projects were being chalked up for him that made his mind boggle – nothing could ever be like this again.

His past was catching up with him in all sorts of ways. He always remembered what it was like to be poor, to think he had no future, even when, in his heart of hearts, he knew that he just *had* to succeed. Somehow, it became all the more obvious when walking through the streets of London that he knew so well. At about this time, he was walking towards The Strand when he saw an old woman shuffling towards him, carrying two bags.

He had £50 in his pocket – and gave it to her. She wasn't expecting him to do that. In fact, she thought he was about to pinch her bags. He was then the one who was embarrassed – and scampered away from her. 'To me,' he said, '50 quid means, maybe, ten. To her it must have meant a thousand.'

It was amazing, even to him, how those values had changed.

How he felt about *Billion Dollar Brain* in relation to values was something that at the time he kept to himself. It was the third Harry Palmer role, the third in what would turn out to be a trilogy for the present, followed years later, by some more. He didn't want any more of Palmer after the first three, he said at the time, and on the whole, the public were with him on that.

Saltzman produced the picture again, but this time Ken Russell was directing – a job that Michael himself had got him. It was a way of saying thank you for the voice-overs that the director had found for him in the bad old days. *Billion Dollar Brain* was the worst of the first three Palmer films and by all accounts did Michael much more good than it did the director, who, according to another of the film's stars Karl Malden, who played a megalomaniac intent on blowing up the world, was 'crazy'. Malden admired Michael enormously, he told me. 'I always admire actors who go over their lines the night before and then come in and do it the way it should be done next morning. That's him. He's not a selfish actor. There *are* selfish actors. But all they know is their own character. Michael, you felt, wanted to know, "What are we trying to accomplish? That's what you try to go for".'

Trying to work out what they were hoping to accomplish was just one of the mysteries of this movie. Nevertheless, and perhaps because of that, the relationship between Caine and Malden was one of the nicer things about the film. The relationship between Karl and the director was not. Nor was the weather. 'It was freezing all the time,' Malden told me. 'It was so cold that you could actually see your breath. You couldn't put enough clothes on, yet we were out there eight or nine hours at a time. The director had us running out of the train, falling into the snow – but we did it. Of course, we were young then,' said the now 87-year-old actor.

'We had one of your directors, not one of ours,' said Malden. Caine told him: 'Let's get on with it and let's get out of here.' Michael's attitude to Russell was one of amazement as well as gratitude. 'We never realised we had this lunatic genius on our hands,' he said. 'He was the least ideal man to do a thriller. What he has is this passion to make thundering great messes.'

Some of the film was shot in the studio, but all too little of it. 'Two weeks in Finland was hard,' says Malden, forced into remembering a film he would rather forget. 'We were in Finland for two weeks in February when it was bleak, the days are short and it's always dark. And something that I've never seen before. The Finns, they would drink! And we'd see how drunk they got, so pissed that they would fall over in the street. Their clothes were drab clothes. Then when it started to snow, ashes were thrown over the sidewalk so that you wouldn't slip. Then when the snow would stop and you'd move away, they would put them in a pile ready for the next snow that came down. It was dreary all day long and there we were, crossing an ice flow, a frozen lake with vehicles – which was dangerous.'

But Michael was happy, the veteran actor remembered. 'He was in a very good mood. He had just met the most beautiful, wonderful girl.'

Caine and Malden got on well. They talked about their origins, which were not too dissimilar except that Malden's father had worked in a steel mill, not in a fish market. 'He talked about his mother washing floors. He told me about his repertory company. I went to work in a small theatre too.'

And they talked about what was already a prodigious output. 'I think that he's an actor who just likes to work. That's a lot of film he was turning out at the time. I, too, always felt that you're not an actor unless you are acting. Being an athlete, I think you can't score a home run unless you get up and play. He might say that he wanted to make the money. I don't think that. I think he is a craftsman who wants to do it. A violinist, a cellist, a pianist practises every goddam day. They may only do a concert, once a month, but they have to practise.'

Michael Caine decided he had done enough practice as Harry Palmer. By mutual agreement, plans for a fourth Palmer film, *Horse Under Water* were shelved. Not surprising, considering the reviews for *Billion Dollar Brain*. 'Incomprehensible spy story smothered in the kind of top dressing now expected from this director,' said Leslie Halliwell.

Caine said that Ken Russell was one of his favourite directors. 'This is the most shocking sort of review that I read for a picture. A lot of it was very beautifully directed. It might have been confused – all right, bloody well say so.' Well, they did. And he still didn't understand why *Carry On, Follow That Camel*, out at the same time, got better reviews than did *Billion Dollar Brain*.

As it was, the third and, for the moment, final Palmer film, representing the end of two years inside the skin of Harry, made enough money to finally pay for his mother's house. He had gained two personas. With his glasses on, people would stop him in the street and say,

'Hello, Harry'. Without the glasses, they would call from across the road, 'Hey, Alfie'. Both personas would find places in the movies that would follow.

Sixteen

Too Late, the Hero

Caine said he was 'about ready to take an hour off for a lie down'. To most observers of the Caine career that seemed like an unnatural luxury. There had been four pictures in a row and more were on the way. Dennis Selinger's injunction to do whatever came his way and hope for the big hits was being taken very seriously.

'I know the problems of making rubbish,' Selinger told me, 'but you have to realise what this business is all about. I can list a dozen big stars who get too big for their boots and turn down work. Before long, the scripts don't come to them any more. What producer wants to waste his time, all the time? So people start forgetting the stars, who just become actors. After a short time of this – and believe me, it can be a very short time – nobody will be interested. When the actor puts out the word that he is ready to work, the scripts are being sent to other people. I know for a time this worried Michael. I told him that, providing *some* of the output was good, he should take what comes. It'll be the good stuff that people will see – and what they will remember.'

The exhibitors liked him and so did NATO, who launched a Kosovo-style onslaught on his behalf. This was not the North Atlantic Treaty Organisation, but the National Association of Theatre Owners, who declared him to be the 'Star of the Future'. Since they were the organisation most concerned with the necessity of keeping bums on seats (and in American parlance, keeping them *off* the seats), this augured very well indeed for his career.

They had to be excited, they agreed, about an actor who had had five films showing in American theatres in as many months, *Alfie, The Ipcress File, The Wrong Box, Funeral In Berlin, Gambit* and *Hurry Sundown.*

Deadfall, directed by Bryan Forbes, was another of the mistakes, however. A story about a cat burglar who falls in love with the wife of his gay partner didn't have the excitement about it that had been evident in *The Wrong Box*, the earlier Forbes film. But it didn't affect their relationship. 'We get on very well,' Forbes told me. 'We have a kind of shorthand between us. I don't have to direct Michael, tell him where to stand. All I have to say is, "I don't think you look very good in that, so I'll retake it." I don't have to direct Michael because he's a professional. I'll direct Michael any day of the week.' Unfortunately for them both, it hasn't happened often enough. And there was that word 'professional'. Caine himself didn't dispute the fact. 'An unprofessional actor is a man who is late, who does not know his lines and has no regard for his associates. If you're late, you keep 102 people waiting. If you don't know your lines when you get there, you upset people who have taken the trouble to learn them.'

Forbes also knew about Dennis Selinger's philosophy and shared Joss Ackland's view on the 'crap' Michael sometimes made. 'I think what Michael says is that you'll win two out of three. By that time, they've got so much money invested, they know you can't win 'em all. His whole philosophy has been "Make a film, yea! The last one was a dog. The next one will be a success." Then, they've got to go on with you.'

The location filming for *Deadfall* was done in Majorca, with Caine showing the veteran jewel thief (played by Eric Portman), who had brought him in to do the more delicate jobs that he was now too old to accomplish himself, that he was capable of as much larceny as his mentor had ever achieved.

It made a change from working in America all the time where, one columnist noted, 'Mike had been seen out on the town more often, and in the company of more women, per week than had been witnessed since the heyday of Errol Flynn.'

He loved the playboy image that was now his. Nevertheless, it *did* begin to irk. 'I was making three and four pictures a year,' he said years later. 'You figure it out. I must have spent some time on the set, some evenings learning lines and some nights going to bed early against early calls. So there just weren't that many girls or that much time spent with them.'

But he wasn't going to fight the reputation. 'All that nonsense helped,' he would reflect. 'When I was 18, I stood in front of a mirror. I thought that if I was ever going to make it as an actor, it would have to be on performance. I've never been one of those really handsome "physical" guys.'

And he faced reality. He no longer believed that women should be virgins before they married – which must have made a number of nubile females breathe a sigh of relief. 'I think that would be ideal'; but he didn't like the idea of women regarding 'what they have to offer as a great favour. Because what I found is that while they said it wasn't fair to ask that favour – which meant that they were going to give it away – they wouldn't give it away to me. When I finally got a woman, she'd had 30 lovers. It's terrible to discover the woman had given it to every guy on the block except you.'

But that led on to a piece of sardonic Caine logic, 'I also don't think a divorcée should be a virgin – which is the way they act.' But whatever he really believed, the reputation meant that he was never without the sort of feminine company that was as important to him as a good meal. Girls called him in the early hours of the morning – and in the not so early hours of the night. At parties, they would drop their phone numbers in his coat. But he said there were other sides to that story. 'I had a great deal of fun then, but anything, if you keep on doing it, becomes a bore after a while.'

He went to so many parties that people repeated the old question, 'When do you have time to work?' Fortunately, he had the stamina to get up at the crack of dawn for a 6 a.m. start, work all day and party all night – except, he maintained, that parties didn't happen until the weekends. That is not to say that he wasn't seen out during the week or that his sleeping hours were spent alone. A lot of Hollywood people liked him for that. Jackie Collins told me: 'Everyone here wants to be perceived as getting up at 5 a.m., so that everybody else thinks they're working and have to be at the studio. Michael wouldn't leave at 11 o'clock like the others. When other people have gone, he'd say, "We're sitting here waiting for the parties to begin." ' For that reason, he was on all the worthwhile guest lists. When someone told him something at a social function, he would be ready to pick up on the same subject years later, making the person feel as though they were important in his life. 'He has a photographic memory for people and what they tell him, as he has for his scripts,' said Ms Collins. That was useful as far as his women were concerned. As she pointed out: 'He was quite a ladies' man before he got married. I used to watch him in action.'

Everybody who thought they were anybody in the film community, reported seeing him in action. They measured the durability of his 'one-night stands'. When one of these turned into two nights, then three, then weeks, then months, the gossips really thought they were on to something.

Occasionally, there were other ladies in his life who were distinctly not on his courting list, but whom he treated with great deference. Such as the 79-year-old Dame Edith Evans. He met the great doyenne of the British stage at Pinewood while doing the studio shots for *Deadfall*. She had come to call on Bryan Forbes, who had directed her award-winning performance in *The Whisperers*.

Naturally, an introduction to his current star was essential.

'Why do I always think I know you?' she asked the man young enough to be her grandson. 'I even tell people I do. We've never worked together, have we?'

'I wish we had,' Michael replied gallantly and no doubt telling the truth. 'But in fact I've never had the pleasure of meeting you before.'

'How odd,' she replied. 'It must be because I've seen you so often – and you are so *memorable*.' She said it with the same sort of emphasis as she said '*handbag*' in *The Importance of Being Earnest*. But the chances are that Mr Caine enjoyed it a lot more than did Mr Worthing.

And, of course, he was memorable. And valuable. So valuable that his accountants decided he was giving too much of himself away. With that thought in mind, he was reinventing himself again, this time as a commercial company. From then on, business contracts were going to be made with Michael Caine Productions Ltd, a company formed both in Switzerland and the Bahamas.

He was now most at home in Hollywood where he was feted wherever he went – and where he was sought after too. Wherever he was staying, in a house or in a luxury hotel, there were knocks on the door – a room service waiter who happened to have a script he wanted him to read or a chauffeur who was really an actor and wanted a part in his next movie.

Some decisions were better than others. Making *The Magus* in 1968 was not one of the better ones. In it, he played an English schoolmaster on a Greek island who falls under the spell of a musician and leaves his wife, played by Anna Karina. Caine probably regarded that as rather a silly thing to do. On the other hand, it seemed that Camilla Sparv was still under his spell, but he would say no more than that he was 'with her mentally'. Yet nothing more. They were later seen at the Alvaros restaurant in Chelsea – sitting at different tables and at first trying hard not to appear to recognise each other. Before long, she married Herman Hoover III, heir to the Hoover vacuum cleaner empire.

The Magus was based on a John Fowles novel and had a lot of philosophy and mystery without any answers being offered. Caine has become amusingly scathing of Mr Fowles. The nearest to his work he has ever come (apart from *The Magus*) was seeing *The French Lieutenant's Woman*. He had never *read* any of his books because he couldn't understand them, which must, of course, have meant that they were great works of art.

One of the bright spots in the movie was the fact that he was co-starring with Anthony Quinn, of whom most people were desperately afraid, but whom he liked enormously. When I met Quinn to talk about Michael, he burst into affectionate laughter. 'We talked about not having any money,' he said.

Caine also explains in his book that it wasn't so much money as the lack of it that occupied their attention. The veteran actor said that the sort of poverty he experienced in Mexico made Michael's South London experience pale into insignificance.

The critics didn't understand *The Magus* any more than anyone else did. 'It has much of the fascination of a Chinese puzzle,' said Michael Billington, writing in the *Illustrated London News*. Which was more polite than some of the other critics' statements, nearly all of which amounted to advice to the weary cinemagoer not to bother.

Caine wasn't sorry that the location was switched from Greece itself to Majorca. In Greece the colonels were still in power after the coup that had dethroned King Constantine. 'I didn't like the idea of spending $3 million in Greece. The workers there would have got the money, but I don't like the Greek government – and we might not have been able to finish the movie.' Which might not have been a bad idea.

In 1969, his next movie was shot in Spain, near Almeria, a popular spot at the time for films with desert backgrounds, which was why the famous spaghetti westerns of the period were shot there. It was also useful for war films, those set in the Western desert. *Play Dirty* was one of those – although it seemed that the real dirty was played on Michael Caine and everyone else booked to have some connection or other with it. You get some idea of how much dirt was thrown their way from the fact that Caine and the cinema reference books differ on the story line. Nobody really wants to remember.

Michael says that it involved a group of Israelis (unlikely since Israel hadn't been established until three years after the war's end) and Halliwell, for instance, talks about them being a band of ex-criminals.

Let's say that they were Jewish soldiers from Palestine, some of whom had been jailed for their activities under the British mandate. The playing dirty of the title amounted to the Jewish soldiers being sent to blow up a German oil dump. The trouble was, to everyone's surprise, the British army had got close to the dump just as the fuses were being laid. They wanted the oil for themselves now that they were in a position to get it. So the Germans were tipped off in the belief that they would kill the Jews. By the time 'our lads' got there, they would be missing a few awkward chaps whom nobody liked and would have the oil intact. It was a good storyline, based on a true story. But it didn't look that good on screen – partly due to the fact that the script was changed and the original director walked out.

In Caine's book, it didn't bring back happy memories for another couple of reasons. He and his stand-in had to travel to the location spot in the most uncomfortable train they had ever been in, in stifling hot weather. It was also when he met Brigitte Bardot again. And was spurned by her. She was working at Almeria too – on the Sean Connery Western, *Shaliko*. Caine thought she had the hots for him and was duly impressed. When it became clear that she hoped he would become friendly with her secretary, he was less happy.

There was always the hope that his professionalism would lead to better movies. And indeed, for Michael himself, there was better news around the corner. Another of the good Caine films was on the way. More than that, it would be another of those 'important' movies. *The Italian Job* would be very special. Don Black, who wrote the lyrics for the theme song used in the film, summed up how grateful he had been to work on it. 'It has,' he said, 'become a cult – which is why it's always being shown.'

But not a cult in America, where the emphasis on soccer in the movie left the citizens of the United States stone cold. But since then, America has even fielded a team for the World Cup, so its transatlantic cult status might yet be achieved. Nevertheless, a picture becoming a cult doesn't always mean it makes a lot of money. This one would prove to do both for Michael Caine.

Once again, he plays a burglar. This was beginning to look like type-casting. This one, he said, was 'a ludicrously inefficient Cockney crook' – who makes this his most important work almost immediately after leaving jail, where he had met Noel Coward, the man who masterminded the whole thing from the 'nick'. The very idea of the 'Master', friend of the Queen Mother, toast of café society, playing a criminal was enough to send matrons running for their smelling salts.

The heist of $4 million, in Chinese gold bullion, took place around a traffic jam that Caine's character and his cohorts have staged in order to make their raid possible. The fact that it had a group of actors as disparate as Caine, Coward, Rossano Brazzi, John LeMesurier and Benny Hill shows that unconventional casting could succeed.

The effort of organising that traffic jam – it involved 800 vehicles – *had* to be rewarded and it was. But more than that was the wonderful idea of having Caine in Italy and Noel Coward sitting in jail in England. They weren't very good at the heist. As Michael said, they couldn't have successfully robbed the toothpaste counter in Woolworths.

But presumably Noel Coward could. While the studio shots were being filmed in England, the two actors from two distinct generations – to say nothing of representing two entirely different schools of acting – dined at the Savoy Grill.

It is fascinating to contemplate the reaction of visitors from Mars eavesdropping on the two men planning the heist of gold bullion over their Dover sole. It is a wonder that nobody thought of phoning Scotland Yard. But then, in those days (but not now) the diners at that august restaurant were older and more staid and would have considered it only right to mind their own business. No doubt all that the two actors were concerned with was hoping that no one would recognise them. That certainly would have been Coward's concern as he dipped his long cigarette holder closer to his ashtray. Michael Caine might have been safer. His films were possibly not so popular with the clientele of the Savoy.

That could be the reason why Michael was anxious that it would be the film that people talked about most. He had set up the deal himself and hoped that the traffic jam would be as well remembered as the car chase in *Bullitt*. Well, it wasn't but that didn't matter. It didn't prevent *The Italian Job* becoming that cult and getting a pre-Millennium new cinema release in late 1999.

There were now just two films left on his contract with Harry Saltzman. On his thirty-fifth birthday, there was an envelope waiting for Michael. He opened it – and found lots of bits of paper. It was his contract – torn to shreds. The producer wanted Caine to keep working on his films, but not as part of the lowly agreement they had first signed for *Ipcress*.

One of these films was to be *The Battle of Britain*, which probably cost almost as much as the original battle and threatened to last as long. Actually, it was a braver effort than some of the critics seemed to think. And brave *is* the word that comes to mind. It did convey more than a little of the incredible courage of the pilots of the Hurricanes and Spitfires – one of which was 'piloted' in the movie by 'Squadron Leader' Caine.

Of course, doubles were used in the actual flying sequences – except for one in which Guy Hamilton, the director, wanted realism. Mr Hamilton, after his achievements with James Bond, was not a man to trifle with. But the battles with Blofeld were as nothing compared with this onslaught on Field Marshal Goering. Having Connery at the wheel of the Aston Martin was one thing. Michael Caine behind the joystick of a real Spitfire was rather more worrying.

All he was asking was for Michael to taxi down the runway. Reluctantly, his star agreed. Until he asked what the little red button was for, that is. Then came the big warning – not to touch it. 'If you press that,' said the technical advisers before walking away, 'you'll take off.' That was not something to take lightly, especially for a man who didn't yet hold even a driving licence.

Looking back on it, he would say that every time he thinks about the movie his mind wanders to 'knickers'. Quite possibly his mind often wandered to thoughts of ladies' knickers. In this case, however, he was probably thinking of the scene in which Susannah York was seen in hers, together with stockings and suspenders. It was the only slightly erotic moment in a movie that concentrated on the battle itself and, sadly for Michael, she didn't wear them in a scene in which he was involved, but with her film husband Christopher Plummer.

It was all a huge undertaking, with Laurence Olivier playing Lord Dowding, the head of Fighter Command, ably assisted by Kenneth More, Trevor Howard, Patrick Wymark (a big TV star at the time), Robert Shaw and Edward Fox, to say nothing of the world's eleventh biggest air force.

That was what Saltzman claimed he now ran (even if half of them had iron crosses on their fuselages and the other half blue, white and red roundels); it was a nice publicity line and one he used to great effect when he fought the Battle of Britain all over again with the German technical adviser, Adolf Galland. Galland was one of the Luftwaffe aces. Saltzman's problem was that the German wouldn't accept that his side had lost the battle. Harry insisted that they had and did so with all the venom of a man wanting to get his own back not just for his 'opponent's' view but for the whole Second World War and the Holocaust, as well.

Too Late The Hero might have seemed an appropriate title for that encounter. As it was, it was Michael's next film. This time he swapped his smart blue RAF officer's uniform for the sweaty khakis of a British soldier fighting the Japanese. He was Private Tosh Hearne, formerly a medic (and therefore unarmed), who was recruited for a suicide mission.

The picture, directed by Robert Aldrich, was about the battle for one small Pacific island, one half of which was held by the Americans and British, who were fighting each other, and the other by the Japanese who were fighting them both. Essentially, it was the story of the patrol, in which he was an obnoxious private, and their attempt to capture a Japanese radio station and so broadcast a false message. The true message was that this Cockney didn't want to fight in the war. It was familiar territory for a Korean veteran. So was the eventual outcome of the movie, but we'll come to that later. The picture wasn't marvellous, but it was selected as the official British entry at the San Sebastian Film Festival for 1969.

But there were consolations. Michael was staying at the White Rock Hotel, where there was always music playing in his room, a feature which he enjoyed and which he has come to need. However, there was always the risk of attacks by Huk terrorists who had dedicated themselves to making life uncomfortable to visitors as well as for the opponents of their independence cause. Then there were the people he was working with, like Henry Fonda, Harry Andrews, Ian Banham, Ronald Fraser, Denhom Elliott and Cliff Robertson. But no women. That left him in need of consolation. The cast had been given a notice, on arrival that said: 'No wives, girlfriends or visitors' – which he thought sounded just right – for the Army.

But he made up for it. It was in Manila that he met a girl. Of course, he always met girls but this one looked as though she were going to be special. Her name was Minda Feliciano and she was married to Leo Guild, a Hollywood writer. She would spend much of the next year denying, half denying and possibly agreeing that she would divorce Leo to marry Michael Caine. And he thought he would marry her. He spoke of wanting to have 'lovely Cockney Fillipino babies'. Sheilah Graham, at that time the only real successor to Hedda Hopper and Louella Parsons as queen of the Hollywood gossip mill, noted his friendship with Minda and said 'Michael Caine's "No" [about having met the future Mrs Caine] is getting weaker.' And, she said, Minda 'has proved herself in word – and many a deed – that she is devoted to him.

Yes, he repeated, marriage was a possibility. 'I don't want to be wandering around as a 50-year-old roué.'

For a time, he was back in Hong Kong, a place he had visited before during his stint in Korea. It is fair to say he was treated rather more pleasantly this time. And with more attention (at least from everyone except the military police who, this time, displayed no interest at all). He was followed everywhere by the Press and quoted on everything.

He said: 'Hong Kong is far behind the times, they think that a movie star is someone you insult.' Well, that *was* strange for him.

He also said he could identify all the CIA and MI5 men in the colony. The Secret Services did not take kindly to the idea of Harry Palmer, who might well have done pretty well sorting out the world's security problems in *The Ipcress File*, pretending he knew anything about the real-life world of the spy. And this time they were less considerate than when he inadvertently got mixed up in the Christine Keeler affair.

During his stay the room where he was sleeping with a particularly delectable female was invaded by the police. In his autobiography, he tells the story hilariously. He says that the police were officious – until one man recognised him as 'Alfie' and said that he himself was the Chinese Alfie – he had fucked hundreds of women.

On the way out, he was in trouble again. He was held up by customs. Was that, too, the result of government intervention? No, it turned out that nobody there knew that Maurice Joseph Micklewhite, the name under which he travelled and which was inscribed on his passport, was really Michael Caine. He was only left alone when he informed them that his company was spending nearly $7 million in Manila, so they had better leave him alone. Actually he put it more graphically, 'For that money, you can jolly well shut up the bag, baby.' He only had 200 French cigarettes and five tubes of Coppertone in that bag, but it was the principle that counted with him all the time.

Another problem would haunt him for some time afterwards. Alas for him and his supposedly non-sexist attitude, he allegedly suggested that Chinese women were flat-chested – women needed to have big breasts, he believed – and he wondered if they ever breast-fed their children.

He did not know from any personal experience: 'The truth is I couldn't even get a Chinese girl to go out with me. They are very sceptical about European men. They take the attitude that we're all right, but you wouldn't want your sister to marry one. No matter what

A battle of wits – and of egos, to say nothing of talents. In *Sleuth* (1972) with perhaps the greatest actor of the 20th century, Laurence Olivier. Caine turned in one of his finest performances and was nominated for an Oscar.

In 1972 Caine met and married his life long partner Shakira.

The Wilby Conspiracy (1975) in which Caine co-starred with Sidney Poitier in a melodrama about apartheid. Here with Prunella Gee.

The Man Who Would Be King (1975). Caine's performance was not liked by 'the bible of the movie industry' *Variety* who commented that he gave a 'poor performance'. But Caine's Peachy and Sean Connery's Daniel Dravot was a pairing that the public liked and at the Oscars the film was nominated in four categories.

1975 – Caine starred alongside Donald Sutherland and Donald Pleasance in an adaptation of Jack Higgins' huge bestseller *The Eagle Has Landed*. Caine's performance was celebrated this time and the film was a massive box office success.

A Bridge Too Far (1977) directed by Richard Attenborough.

1978 – the year of *Silver Bears, The Swarm* and *California Suite* and the year he worked with Shakira on *Ashanti.*

Educating Rita (1983) turned into one of those Caine movies that make you want to forgive so many of the others. Caine was nominated for Best Actor and Julie Walters for Best Actress.

1981: Michael Caine, the restaurateur – with partners Peter Langan and Richard Shepherd. He was to go on to own a number of first class restaurants around London particularly with Michelin Three Star Chef, Marco Pierre White.

With Steve Martin in *Dirty Rotten Scoundrels* (1988). Caine played the role as David Niven might have done.

Michael Caine, 1997 – back in London near Tower Bridge, just up river from Rotherhithe where he was born and down river from where he had set up home at Chelsea Harbour.

The family man (1990). Shakira is on the right. Daughters Nikki and Natasha on the left.

The great return to form, *Little Voice* 1998. Caine with his co-stars Brenda Blethyn, Jane Horrocks and Ewan McGregor. He was nominated for an *Evening Standard* Award and at 65, Michael Caine won The Golden Globe.

I said after "the flat-chested" item was printed, I seemed to get deeper into trouble. I didn't mean a *double entendre* when I said, "What a fuss over so little".'

But the local papers defended their national pride – in the most logical way imaginable. Just like a British tabloid, they went in search of evidence to bolster their response – and came up with a gaggle of native women with the biggest breasts their side of Australia. In the end, Michael tried to make light of the matter and hoped that he would not be barred from the area in the future. It was just a 'tempest in a C-cup,' he said. Minda Feliciano didn't appear to be lacking in that particular department – or to resent his comments about her Chinese sisters. And their love affair seemed to be blossoming.

Back in Grosvenor Square, she would cook him oriental dishes, but for much of the time she appeared to be the only 'dish' in which he was interested. Sheilah Graham reported that Michael was 'almost in tears' when Minda threw a surprise birthday party for him at the Tramp disco in Mayfair. This was one occasion when he wasn't about to take a girl to an Albanian film. Even so, the romance didn't last. He somehow felt guilty about his relationships. He said he went to see Joanne Woodward in *Rachel, Rachel*, about a woman whose lover leaves her when she mentions marriage. He said he couldn't bear to watch it and walked out of the cinema. 'I felt it was about me. I couldn't wait to get out. I felt guilty.'

There was now someone on hand to prevent those thoughts getting to a public who might get the wrong idea. Jerry Pam had met Michael once again. Pam was the publicist on *Too Late The Hero* and took advantage of that to suggest again that Caine might do worse than employ a press agent – himself.

'Michael said: "We've met," and I said, "Yeah" and he said, "I thought so. You're a Cockney lad like me." '

The two men, who suddenly found they had more in common than most in the business, agreed to meet for lunch at the Cock 'n' Bull, a restaurant on the Sunset Strip in West Hollywood that liked to think it resembled an English pub. Perhaps they thought that it would be an omen for a successful future together. Caine told him: 'You know I think, from my experience here in America, I might need a publicist.'

It was music to Pam's ears, he told me, but he couldn't understand why Michael had rejected the notion when he had first put it to him. He now knew, with all the publicity he was getting, that interpretations were being put on what he said and he knew that he was in an industry that required people to be in the news – but only the good news – all the time.

'I said to him,' Pam told me, 'that everyone has to have a gimmick.' Was Michael Caine, the glasses-wearing Cockney enough? They agreed, for the moment, that it was and also to let Dennis Selinger in on the idea. The deal was done – at the Bistro restaurant, one of the smartest Beverly Hills eateries of the time. Pam paid for the food 'because I've been wooing you for a client.' Michael paid for the wine. 'I'm a lover of good wine,' he said. It was the first time he had discussed what was about to become one of his trademarks. 'And besides, we'll celebrate your becoming my publicist.'

He realised the value of what was now on offer. Pam was officially appointed and in London, one of the most eminent public relations men in his field, Theo Cowan was given the job, too – with Jerry Pam dictating policy.

Pam went to London to assess his new client and his surroundings. He stayed at the flat in Grosvenor Square and enjoyed the Caine lifestyle. There, they would have steak sandwiches at 3 o'clock in the morning. Michael talked to him about his career and about his artistic tastes, his passion for Tiffany lamps and anything art deco, his fascination with contemporary art.

Pam asked him about his plans. 'I need the money,' he said. 'I'm going broke.' 'I was stunned,' Pam said, 'I don't know if it were bad management or what. But he was spending money very extravagantly.' It wasn't the publicist's place to tell him to change his way of life; that wasn't something anyone could do.

In London, now that Michael's romance was all over, he was still being watched. Jackie Collins noted that he had no time for women he didn't want to be with. This was never more evident, she told me, than at a lunch at the White Elephant Club, a hangout in Curzon Street in the heart of Mayfair, much sought after by Hollywood personalities, in particular. (Sammy Davis junior virtually made it his London home and he was followed by a hundred others.) 'There was one particular rich woman who collected movie stars,' Ms Collins remembered for me. 'It was at the White Elephant Club where this woman tried to come on to him. He was the only movie star who ever turned her down.'

He didn't need her. He had his pad in Grosvenor Square, seemingly lined wall to wall with women as well as with books; it had few windows and wallpaper which one of his girlfriends described as looking like something from the jungle. It was a jungle, however, that most females were still willing to try beating their way through. There were paintings, too, antique furniture and one wall reserved for showing movies.

The fact that he was so happy there was in its way a kind of statement – that no matter how much he liked Hollywood and all that the nearby paradise of Beverly Hills offered him, England was still home. The statement was underlined when he bought another house, some 30 miles away, which would prove to be more like home than anywhere he had ever lived before. It was a small Queen Anne property – actually a converted water mill – built on 750 feet of river frontage near Windsor.

He decided that he was a passionate gardener and set about pulling up things he thought had been planted wrongly, clearing land for the grass and trees that he saw as his true heritage. The garden, he said, was his psychiatrist. It was a novel way of going into therapy and was a lot more inviting than a stranger's leather couch.

He would reflect for years on his good fortune – not luck; his fortune had come from hard work, nothing less – in having a place like that. More than just the house and the outstanding views of the river, it was the proximity to Windsor race course. Not that he ever used it himself. But there was a gate close by. Every time he saw it, he imagined what his father would have given for such an opportunity. The man who wasted so much of his money on lost bets and on the fares to get to the course would at least have saved on the cost of getting on a train or bus. The chances are that his son would have given him the money for the bets too. With Michael in charge, there's no knowing how old Maurice Micklewhite's luck might have changed.

As for his son's, he acknowledged that his career was at a crossroads. 'You reach a point where you may go up and become one of the very big names like Taylor or Burton. But there's nothing you can do about it. I carry on as I have been, but for me production is the goal. I want to be my own producer and not only myself as an actor in my own films.' He also wanted to direct films. He should probably have been content with the goal of producing, something he was already on the way to achieving. Production was more in his line, but not directing. He planned to direct a picture called *Written In The Sand* – but it never happened. He said he got the idea after being invited to direct a commercial – for an ice cream firm. They wanted to plug five new flavours, each one enjoyed by a different girl. The company thought that Caine would be ideal casting for that job, even though he had never directed anything in his life before. He thought about it and rejected it. Anyway, he always believed that it was easier to be an actor than a director. 'A director has to come in every day. Actors get days off.'

Nevertheless, given the right opportunity, he said, he would 'jump at it'. And he explained: 'There never was a property that I would have wanted to direct yet, but there will be. And also I would rather grow old disgracefully behind camera rather than wearing wigs and having my face lifted and doing push-ups all afternoon.' Another time he put it more colourfully: 'I don't want to wind up an old poop cadging pink gins off young actors in pubs.' Nobody would see the push-ups – or the wigs or the facelifts. They were happy he was an actor. He was much too young to think about growing old, anyway.

His fans were becoming content to have him as a superstar – even one who sometimes made films which people like Joss Ackland would refer to as crap.

Seventeen

The Male of the Species

People wanted to know whether Michael would have made it in the age when Cary Grant would have been a natural choice for all those romantic burglar roles that were now being earmarked as Caine territory.

Even Jerry Pam told me he thought Michael might not have succeeded when stars had worn white tie and tails. No, he was the perfect example of someone being at the right place at the right time, no matter how long it seemed to have taken to get there. 'The timing was perfect for him.' The 1960s were turning into the 1970s and Caine and the Beatles and the Rolling Stones and Carnaby Street represented that exciting place called England. In America, where Grant and Ronald Colman had epitomised a sort of British Royal family in exile, people had suddenly found that Britain had stars they liked to think were like themselves – aristocrats who had come from working-class roots.

In the United States where the only effective class barriers were delineated according to money, these were people who could sit with kings and queens – and, of course, did.

Nobody in Britain had ever made so much of these roots. In truth, few would have wanted to do so. A previous generation would have covered them up, invented pedigrees to match those of the thoroughbred horses and dogs with which they liked to pose. They invented names for themselves, not at the whim of some producer or press agent, but because they wanted to be those names.

America helped Michael Caine all along the way. In Britain, that Elephant and Castle accent might have been seen as a quaint form of revolt, but if he hadn't worn it as a kind of second skin, audiences would have tired of it before now. America liked it. For people in the sticks as much as in the big cities, it had the same sort of effect that transatlantic voices had for the British after *The Jazz Singer* in 1927, the film which showed that the motion picture screen could talk. Most British people had never heard an American accent before then.

After Michael Caine, Cockney – real Cockney and not those Dick Van Dyke or even Eliza Doolittle vowels – was not just acceptable, it was the English norm. Hollywood society took to him for his novelty value as much as for his talent and discovered that they also liked to be with him. There was also the fact that he had crossed those class barriers. People who had money didn't normally mix with common people. No one in America thought about the accent making him common.

For Michael himself, it was a kind of reverse snobbery, a charge that he has never effectively been able to deny. 'Meritocracy,' he said, 'is taking the place of aristocracy.'

There was another factor he probably never gave himself a moment to think about – his background at the Grocers. He was amazed that day at the Cock 'n' Bull to discover that Jerry Pam had been to the same school. Others in the Hollywood community were equally amazed to realise that he wasn't Jewish. 'Of course, he is, isn't he?' Karl Malden asked me again. 'My wife is Jewish and he talks to her in Jewish.' 'Jewish' in this case being Yiddish, almost the lingua franca of the Hollywood hierarchy in the 1970s as it had been 40 years earlier when Jack and Harry Warner used it to talk about their actors in their presence – until they realised that the Irish–American James Cagney spoke it as well as they did themselves.

Since then, many Yiddish terms have entered the general lexicon. In the 1970s, it was, outside of elderly or strict religious Jewish communities, mainly a showbiz language. But it was more than just the words that Caine used that made producers, agents and others in the business feel as though he were one of them. There were gestures, attitudes, which appeared to make a difference. Nearly all his friends were Jewish. He was able to communicate. Other English actors had stumbled at such fences. Again, these were barriers that didn't exist for him.

But all this was as nothing compared to that other factor in his make-up which made him the ideal dinner party guest as well as a seemingly unassuming character to have on a movie set. 'He's very, very bright,' says Pam today. 'He can discuss so many subjects on which he is so knowledgeable. He has great reasoning power. Not just the stuff he reads, but he can analyse everything. He has a fantastic memory.'

He would talk about the war in Vietnam, the favourite topic of conversation among what were not yet known as America's chattering classes. But what they liked about him was his willingness to listen – a compliment other successful people were not always so willing to extend. And when those people – frequently beautiful women – asked if he remembered an event in their lives which was clearly more important to them than it could possibly have been to him, he would always say that he did. Because it was the truth.

That memory was useful. It is, of course, one of the greatest and most important tools of an actor. Without a memory, he is not going to be able to function as effectively as Caine always has – even in those terrible pictures. Not for him the idiot boards that became as essential to performers from John Barrymore to Bob Hope. Barrymore once said: 'My mind is full of the wonders of Shakespeare, I'll not sully it with this shit,' and looked for his next line scribbled on to a piece of paper dangling from the camera.

Caine knew his lines. But he also knew how to train that memory, to get it to work for him. Once a scene was locked in the can, that was it. The speeches were gone. He didn't need them any more. There was a vacant place for those he would use in the next day's shooting.

But the memorising operation was essential for the Caine character. Not just for working on scripts or even for being able to recall the conversation he had with some girl or other, but because it enabled him to pursue arguments that suited his stance on so many matters. Pam told me: 'If I say anything to him, he will reply, "But six months ago, you told me . . ."' Plainly, you got into an argument with Caine at your peril.

It was also sometimes at his own peril, of course. The man who had vowed not to do theatre or television again – he was now a man of the cinema above all else – had succumbed to another TV play. Not that it was surprising. Laurence Olivier, Paul Scofield and Sean Connery had done so too. The play was called *The Male Of The Species*, a three-parter in which the three men other than Olivier – who acted as narrator throughout the series – each vie, in their own way, for the attentions of Anna Calder-Marshall and show how they have affected her life.

The writer Alun Owen had described his work as 'a moral fable for our time'. The fact that a dozen other writers had called their plays precisely the same thing was not intended to diminish the importance of a largely amusing trio. Caine's role was said to be 'an Alfie without tears'. Connery played Anna's father (a brave move in an age when he was still identified with James Bond) and Scofield, the older man in the story, a barrister who wouldn't have dreamed of spending a moment with the likes of Alfie, which, of course, he didn't; in the play the three never meet.

There was prestige in being sandwiched between Olivier and Scofield and, once again, demonstrating his equality with Sean Connery – all good reasons for agreeing to do television again. But there was a third reason. The films, shot at ATV's Elstree studios, were all in aid of charity – for rebuilding Denvile Hall, a home for elderly British actors and actresses.

'I wouldn't do a television play for money,' said Michael, which showed that he really did believe he had arrived. In the old television days – the good days, as they had appeared then, at a time when there was a rush of good work, some of it winning awards – money was what he wanted, although there had never been enough. After all, this was the bloke whose memory of borrowing money from his mother was still agonisingly fresh.

The new plays won an Emmy and most people connected with them seemed content about that.

He admitted that TV was something to be used, not to figure in his career. That was certainly how he saw it in America. 'I use television as a marvellous communications system, as publicity. The *Johnny Carson Show*, *Today*, the *Merv Griffin Show*. I've done them all five times.' He would do similar programmes in Britain too, but the idea of the talk show hadn't yet caught on to anything like the same degree. Television plays were very different.

After all, this was the man now being called 'an English Humphrey Bogart' – Angie Dickinson's term for him. He would have had to be super-human not to have been flattered by that. After all, Bogart was one of those heroes, a man he used to play truant to see at the local Odeon.

The past kept his feet on the ground. And so did his own definition of morality. On his wall was Kipling's poem 'If'. 'I've always had Kipling in my philosophy. There are things in that that I live by. It's like a mini religious sort of thing.'

The other 'mini religious sort of thing' was not falling into the traps that had ensnared his father. He still didn't gamble. He loved his wine, but never got drunk. The only spirits he enjoyed were camouflaged into cocktails like whisky sours. Before long, that would change to an alarming degree, but in the early 1970s he was totally sober and able to remember how it was when he had started out in the business.

After all, he had seen the effect of drink and not just among some people he knew in the early days. They were sometimes close to paralytic but he never was. 'I used to stay sober long enough to hold a decent conversation in case the police arrived. By the end of the evening, I'd be looking for women but everyone else would barely be starting their drinking. They would drink until dawn, sleep in the afternoon and go to the theatre at night. I went home early. I guess that's the reason I was the last of the group to become successful. I remember one night I left early, which was three in the morning to the group. One actor got drunk and took off his clothes. He sat on top of a police car that had been summoned to the pub we were at.'

No. That never happened to Michael then. But before long, he did start drinking – and his smoking turned from a regular habit into an obsession. He smoked so many cigarettes that it was noticed. Once, at a party, Tony Curtis spotted the habit and grabbed the packet from his hands and threw it in the fire. It made such an impression that he actually did decide to give up – not the 'weed' entirely, but cigarettes. There were no more foul-smelling French fags for him. Instantly, he switched to cigars. They remain his weakness to this day. But just as the smoking habits changed, so did his attitude to booze. He started drinking vodka, at first just a little, before long, a whole bottle a day.

There were those who thought that he used to drink to fortify himself against some of the work he was having to do – or perhaps that he should have done. But that was wrong on two counts. He knew when films were not going to be particularly great, but he was still able to turn work down – and, besides, the drinking didn't seem to have any noticeable effect. It was just a pleasurable thing to do.

Nevertheless, there are those who wished that he was as discriminating about his movies as he was about the products of his cellar or the food he was served at restaurants.

In his autobiography he says his rule of thumb was simple: he chose the best script available at a time when he 'needed' one. None of that nonsense about artistic integrity. I asked Karl Malden about that. He was the actor who said that he and Caine had to work because they were workaholics. It was what they did. Michael also believed that it was a muscle that had to be constantly exercised. 'It's a muscle up here,' Malden said, pointing to his head.

There were certain other muscles he was not prepared to exercise as an actor. In 1970, he was asked to play in *Women In Love*, based on the D. H. Lawrence novel. He could have either of the two main male roles opposite Glenda Jackson. The director, Ken Russell – proving, despite what Karl Malden had said, that he and Caine had got on very well indeed during *Billion Dollar Brain* – believed he was what was needed in the earthy story.

Michael, who as we have seen, rarely turned down a meaty part, thought this one was too meaty by half. The script showed that there was a nude scene – not just for the women in the picture, but for the two men who wrestle in front of a giant fireplace. Michael didn't mind the wrestling – Wilson's school had prepared him for that. He didn't even object to the fireplace. But the nude scene he wouldn't tolerate. So he took it out of the script, presented the revisions to Russell and said that either the nude scene stayed out or he stayed out himself. The director insisted and the parts went to Alan Bates and Oliver Reed.

Caine was unrepentant. 'I think nudity's undignified and I think the worst enemy of an actor is ridicule. I think nude men look ridiculous. I really do. I didn't spend 20 years learning how to do something in order to have people staring at my ass.' His real worry was that people would be staring not so much at that ass but somewhere else.

The film would indeed always be remembered for that scene. 'That's one instance where I turned down a good film that was very successful and very good for the two actors who appeared in it. It was a wonderful film, probably better off without me.'

There was another picture that was probably better off *with* him. *The Last Valley*, made that same year, had all the marks of one of those films he should never have made and yet it turned out considerably better than he or anyone else had a right to expect.

Actually, he liked making it. At least, he liked a lot of it. He liked the idea of John Barry – the composer who was not just a close friend, but whose home he had shared after he left Terry Stamp's flat – writing the score.

What he didn't like now, any more now than he had earlier on, was riding a horse. He and the equestrian life were not made for each other. This time he had a horse that would have been more comfortable under a jockey in the Grand National. Michael's problem was that the animal liked to go fast without any encouragement from a human being. The horse's problem was that encouragement was precisely what Caine was giving it. It turned out that the sword he was wearing was giving the horse a message – without his realising it. Every time the sword knocked against the horse's side, the animal took it as an invitation to advance. The faster the sword went, the faster the horse ran. It was no more than reasonable. It hadn't been told that its rider had other ideas.

The picture was set in 1641 and also starred Omar Sharif, neither of which, on the surface, seemed to augur well for him. Sharif was every woman's pin-up of the age and playing with him was rather like defying the old Hollywood adage of never making a movie with children, animals or other people's screen idols.

What was more, it was a film in which the actors were likely to be more overwhelmed by the action around them than they had been in any Caine film since *The Battle of Britain*. Imagine every nasty thing that could have happened in 1641 and then add pillage and rape, executions by being tied to a stake while fire danced at your feet, and a few additional examples of torture, plague and throat slashing and any sense of competition between two male film idols doesn't really seem all that worrisome. The *Washington Post's* critic Gary Arnold said that Michael was 'wonderfully convincing and satisfying' in a film that is now largely forgotten.

The more recent past occupied Michael in a rather different way. He went back to South London. He regularly went there, of course, to see his mother. He had bought her her own house in the South London suburb of Streatham. Mrs Micklewhite wouldn't have felt comfortable near Grosvenor Square. But Michael knew that she liked to have people, her own people, close by. So he had flats built in part of the house so that she could put in whichever relatives she might fancy having nearby.

This particular visit wasn't just to see Ellen, but to be close to his roots near the place where he was born and where he went to school, near the sewer culvert where he practised speaking 'posh' and where the cinemas used to be, the ones where he went to see all his heroes. It was one of those nostalgia trips to which, no matter how glad he was to get away from it all, he still felt drawn. It was an astonishing visit. He wasn't alone. Making a similar kind of return to his origins was another personality who had made a name for himself in Hollywood – Charlie Chaplin. They were born in different ages but just two blocks away from each other. Chaplin wasn't terribly sure who Caine was, but that was a purely one-sided observation.

It was also a sad day. It was while he was in the neighbourhood that he saw a gang of workmen hard at it – pulling down the Kennington

Regal, the scene of many a day playing truant. 'What a thing to do,' he said at the time.

That sort of thing made him think about where it had all begun, physically and philosophically and about his own political stance at a time when wealth meant a total change in politics.

He said he was going to become a Liberal. He would be a Labour supporter if Roy Jenkins, Home Secretary and Chancellor in the Labour Government, were premier. But Harold Wilson was in Downing Street and he had talked about 'the white heat' of technology. He didn't like the white heat – any more than he liked communism, the attitude of the trade unions or East Germany. The white heat, he decided, was something that might burn up people like him.

He was, he said again, 'a product of the meritocracy', a word much in vogue at that time. 'The day of the working man has come. I really don't mind what they do, but it does seem as if the present Labour Government is set on a policy of punitive taxation. This is entirely political and has nothing to do with economics. It just ensures that large amounts of capital will be moved out of the country.'

He was talking now of moving out of the country himself. At least he said so in America, which a lot of people thought was not cricket. He should speak well of his native land when abroad, not knock it. 'I'd hate to leave England, but I wouldn't stay if it meant I'd be destroyed financially. I suppose I'd come to Los Angeles, it's a very relaxed way of life and it's the centre of the business I'm in. The weather's good too but then I'd miss the seasons. Altogether, I wouldn't be very happy.'

The story got out that he said he was going to leave the country. All hell broke out, with British newspaper leaders declaring that he was biting the hand that was feeding him very well indeed.

'That was not quite what I said,' he responded to London journalists. 'There really is no way of getting me to quit Britain, not unless they drive me out by force. I'm so bloody English, it's ridiculous. I'm a very loyal supporter. I believe in staying with a team even when it's doing badly.' But he hated the tax proposals which he said amounted to 'hammering nest eggs'. Particularly, as he said: 'I pay the bloody things, that's what I do.'

He described himself, in terms similar to those used by the future prime minister, Tony Blair, as, 'A New Londoner – with the Cockney lilt still in the speech patterns, still Cockney, but well dressed, working into a new class.' He was now talking about his political stance more and more. 'I'm a right-wing socialist,' he explained. 'If not 'a champagne socialist', another label to which he owned up. Socialist enough to believe that people who can't help themselves needed to be helped by the state. Right-wing enough, he said, to be willing to pay tax to cover that need, but to believe that he should then be left alone.

Fortunately for him, nobody was leaving his career alone.

Eighteen

Get Carter

Perhaps people were talking a little too much about the poorer Caine films. It was about time to remind audiences and critics alike what he could really do in a good movie.

In the coming five years, sandwiched among the ones he hoped nobody would remember, would be two pictures that he might like to have engraved on his tombstone. Both became serious markers in his life. Milestones rather than tombstones. They point the way to understanding what was so special about him.

Get Carter in 1971 was not everyone's cup of tea. Judging by the eminent critic of the *New Yorker*, Pauline Kael it wasn't her cup of coffee either. 'There's nobody to root for but the smartly dressed sexual athlete and professional killer (Michael Caine) in this English gangland picture, which is so calculatedly cool and soulless and nastily erotic that it seems to belong to a new genre of virtuoso viciousness,' she wrote.

But if you analyse the words she wrote you realise that beneath that 'nasty eroticism' was something more. You didn't have to like a picture to realise that it had something strong behind it. Even she went on to say: 'What makes the movie unusual is the metallic elegance and single-minded proficiency.'

Peter Schjeldahl wrote in *The New York Times* that Michael's performance 'ticks and glints like a bomb encased in stainless steel'.

It was more than a gritty performance by Michael Caine. He chalked up yet another first. He produced the picture too. It was also a milestone for the British film industry. For the first time since *Brighton Rock*, almost a quarter of a century before, gangsterism was attacked by an English studio the way Warner Brothers used to deal with Chicago in the 20s. It was more than the once-tried British formula of the unpleasant man in the brown trilby who fiddles his way to the race track and slashes the face of a girl or two before he finds a pair of handcuffs clamped on him.

This had all the sadism of the 1947 picture and then some. It possessed a strong storyline and it portrayed sex that would have made the old Hays office spin in its corporate grave. Now you saw naked breasts in a British film and terrible things being done to women. You also saw pretty nasty things being done to men too. Above all, however, you saw Michael Caine, who had had quite a track record playing men who were on the wrong side of the law, usually overseas. But now he was operating in his own country and you didn't have to laugh at his lines if you didn't want to.

He knew a bit about gangland. He had run a gang at the Elephant, the one he now admits he left because he was afraid it could have led him into a serious life of crime. Jack Carter made no such decision. 'Carter is the dead-end product of my own environment, my childhood. I know him well. He is the ghost of Michael Caine.'

Even so, he had to make the real facts of the matter clear. 'I'm not playing Michael Caine and I'm not playing Humphrey Bogart. I'm playing Jack Carter.'

He felt that he was a kind of combination of Spencer Tracy in *Bad Day At Black Rock* and Lee Marvin in *Point Blank*. But then that wasn't really true either. 'When you get down to it,' he said, 'Carter is unique.' What is more, compared with the likes of *Lethal Weapon*, it was all fairly tame stuff. The cost of the movie hardly matched either, but this was the early 1970s.

The statements about playing his own ghost were frank words, not necessarily chosen by his publicist. 'I'm there to tell the truth,' protested Jerry Pam, 'to show Michael in the best light – which isn't difficult.' But the admissions, the genuine ones, out of Michael's own mouth made him seem all the more human. They also showed the seriousness with which he judged one of his most significant roles. The fact is that the dapper Michael Caine seems very much at home in the picture toting a rifle behind a crumbling wall in Newcastle.

And if you wanted to know just how significant it all was, Caine was ready to underline the sentences he had already uttered a dozen times to a dozen reporters. 'Carter was part of my childhood folklore. Where I came from there were a dozen Jack Carters. All folk heroes. The status quo was to be violent and crooked, not decent and respectable.'

It was a lesson on how to bring that childhood to bear on the future.

James Cagney once told me how he grew up with kids who 'ended up in the Chair – or in the Hoosegow, as we used to say.' He came from Yorkville, in New York, where carrying a gun was as usual as having a baseball bat (also used as a weapon). Caine was the first English actor to have had that 'advantage'.

He added to that experience by building up a dossier of what happened to people who had not travelled along a path as peaceful as his; the only action he had taken against a fellow human being was to tell Otto Preminger, and a Rolls Royce salesman, to please be kind enough to 'fuck off'.

'It made me realise that when you go the other way, as I did, it doesn't destroy the old lessons, not quite. It simply suppresses them. It is hard to take the milieu of youth out of a man. It's not like removing an appendix, not like cutting out your tonsils.'

But the film was intended to tell people that there were men around who weren't beyond cutting out another person's tonsils – in less than hygienic conditions and without the aid of an anaesthetic. 'It is completely abhorrent to me to contemplate my fist going into somebody's face, making them bleed. It is even more abhorrent to contemplate somebody doing it to me.' Perhaps that explained his suggestion that *Get Carter* was performing a public service.

The fans loved him – and got him to sign his autograph on whatever was to hand. He hadn't yet, like Errol Flynn or the youthful Frank Sinatra, reported experiencing the delights of young women opening blouses for him to sign his name on their bras, but there was almost everything else presented to him – anything from newspapers and bus tickets to brown paper parcels. It proved what Jerry Pam told me: 'He's always co-operative. He doesn't refuse autographs or to have photographs taken.'

But sometimes he had to suffer unanticipated reactions from the fans. It was while he was signing autographs in Newcastle that a girl went up to him and gave her opinion: 'Me mum said you were good-looking. But I think y'er ugly.'

The picture was received in much the same way, certainly not as he would have liked it to have been. At the time – long before it achieved the following it now has (like *The Italian Job* rereleased on the big screen in 1999) – he said it was seen as just another violent film. 'Hoist on our own petard, we were.'

What you decide after watching *Get Carter* is that this is the star's movie. As nothing he had done since *Alfie*, this was all Michael Caine, even though John Osborne and Ian Hendry were there with him in the acting credits.

But he didn't see it like that. To him, it had become a director's picture and he was not at all happy about that. Michael maintained that Mike Hodges, *Carter*'s director, was one of those who wanted to put his stamp on the film above everybody else's. As he said, 'Half the films I've made have been "Look ma, I'm directing". And you sort of put the actors wherever you want, to prove you are directing.' He went on: 'Bob Aldrich never sacrificed actors on the altar of direction. But Sidney Furie used to do "Look ma, I'm directing". Mike Hodges did it. I mean they never sacrificed me either deliberately or accidentally, but you got the feeling that had it been someone who might have disappeared a little easier, they would have done it.'

But then, Michael Caine never had any intention of disappearing, easily or otherwise. And to prove the point – before the next milestone picture a few years later – he showed he could still make the less remarkable movies. Not that *Zee and Co.* later that year was at all bad. It just wasn't all that good. (It was called *X, Y And Z* in America; but since 'Z' in England was pronounced 'zed' it didn't have the right ring about it.)

This latest film featured Susannah York, who always looked lovely. Margaret Leighton was there too, and she always looked elegant. And Elizabeth Taylor was his co-star. In the 50s and 60s she was the most beautiful woman in Hollywood. Some said she was the most beautiful woman in the world. She was beautiful in a way that Marilyn Monroe was not. Elizabeth was a wonderfully sophisticated woman of the world who purred at her lovers when she needed to but could be tough. When she stood in her satin slip in *Cat On A Hot Tin Roof* she oozed sexuality, but even as a call-girl in *Butterfield 8* she had class. Monroe was magnificently gorgeous, but you wouldn't have cast her as a lady. Elizabeth Taylor always seemed to be that – until this period in her life. Now, age was taking its toll. She was fat and dressed not so much in frocks as in tents and, as one critic remarked, 'Miss Taylor is rapidly turning into a latter-day Marie Dressler.' In this film, she was also playing *Virginia Woolf* all over again.

Michael played an architect. An architect with wife problems – and, thanks to a great deal of intent on his part – mistress problems. Audiences were shocked, although more by the bad language than anything else. Michael, who has never failed to call a spade a fucking shovel when the opportunity presented itself, didn't seem to have any problems with that aspect of the picture. (Michael once told *People* magazine, 'Someone said to me at a dinner party, "You're swearing in front of the ladies." I replied, "Did you notice they swore first?" I was trying to make them comfortable. My mother told me that; always make the ladies comfortable.')

There were, however, critics who did not conclude that *Zee and Co.* made *them* particularly comfortable. It certainly wasn't a gift to film history. Martin Knelman writing in the Toronto *Globe* said it was all 'engagingly trashy'. But most were less kind. As Judith Crist remarked: 'The distinction of this film is that its characters are repulsive, its style vulgar, its situations beyond belief and its dialogue moronic.' She didn't seem to like it. The writers got the wrong end of the stick, Michael protested. 'It was supposed to be fun. But a lot of the reviewers took it seriously.... It's terrible to make a movie you think is very funny and get bad reviews because the audience laughed.'

That was when the film was new and potentially ready to make him money. Later on, he was more objective, but he still thought it wasn't so bad: 'We made what we thought was a comedy, and everybody thought it was a drama. I thought it was a good movie, but then I don't have to pay to see it. When you work with Elizabeth, none of the women look at you. They spend the first part of the picture seeing how she looks and is she wearing *the* ring [the huge diamond bauble that Richard Burton had famously given her] then about half way through they realise there's somebody mumbling and droning in the background – and it's me. I did a lot of pictures nobody is going to do a remake of.'

Joyce Haber, the American columnist liked it a whole lot more. It shouldn't have been taken, she said, 'as a kind of Monday, Bloody Monday *ménage à trois*.' It was, she said, 'great fun and hilarious'. So you saw the reviews and took your pick.

Besides, Michael had made a million dollars in five years, an astonishing amount even for film actors at that time. 'Now I want to try and make $5 million in one year.'

A remake of *Kidnapped* in 1971 didn't bring much joy. After *The Wrong Box*, it might have seemed obvious that Michael Caine and Robert Louis Stevenson were not exactly made for each other. But, once again, this was a movie with an interesting cast. Trevor Howard, Donald Pleasence, Gordon Jackson and a sad, sad Jack Hawkins – minus, since his cancer operation, that wonderfully distinctive voice. Caine was the star without any doubt.

The film was terrible, most people agreed. However Pauline Kael said that Michael's portrayal of Alan Breck was 'a wonderful mixture of swagger and intelligence that keeps the movie alive.' However, it didn't help his recurring drink problem, which went from the one bottle of vodka a day to sometimes as many as three. There were ways of trying to get over some of the difficulties. One was to leave not just the producing to someone else, but some of the acting as well.

Later, in *Pulp*, he gives away most of the best scenes to Mickey Rooney, which couldn't have been an easy thing to do at all. But then he was producer of this picture as in *Get Carter*, with his friend Michael Klinger, he could be generous to whomever he pleased. Rooney, once the darling of the MGM *Andy Hardy* movies, hadn't done anything for years. For him, the role was a huge boost to his ego, to say nothing of his bank account. It was set in Malta; the story of an undertaker who switches to writing the kind of fiction Michael Caine would always say he never read. Rooney played an old Hollywood actor who wants the Caine character to ghostwrite his autobiography.

But it was now 1972 and for Michael Caine there were bigger, stranger things about to happen. Laurence Olivier, who had played those great roles with Vivien Leigh, Joan Fontaine and Claire Bloom discovered that his next co-star was going to be Michael Caine.

And then, at the American premiere of *Zee and Co.* – sorry, *X, Y And Z* – there was a new girl on his arm. There was nothing unusual about that. She was dark and he was known to quite like dark girls. She was foreign and he had always seen something in ladies from overseas that he never saw in British or American women. And she was a beauty queen, Miss Guyana to be precise. Her name was Shakira.

Nineteen

Tonight, let's all make love in London

He fell in love with a girl on a television commercial. It was as simple as that – an exhausted film star actually having an evening off and wanting to do nothing more than watch TV.

That was when it happened. It was a commercial for Maxwell House coffee and there, dancing among the coffee beans, was the woman he decided was the most beautiful he had ever seen. That being so, he was going to find her.

Now, other men have had similar moments of apparent madness. But other men are not Michael Caine. The commercial was set in Brazil. That being so and with no new film on the Caine calendar for a day or three, he decided that the next afternoon would be an appropriate moment to take a plan to Rio De Janeiro. He was going to find this beautiful, magnificent Brazilian girl. Perhaps he also decided that he was going to marry this beautiful, magnificent Brazilian girl.

Before telling his driver to speed to Heathrow airport, he met a television advertising executive friend and told him that he had just seen a television commercial and was going to Brazil to find the girl starring in it. The executive told him that, coincidence of coincidences, the commercial was made by his own firm. Would Michael like him to find out more? The answer was pretty obvious. But the commercial was not made in Brazil at all (funny that a film man like Michael Caine didn't spot when a location was not a location; it must have been a pretty good advert). It was produced in Britain. His friend made inquiries. The girl wasn't Brazilian either. She was Indian. OK, said Caine. He was off to India. What part? Try the Fulham Road, his friend responded, in London. The young lady's name was Shakira Baksh and the friend got Michael her phone number. The wonder is that when he phoned, the woman at the other end didn't think it was somebody playing a Peter Sellers-type trick. She was a friend of the coffee girl and promised that Caine's call would be returned.

They eventually spoke. Shakira returned his call and, probably to his amazement, agreed to go to the Grosvenor Square flat. She realised she was being a bit forward but.... Michael Caine was Michael Caine. Actually, she didn't want the other five girls who shared her flat to meet him. It wasn't that she was afraid that they might steal him from her – she probably was, but would never have admitted it – but thought it would be easier that way. So they met and kept on meeting.

He found her as enticing off screen as he had on. She was a former Miss World contestant. Although Shakira came from an Indian family from Kashmir she had been born in Guyana. She came to London for the Miss World competition, representing her country. But she had wanted to get out of Guyana long before she put the sash over her white, one-piece bathing suit. The idea of leaving had come to her when the American Library in Guyana, where she had been working, was blown up.

Mr Caine and Miss Guyana found themselves in love. It sounds terribly corny and old fashioned, but sometimes terribly corny and old-fashioned stories turn out to be true.

Later she would say: 'I expected somebody who was terribly spoiled, somebody who was very affected, all those things you read about a movie star. He was quite unlike that. Somebody who was very natural, very easy going. I was won over by his sense of humour. He has the great ability to laugh at himself too. We fell madly in love.'

They only separated when he went to Malta to make *Pulp*. Then she flew out and joined him. It seems that Shakira was much more on his mind than the picture, although he manages not to mention her name on screen. He insists that they haven't been apart for any length of time since.

The writer who had made the point about Michael Caine not going for British or American girls seems to have known what he was talking about.

They didn't marry at first. But she took up residence in Grosvenor Square with him. Then, when the lease on the flat expired, he said goodbye to the American eagle, and the statue of Franklin D. Roosevelt below his window, and moved lock, stock and paintings and records into what was now known as Mill House. Friends would say that the house changed when she came to live there.

'It was obvious from the start that they were made for each other,'

Jackie Collins told me. 'She brought great happiness to the house and we could see it every time we were with them. She was very, very shy, but we were very impressed how bright she was as well as beautiful, and just how nice she was.'

That, coupled with the fact that Michael is a 'very good and very loyal friend who you don't have to see for years,' convinced her that there was something very exceptional between Michael and Shakira.

Nearly always, in those early days, his mother was there for Sunday lunch at the Mill House, where Michael was the one in charge of the cooking. Sometimes, Stanley came too. Jackie Collins came whenever she was in England. 'There were always the best wines there and he cooked a mean roast beef,' Jackie recalled. 'He taught me how to make Yorkshire pudding.'

Before long Shakira would also bring a new baby to the house. They were happily settled into the Windsor life and Michael was in the middle of his next big movie when Shakira gave him the news: she was pregnant. That was when they decided to get married. It wasn't, he has said, 'because I was tired of being a bachelor. I [wanted to get] married because I wanted to spend the rest of my life with the woman who's now my wife.'

There were plenty of churches in Windsor where they could have had a nice, tasteful wedding. Except that that wasn't what they wanted to do. Instead, they chose a wedding chapel in Las Vegas. It wasn't that they were cocking a snook at convention. Michael liked Los Angeles, where they would go first to prepare themselves for the ceremony. Shakira had never been there before and Michael introduced her to the town (although she was upset that it took so long before he also showed her off to any of the other film stars).

So Vegas, a place famously free of any inconvenient pre-marriage requirements, would be a convenient spot for the nuptials. Nobody, he thought, would imagine that they weren't going to take it all very seriously. They weren't in search of something terribly tacky. They wanted to get married without any fuss. Since Vegas specialised as much in instant marriages as it did in instant jackpots (and instant lost fortunes) it appeared to be an obvious place for them. One photographer was there to take the pictures. He wasn't invited, but he found out and promised not to tell anyone else, which suited them both. Dennis Selinger was there to give the bride away. Jerry Pam was best man.

'I suppose it was the strangest wedding I've ever been to,' Dennis told me. 'But I think it was also the happiest.' The 'reception' was a dinner in a fish restaurant on Sunset Strip. 'We spent our honeymoon at the Hilton listening to Louis Prima,' Michael told *Variety*.

They stayed in Los Angeles for a couple of days and then returned home to Windsor. Everything about the place was wonderful for them. He says that there was nothing he liked better than loading up a station wagon with produce from Harrods food hall – not a place much known by the inhabitants of The Elephant – and then driving up to Windsor 'with the castle battlements etched against the sky'.

The next spring, Shakira gave birth to a daughter. They called her Natasha. It had been a nerve-racking time. There had been no real preparations for her arrival. 'It's an old Cockney superstition: do nothing for the baby until it arrives in case you put the mockers on it.' He was there at the birth and it all seemed to go fine. But then, soon afterwards, the baby was rushed into intensive care. Her lungs had collapsed. Then Shakira was taken to hospital herself with peritonitis. It was a traumatic time but both soon recovered. They were both the apples of Mr Caine's eye.

Twenty

Sleuth

There were actually two babies for Michael Caine now. Natasha (Natasha Halima Mickelwhite on her birth certificate) and another that, like her, seemed to get under his skin. This one was called *Sleuth.*

It was a film that proved to be important for more reasons than that it was well directed, well written, well photographed – and, yes, well acted.

For one thing it was highly unusual, a film featuring just two actors who set out to torment each other. It was a movie chess game, a kind of *Who's Afraid of Virginia Woolf* performed by two men. Gay activists might have tried to find some kind of homosexual undercurrent to it. It wasn't there. It was a duel as well as a duet. But the real significance is that this was the movie that pitched Michael Caine against Sir Laurence Olivier. And that is how it must be seen. Both in real life and in the picture itself Olivier was the unassailable fortress in the acting business. On the surface it was as if Michael was a hand grenade repeatedly thrown at the main wall of that fortress, but which simply bounced off every time.

Caine was by now one of the best established of all British actors – certainly, Sean Connery and Olivier himself apart, there were few who were more so. And yet he had not felt more inhibited since the first time he faced a movie camera. Here he was playing opposite Olivier and he not only had to impress his audience, he also had to show that he was every bit as good as 'Larry' was himself. That was a tall order. Harder still was convincing Olivier that he was up to his standard. At the front of his mind, not merely at the back of it, was a feeling of inferiority that suggested that the grand man would never accept him.

All those problems were real. The strange thing is that perhaps Olivier felt inhibited, too. He may have known that while he was getting $200,000 for his role, Caine was earning $50,000 on top of that. Here was a highly successful actor from a new generation who looked as if he could act him off the screen – just like he himself had with so many others. In short, they both felt threatened. Very threatened indeed.

Fortunately, it was Olivier who made the first move and tried to show that he was welcoming the young pretender. 'Call me Larry,' he said. That immediately got them out of a problem. Olivier was now Lord Olivier, the first actor ever to get a seat in the House of Lords. The kid from the Elephant hadn't fancied spending the months they would be together addressing him as though he himself were a butler holding a silver tray. No, 'My Lord' would have been difficult every time he wanted to break off to go to the loo. But he said: 'Snob that I am, I was impressed that I was appearing with a real-life lord.' The actor peer was the first of the two men selected for the picture and, therefore, must have approved Michael as his co-star. It was one of the more intuitive decisions of his long career.

The suggestion about names when they met confirmed a telegram he had sent off as soon as he knew who his co-star would be. 'I'M DELIGHTED THAT WE ARE MAKING A FILM TOGETHER. LET US GET ONE THING SETTLED AFTER THE FIRST INTRODUCTIONS LET US USE FIRST NAMES ON THE SET.'

When those introductions *were* made, Michael said he thought it was very considerate. 'We meet at last,' said the older man and they sat down to discuss strategy. It turned out to be something like a drama lesson, with Olivier telling Caine how he intended to act out every scene. It was as though he considered he was the only one there in front of the cameras – a situation not helped by the first scene that was shot. 'Larry' arranged it so that only his profile was in shot; Michael's was in the background. On other occasions, he was not beyond cutting Caine's lines – if he thought they were too good and likely to outshine his own.

But Michael knew how to deal with him. As the younger actor said: 'He never gave any concessions. I mean, if you relaxed for one second, that's when he would let you have the knife – a very sharp knife indeed. It wouldn't hurt very much. Not dull, no blood, but you'd know you'd been done.' Early on, he told Olivier: 'As far as I am concerned, you are the greatest actor in the world. Now, there's no way I'm going to overpower you, but I won't back off. OK, Larry?' Olivier replied: 'What a good idea, Michael.' That couldn't have been an easy thing to say or to contemplate. As Michael said about Olivier: 'He is a very great and powerful actor. Very deadly.'

There were not many actors who were so described by their co-stars. 'If you relax for a moment, he's got the scene from you. While I figured I couldn't make him back off, I made sure *I* wasn't going to. If you're not absolutely centred in your part, and if you don't pick it up quickly enough, he'll move in and start adding to his own character in the spaces left by your dereliction.'

Indeed, Olivier soon realised he was not dealing with an amateur here – or a young man who considered himself to be an inferior, no matter what Olivier believed him to be. Thereafter, Michael made sure that giving 'Larry' a chance to overpower him would never happen and the most celebrated British actor of the twentieth century took note. Later, he told him: 'When we first started, I thought of you as an assistant. Now I consider you my equal.' Michael did too. But it was nice to hear it.

OLIVIER: It's a good thing, I'm pretty much of an Olympic sexual athlete.

CAINE: I suppose these days you are concentrating more on the sprints than on the long distance.

OLIVIER: Not so. I'm in the pink of condition. I could copulate for England at any distance.

Olivier, of course, shone as the author who plots his visitor's destruction as though he were mapping out a new novel. Years later, Michael hosted a master-class on movie acting broadcast on BBC television. He referred to the great anomaly in *Sleuth*. 'Usually, I play the character who terrifies other people. So in *Sleuth* it was rather an unfamiliar experience for my character to think that he was going to be killed, and to be abjectly terrified.

It was a case of trying to get under the skin of his character. He let his 'nerves take over' – and was amazed how nervous he actually was as a result. Not of acting with Olivier, but of being put in a position in which he might be killed. Some might say that was carrying acting too far. But that was what he meant by acting.

Lewis Gilbert told me: 'Seeing *Sleuth*, you realise how different the two actors were. Olivier was totally theatrical, yet you didn't think that

Michael was being swamped by Olivier. Michael was totally holding his own.'

Indeed, 'Larry' was a man from a different school of acting. And that accounted for the fact that, once settled in, Michael wasn't intimidated at all. As he said: 'I was a very experienced film actor and Larry hadn't made a film for a long time.' But Olivier was not just surprised at the way Caine performed but by the ease with which he did it. During every break in the filming, Olivier would retire to his dressing room. So did Michael. But it was passing the Caine room that the differences between them became most obvious. 'What are you doing?' Olivier asked. 'Watching Wimbledon on television,' Michael replied. Olivier was astounded. Hollywood gossip had it that only Frank Sinatra ever had a television in his dressing room. 'Aren't you learning your lines?' he asked in amazement. So amazed was he that he put his script away and sat down with Michael to watch the women's finals. Legend has it that Lord Olivier then requested a TV for his own dressing room.

As far as Caine was concerned, *Sleuth* was a breakthrough in a career that in less than a decade had seemed to go wherever he wanted to take it. He could sign his name to almost any part available – except perhaps a remake of *Lassie Come Home*. But the cheeky chappie or the Cockney or the posh fop – or any combination of these – had a certain link with each other. *Sleuth* was something very different – as the link with Olivier indicated. Caine himself has said that it was the best thing he ever did – up to then.

'And why shouldn't it be? I'm more experienced now that I've ever been. I've worked on the best script I've ever worked on. With no detriment to anyone else, I've worked with the greatest actor you can work with.' He was, said Jay Cocks of *Time* magazine, 'not in the least daunted by acting with a legend incarnate.'

Nevertheless, when Anthony Shaffer wrote his stage play, he could not have imagined Caine in the part of Milo Tindle, the beautician who works for Olivier's wife and who comes to Olivier's house, plays billiards with him and ends up weeping for his life. It was very different from anything he had done before. But by the time that the film was in circulation, with a screenplay written by Shaffer, Caine had made the role essentially his own.

He actually played two roles in the film – or, at least, wanted it to be thought of as two roles; the second was as a police inspector. And it was that which gave the director, Joseph Mankiewicz, his biggest problem. Ossie Morris, one of the great British cameramen, who was in charge of photography on the picture, remembered it for me. 'Before the film started, we had to do various tests to get the character established. The role of the hairdresser was fine. The difficulty was making the inspector seem someone totally different, without the audience realising it was Caine. 'Joe Mankiewicz got very worried about it, because every time we did the test, the inspector still looked and sounded like Michael Caine. Joe said that unless they could get that right, we had no picture.' It was Michael who came up with the solution, recalled the cameraman. 'Instead of reading the part to a stand-in, we got Larry to be there, as he would be in the actual film. And that worked – perfectly. With the real man there, he was able to get into the character. It was wonderful.'

At the end of the filming, Michael said he was totally drained. 'I could hardly speak. And 16 weeks of trying to talk Larry out of stealing the scene.... I'd love one day for another actor to do a picture like this with him, to find out what stretching is really like.' At the time he was not volunteering to do it again himself. But he would.

The New York Times's critic Vincent Canby said that Caine made Tindle 'a perfectly unstable mixture of fury and foolishness.' Pauline Kael reserved most of her comments for Olivier – and they were not as flattering as the great man was used to receiving. 'At first,' she wrote, 'the elation of seeing Laurence Olivier in a big role is sufficient to give this Joseph L. Mankiewicz transcription of the Anthony Shaffer play .... a high spirit and Olivier seems to be having a rip-snorting old time [Americans at this time loved to adopt what they considered to be very 'English' terminology when they referred to very 'English' institutions]. But the cleverness .... wears down and the stupid tricks that the two characters play on each other keep grinding on. It's Olivier in the kind of material he outgrew more than 30 years ago. It's Olivier in a George Sanders role.'

When the film was released in America, Michael went on a national tour, sometimes having a great time, at others isolated in lonely hotel rooms with no one to talk to – even now. In Georgia he was marooned in a hotel room in a dry state; he couldn't even get a drink.

He went on the *Tonight* show, guided by Jerry Pam. Pam was finding that, 'he always said the right thing. Carson asked for his definition of the ideal woman. He thought for five seconds and said, "The woman who thinks I am the ideal man."'

He ended up with an Oscar nomination – as did Olivier himself, the director, Joseph Mankiewicz and John Addison, who wrote the music.

In the wings at the Academy Award presentations, he was talking to Jack Lemmon. Lemmon noticed: 'There are 80 million people out there watching this show on TV and you're not even nervous. How do you do it?' 'Easy,' Michael replied. 'I'm not getting paid for it and they can't fire me, so why should I worry?' He was asked when he had stopped worrying 'From the beginning,' he answered.

To this day, *Sleuth* is mentioned whenever anyone talks about the careers of either Caine or Olivier. Athelhampton House, the stately home in Dorset where much of the film was shot, still celebrates the fact. The maze became a local attraction for years afterwards – although it had never previously existed. The bushes making up the intricate pattern – and the one that moved like a revolving door – were placed there by the film's designers. Location scouts had, however, already picked out the house and grounds, a few miles from both Dorchester and Tolpuddle, the home of the martyrs, as the ideal setting in which the maze could be created. It was a beautiful garden, full of the most exotic and rare plants. Olivier, a man with a considerable knowledge of horticulture, explained them – Latin names and all – to Michael who was at the time developing both his own garden and his gardening skills. There are still pictures of both the stars – and the billiard room – as one of the central attractions of Athelhampton.

His lifestyle now, he liked to think, was nothing out of the ordinary – except that he couldn't imagine anyone having an ordinary life that was so contented. Shakira went everywhere with him and so did Natasha when that was possible. He has said he was always convinced that she would become an actress. He had to be aware of his responsibilities to her. 'The children of the rich are more inclined to get psychologically screwed up than the children of the poor. I had no expectations at all, so I couldn't get screwed up because I didn't get anything. There's something to be said, only in retrospect, I must admit, for having nowhere to go but up.'

It was something that both Michael and Shakira recognised as important. It seemed to start with being right for and with each other. 'At first I was awed by her beauty,' he told *Cosmopolitan* magazine who selected the Caines as their 'Couple of the Month'. 'But what's more remarkable is Shakira's incredible serenity. I'd had it with women who wanted to be seen on the arm of a star. My wife is a home girl who wants a bundle of kids and to be *out* of the limelight. She's totally non-competitive.' They liked staying home, although they occasionally went to discos, the big 'in' thing in the 70s, and they tried to have weekends away from everyone, 'Second honeymoons' he called them.

Occasionally, Shakira would do some modelling and she had small parts in films. She always kept her own money. 'Pin money,' Michael called it. His mother would have scrubbed a couple of hundred floors for that sort of pin money. But then, things and values had changed. He once worked out that he made more money in ten weeks than his father had in his entire lifetime, and that included the cash he had gambled and spent on booze.

They entertained at home a great deal. 'Michael is a wonderful host,' said Jackie Collins, and over the years hundreds of other privileged people have testified to that. Friends came to the house for dinner and, afterwards, there would usually be a new film to see. But not his film. 'I figure my guests get tortured enough with my dinner conversation that it would be pressing my luck to show my films.'

He liked to think that it was a 'rustic' life he now led – 'but with plenty of built-in expensive appliances to make life simple.' Of course, there's rustic and 'rustic'. It was hardly farmer's boy territory that he lived in. When a thing was expensive, he still knew it was expensive and bought it just the same. But he wanted other people to know it was costly too. He staffed the house with a butler, a cook, a nanny and a cleaning lady. But he liked to think he treated them all as friends. He also did the cooking when he didn't want the cook to do it. It was part of his view on the place of women in his home.

He conceded that Shakira had 'an iron will'. She was, he said, 'a very strong and efficient woman. She's never any threat. She's never eyeing anyone's husband or boyfriend.' In his circle, that was rare indeed. Few people suspected that he ever eyed up anyone else's wife or girlfriend either.

As for himself: 'I'm a male chauvinist in the nicest of ways. I agree that women should get equal pay and I agree with the [American] Equal Rights Amendment. I don't think women should be stuck in the kitchen. But if we're going out, I make the decision where and then let the woman change it, if she wants to. I don't want to stand there like a bloody jelly waiting for the woman to make up her mind.'

He planned the house too – with its masses of books and the paintings that he acquired the way he once collected comics. He had a tennis court and a swimming pool. There were always dogs and toys around the place.

Everyone knew that Michael Caine was happier now than he had ever been in his life. 'I joke that if ever we got divorced, I would sue

Shakira for loss of status. That's how I feel about her. I would lose status in Hollywood.' It wasn't meant as an unkind statement. He did worry about his status, but he cared about his wife just as much.

All that he had were the perks of a super successful life in his chosen business and he would never forget it. And there was still a magic about films in general for him. He was as fascinated by the business of film making, the technicalities, as he was by standing in front of a camera himself and performing. 'I enjoy the wheeling and dealing and the villains. I don't let anyone get away with anything. I'm in there fighting from the word go, I'll take on anyone.' That was not much of a surprise to those who knew him. 'I'm not temperamental. Sometimes I'll blow my top at unpunctuality or inefficiency. But then it's over. No malice.'

There were, however, four actors with whom he would never work (none of which have been mentioned in this book); their identity a secret shared with only Dennis Selinger and usually Jerry Pam. He had good reason, he believed, to maintain the ban and when he thought about those four men, his blood boiled to the kind of temperature he had experienced long before in Korea. 'When I was a bit player they treated me like dirt and you remember those things. They don't remember *me* because if you treat someone like dirt they don't have names or faces. To this day those actors don't know why I won't work with them. It's not a vendetta. It's just that I wouldn't feel comfortable on the same set.'

But he didn't feel that way about most of the people with whom he came into contact. 'Movie people have a kind of joy about them, as though they feel privileged, as though someone had done them a big favour just allowing them to be there.' And that was why he preferred working for the big screen. 'In the theatre, it's the other way round. They're doing you a big favour if they deign to show up.'

But now he wanted to extend the ever-widening Caine horizons. There was one other profession for which he now had ambitions. He fancied himself as a writer. A successful writer, after all, need never leave home and that idea appealed more than a little. But it would also be a profession he could pursue when his acting days were over. He now thought a lot about that time and what he would do when it came. He didn't want to become 'one of those doddering old embarrassments they wheel on every now and then because they still need to earn a few bob.'

No matter what his mother might think, he didn't need those few bob any more and hoped he never would again. That was a lesson that was still very hard for Ellen to appreciate. 'She can't conceive of the money at all. She told me that milk had gone up a penny – since I was paying the bills, she wanted me to know just how much I was going to fork out.'

Others wanted to know about his spending habits too. But that was all part of being a film star.

Twenty-One

The Romantic Englishwoman

Analyse what Michael Caine was doing now and the definition of what he always claimed to be above everything else – a professional actor – becomes clearer. Yes, he was a workaholic. Yes, he knew that not every picture was going to be a huge success. He liked to say that he happily took scripts other actors had turned down – because he saw something in them that they hadn't. Sometimes it was the other way round.

In 1973, Fred Zinnemann was about to direct the movie version of the Frederick Forsyth best seller *The Day of the Jackal*. 'People wanted Caine for the role,' he told me. 'They saw him as the assassin. It was the kind of role he did well. But I didn't want Caine. I wanted an unknown.' The unknown he picked was Edward Fox.

But acting was what Caine did, what he got paid for doing. He undertook work in films the way portrait painters agreed to put ugly industrialists and their wives onto canvas. That was his profession. If the film was very good, it was a bonus. If it fitted his own idea of his persona, it was a gold-plated gift.

The Marseille Contract, known in America as *The Destructors*, was not one of the pictures in the 'Great Caine Films' list. It involved an American narcotics agent in Paris who hires an assassin to kill off a drug smuggler and so it was right up his street. Assassins, Paris .... *The Day of the Jackal* had those ingredients too and would have suited him better.

But this film featured Anthony Quinn again, assisted by James Mason. 'We're old friends,' said Caine at the time. 'Both of them have marvellous confidence in their own ability .... I love working with pros.'

The Black Windmill directed by Don Siegel was a remake of a classic – Hitchcock's *The Man Who Knew Too Much*. Hitchcock had himself done a remake of the film in the 1950s. The second version of his story about the search for a kidnapped child was a mere shadow of the original film 20 years earlier. This third one should never have got as far as a movie studio. The picture made so little impression on Caine that in his memoirs he says he has forgotten almost everything about it. But two people working on the film with him told me how much they appreciated having him around. For both Joss Ackland and Janet Suzman it was a time to treasure. 'He was always making everybody on the set curl up with his jokes,' said Mr Ackland. 'I remember pointing out that a certain actor was a Black Belt. "Yes," said Michael, "a Black Belt for boredom." '

Ms Suzman told me that he treated her better than almost any other actor she had worked with. 'We had one scene in a London bus,' she recalled, 'and we had to go round and round the Aldwych while they were setting up the shot. He spent that time telling me about his childhood in London. I had heard those stories before, but I was very moved by the way he did it. Other actors complained about being kept waiting. Michael never did. He was always totally patient and good with the crew. There are not many star actors you can say that about.'

He was also free with advice for other actors. No film performer should be too fussy about what he did. 'You've got to put your face on the screen,' he said. He had certainly practised all that he preached.

Natasha was the one whom he hoped would take all the best advice around. The sun, moon and stars glinted in her eyes as far as her father were concerned. He wanted to do everything for her that he had been unable to do when Niki was at the same age. He looked on his elder daughter, now 15, with love and admiration. He said of her: 'She's blonde and she has a mouth like her mother's. But her eyes and hair are like mine.' Niki, he seemed pleased to note, had no interest in acting. She was a showjumper. Considering her father's antipathy to horses, his mouth was obviously not the only thing she had failed to inherit.

There were no horses for him to ride in *The Wilby Conspiracy*, the 1975 film he made in Africa with Sidney Poitier as his co-star. The picture, about a British mining engineer who helps a black South African in the heat of the apartheid era, had to be shot in Kenya. It was either that or risk making the picture in South Africa and then be locked up for a few years in a Johannesburg jail. Poitier was glad they chose Kenya. He was treated like a respected elder statesman in that country. Mr Caine, however, only occasionally met anyone who recognised him. Perhaps the old slander was being reversed and to the Kenyans all white men looked alike.

Saeed Jaffrey, the eminent Indian actor, saw a side of the Caine character that he has always appreciated. 'I was struck by how kind a man he is,' Jaffrey told me. 'I had been going through a very bad time. My girlfriend at the time had suddenly stopped writing and it was affecting me very deeply. Both Michael and Sidney Poitier were sympathetic. But Michael offered practical help too. He said, "Saeed, you look all done in. Get down to the Missus and she'll give you a large brandy." ' Shakira did just that. 'I appreciated it. He then saw that I was sent back to London and that solved my problem.' But there was something else. Michael said he was going into a very big film the following year and that there would be an important part in it for him. But it was not a promise he felt he should depend on.

Part of the filming for *The Wilby Conspiracy* was done in London. While that happened, Caine and Poitier went to the same restaurant in Marylebone each evening. It was on one of those evenings that a man, slightly the worse for drink, introduced himself. His name, he said, was Peter Langan.

Michael, at the time, could have had no idea how important that meeting would be – after all, he had met any number of drunken Englishmen in his time and had played the part himself on more than a few occasions. But before long, this man would be, for better or worse, his business partner, the key to the door of becoming a restaurateur and part owner of Langans, the 'in' place in London's Mayfair.

At the same time he was concentrating on the friendship that Shakira and he had with Sidney Poitier and his wife and there was much still to do finishing off the work on their film.

There was also the little matter of another picture to think about. Caine said in *What's It All About?* that he hoped this would be his last 'artistic' movie. It was also his first. *The Romantic Englishwoman* had him married to Glenda Jackson, but part of a love triangle (the third principal was Helmut Berger) that develops into a thriller. Not that many people knew what was going on. *Current Biography* described it as 'an ambiguous disquisition on infidelity'. If you understood what that meant you stood a reasonable chance of understanding the movie, but there weren't many who did either.

Ms Jackson is a Labour Member of Parliament and former Government minister. At that time, she was frequently to be found in the beds of screen lovers – as in *Women In Love* and now with Michael, who found numerous opportunities to impose his own dialogue and 'business' as he went along. It gave him a chance, he thought at the time, to develop his own ideas of 'Method' acting. There was one scene in which he had to shout at everyone around him. It was a gift to any improviser. Every little thing that went wrong that morning was allowed to overtake his normal good judgement. He quibbled at the slightest difficulty and was convinced that the scene benefited from him not being his normal kind, considerate, pliant self.

There *are* people who think that a little rage in Michael Caine helps him. 'I don't lose my temper often,' he insists. 'But there *is* a lot of fury inside me.' When he has had to lose that temper on screen, it comes from real anger. Frequently, he remembers his childhood and the physical abuse from the policeman's wife. 'When I think of that, I hate all adults and go BANG.'

Caine finally overcame his resistance to nude scenes. But he said he still didn't like them. The great thing about film acting, he believes, is the attention audiences can pay to performers' *eyes*, which is another good reason not to blink when standing in front of a camera. In those nude scenes, however, the public's own eyes were likely to move elsewhere and that worried him. The truth of the matter was that he was totally embarrassed by the whole thing.

Caine was a lot more enthusiastic about it all before the film went into the studio than he would be afterwards. But even then he told *The New York Times*: 'I don't find it easy to describe. It's essentially a contemporary triangle.' But more than that, 'as far as Glenda and I are concerned, different from anything we've seen in movies before.' He made the movie in the first place because Joseph Losey, the director of *Darling* and *Accident* and so many of the other 'in' pictures of the 60s, asked him to do it. He had been wanting to work with Losey for some time and this was the first suitable occasion. Also, to use a phrase current 20 years later, he had a 'window' in his schedule.

The man he played, he has said, was someone he completely despised – a husband who was without backbone. Anything less like the Michael Caine whom people had come to know – or like the man he knew himself – would be difficult to conceive. Here was one who loved his wife – well, that *was* him – but who because of that love, tolerated her adultery, and that certainly was *not* him. He said: 'There was nothing of myself I could bring to that role, so I had to construct the character from the ground up. It was pure performance.'

He said he was disappointed with Glenda – who didn't want to tell me how disappointed she was with Michael. He enjoyed working with her, 'but only professionally. She doesn't go out to lunch, if you know what I mean.'

The picture proved what any number of people – now wise after the event, of course – could have told him: Tom Stoppard – who wrote the screenplay from a story by Thomas Wiseman – and Michael Caine were not natural bedfellows.

Michael Billington described it all as 'an itsy-bitsy fragmented film that seems less than the sum of its parts'. Most people would have said that was being very kind.

Perhaps, he wondered now, it was time to start writing scripts himself. His brother Stanley had gone into writing but had never done anything with it. He had written screenplays that were 350 pages long and not usable. So why didn't Mr Caine go into the writing business seriously himself? He had once said that he 'was writing scripts and tearing them up like yesterday's newspapers'. Now, he was doing something else – 'tearing up scripts that other people send me'. So it might be worth thinking again of writing his own screenplays. But it didn't happen.

The time had come once more for a picture that no one would make the target of insults. It was going to be another of the big ones.

Twenty-Two

The Man Who Would Be King

The Man Who Would Be King was a duel monarchy movie. Michael Caine and Sean Connery were showing that between them they *were* the kings of British cinema. There was no question of either of them being a pretender to the throne. They shared it just as they shared the credits above the title.

There were so many things right with the picture. The fact that they were close friends helped. That after the event they remained close friends was a bonus. There was one other factor that made it an important film: Shakira was in it, too.

It was partly to do with Dennis Selinger, who was Sean's agent as well as Michael's. 'It was my idea to put him together with Michael,' he told me sitting in Langans, where he had his own table.

There was one other dream that came true. Getting his two men to work with John Huston. One of the principal qualities of a good agent, one that singles him out from the others, is having the contacts that tell him what's going on. Selinger knew that Huston was trying to put together a movie based on the Rudyard Kipling story, the tale of two con men who end up with rather more than they had originally planned.

They were two renegade ex-sergeants and Selinger knew that his clients fitted the parts perfectly. 'Huston,' he told me, 'was talking about wanting to make that movie and I said that as far as I was concerned, there were only two people who could play the parts – Michael and Sean. One's a Scotsman and one's a Cockney and that's exactly how it had been written.'

In the territory of Kafristan, supposedly in the foothills of the Himalayas, the character Connery plays is worshipped by the monks of the country. To them, he is more than just a god. They make him their king, which for the sake of the story is more important. Caine is the one who sets it in motion, virtually destroying the Raj and the British Empire in the process.

Huston himself had suggested to Caine that he play the part of Peachy Carnehan. He was in Paris at the same time as Michael and had invited him for a drink. Caine said yes. He had always wanted to work with the director, a man's man of an executive whom he thought he could trust. He was also a Kipling addict.

Ossie Morris was working with Caine once again. He was brought into the production at the earliest stage, and told me how Huston had come round to the idea of making the picture in the first place. 'Twenty-five years ago,' he said, 'I had a call from John. "Kid," he said, "I've got a great story, *The Man Who Would Be King*. Ever heard of it?" '

Morris hadn't. It wasn't one of the better known Kipling stories, but Huston had discovered it in a collection of tales called *Wee Willie Winkie*. He said he was going to do it with Humphrey Bogart and Clark Gable. 'Fade out and ten years later, he said: "Kid. We're going to do *The Man Who Would Be King* again. With Peter O'Toole and Richard Burton." ' But they didn't. 'Exactly ten years after that, I had just come in from shopping and there was a message to ring him at the Beverly Hills Hotel. "Kid," he said, "Wonderful news. We're going to do *The Man Who Would Be King* again." ' 'Yes?' asked a now incredulous Morris, 'Who with this time?' That was when he heard it was going to be Caine and Connery.

It was when the director told him that he had originally planned the movie for Clark Gable and Humphrey Bogart that Michael really got interested. 'Who was going to play my part?' he asked. 'Bogart,' the director replied. There was nothing more to be said. The old Saturday morning pictures had finally come home and landed on his doorstep.

Actually there *was* more to be said ... a great deal. There was the question of the location for one thing. The story was set in India, but Huston wasn't sure that was where he wanted it to be shot. Ossie Morris told me about how the location eventually became Morocco. 'Huston always wanted the movie to be shot in the Hindu Kush of Afghanistan where the scenery was so marvellous and one of the reasons why the first two films were never made was because the insurance companies wouldn't go for it. They thought it was much too risky there. Somebody convinced him that it could be done well enough there in the Atlas mountains.'

And that was why Morocco was chosen as the location for Kafristan.

It had nothing to do with the fact that they would be accommodated in one of the world's greatest hotels, the Mamounia in Marrakesh. It is well-known that Sir Winston Churchill used to stay at the hotel regularly. It did wonders for his painting, he always said. The accommodation and the service did wonders for Sir Winston himself. In the 35 years since Churchill's death, it has not only come to be regarded as the best place to stay in the Middle East, it has also developed into a place of pilgrimage – people who could never afford the hotel (also featured, incidentally, in the Hitchcock remake of *The Man Who Knew Too Much*) would go there just to see what all the fuss had been about.

The fuss in making *The Man Who Would Be King* was in trying to survive the weather and the travelling to less enticing places. But there were other things to contend with, not least the nude scene that Mr Connery had to do. Not the conventional bedroom scene, but when con man Connery was crowned as the local king he had to be divested of all his clothes before the new robes of office could be draped around him. He was completely naked, but the picture was shot – ever so tastefully – from the back. Perhaps that was another reason Michael wanted to play the other role.

But there were other difficulties. At the very beginning of the movie, Caine is seen holding a box – supposedly containing Sean Connery's head wrapped in muslin. He had been hanged by the marauding natives. Michael was supposed to look harassed. But Huston told him, 'Kid we've got a bit of a problem, you don't look as though you've been through the mill.' Ossie told me: 'John Huston was very worried indeed. We couldn't get the make-up right and this time he couldn't get in the mood simply by playing to Sean – Connery was supposed to be dead. Eventually by sheer hard work, trying one idea after the other, he got it.'

John Huston worked hard, too, to get into the spirit of the movie early on. In one scene, Peachy had to throw an Indian off a moving train. Michael was unhappy about that. Huston said they had to learn something about Victorian values – or the lack of them. They got on well together. Only once did the director stop him in mid flow. 'You can speak faster,' he told him. 'Peachy is an honest man.' That was what was so clever about him. He saw – just as Caine had done while making *Zulu* – the inferences that could be read into the speed of speech. 'If you ever heard God speak,' said Caine at one time, 'he would sound like John Huston.'

Shakira came into the picture when the actress who was booked to play the part of the Indian princess had to back out. Michael was the first to try to persuade his wife to take the part. No, she said, she wasn't an actress. John Huston tried too – and succeeded. It was only a small role but she had some complicated business to do, including going into a trance. Caine said he was very proud of her. Perhaps never more so than when she and the Connery character were married. 'I never thought I'd end up being best man at my own missus's wedding,' he said.

He was on hand for her whenever she needed him. Too much so, thought the director. He was on the set all the time that she was, giving her advice. 'I was so nervous for her, I became a pain in the neck,' he said afterwards. So much so that Huston sent him off.

But no one seemed to object to the way the two stars of the film respected each other. 'It was something I had never seen before,' Jerry Pam told me. 'They not only never competed, they would make sure each other had the best close-ups when they were speaking. It was as if they choreographed what they were doing.'

What struck people in the *King* company was the relationship that Michael had with others in the cast. Saeed Jaffrey appreciated it, as he had in *The Wilby Conspiracy* for this was the film in which Caine had said he would find him a part. He had been true to his word.

Jaffrey played Billy Fish, a Ghurka soldier. He was an experienced actor, but he was not beyond learning new lessons. There, in the heat of Morocco, Caine was very good as a teacher – as all the students of his master-class on BBC TV would discover.

'He would say to me, "Saeed, have you learnt your lines yet? Have you seen the script. You've got to know the *whole* script." It was something I hadn't thought of before, the importance of knowing everyone else's part, not just my own. You get a much better picture of the whole thing that way. Before that, I tended to just know my own lines, my cues, that sort of thing. It was a whole new thing to learn. I think he wanted me to concentrate more. I think that was why he said it. He used to go over his own lines quite loudly, just walking up and down.'

It was his relationship with the other actors that made the biggest impression. Christopher Plummer was the third star of the movie, playing the part of Kipling himself. But it was the lesser performers and others on the set who particularly appreciated the relationship they had with Caine. Said Saeed Jaffrey: 'He seemed to think that if you are in a starring relationship, you have to make the whole company feel like a family. He made sure he knew the first names of everyone – even the people who bring the tea and coffee, the camera assistants. That was a very good lesson.'

Jaffrey made his own contributions to the movie. He invented a language for the Kafristan soldiers. 'I used the grammar of Urdu, my mother tongue, and used a lot of Arabic which the Moroccans in the company could understand. It seemed a lot more sensible than getting these people to say, rhubarb, rhubarb.'

He appreciated Michael for other reasons. 'Maybe it was his working-class origins, but he had a consideration for people like me that others didn't.' That consideration became clear early on when the stars and the director settled into their canvas chairs with their names on the back. But Saeed did not.

'Where's Saeed's chair?' Michael asked.

'We had a very sycophantic gofer on the set. He only cared about the stars and didn't want to get me anything more than a stool.' When Caine asked about the chair, the man replied: 'Oh Michael, don't worry about it. These guys can sit anywhere, you know,' and laughed. Michael didn't and said nothing for another two days. Then Caine asked him again – this time more severely. 'Where's Saeed's fucking chair?' he demanded.

'Within half an hour my chair was brought. How can you forget something like that? I'll always be very grateful. The man's attitude was deeply racist. Michael, so much in love with Shakira, resented that.'

Caine wasn't just a considerate star. He was also a very funny one. Particularly when he 'remembered' John Wayne's recitation of *Hamlet.* With perfect Wayne-like diction, he pronounced the famous words, 'To be or not to be? .... Who wrote this shit?' He made up words for Richard Burton, sounding like a Cockney version of the Welsh thespian.

All his friends talk about the Caine sense of humour. Jerry Pam told me: 'Michael belongs to a breed of actors that really don't take themselves that seriously. They are very serious about their work, but actors like him don't believe most of the publicity about themselves.' 'What I loved,' said Jaffrey, 'was his French. He spoke the language very well – but not with a French accent, with a Michael Caine accent.'

Michael was now planning his restaurants. He was very serious about the suggestion that he should go into partnership with Peter Langan, although he had every intention of running his eateries more seriously than the professional restaurateur had done.

For now, he was concentrating on the etiquette of serving food properly. Jaffrey poured the wine at one dinner – from the left. Caine corrected him. 'Saeed, that's not the way to pour wine. You have to pour it from right to left.' That was just another Caine lesson. Saeed Jaffrey says now: 'I like to think there's a truth between us, a rapport. I didn't feel it was there with Sean. He was much more reserved. But I respected that.'

The film itself got a great deal of respect. Caine said that it would always be one of his favourites. 'It's the only film, if any film would, that might last after my death. I think it's the best performance I ever gave.' Pauline Kael seemed to agree. She said it was a 'wonderfully full and satisfying movie with superb performances by Connery and Caine and also by Saeed Jaffrey.' Caine was prepared to accept the accolade. He felt he had deserved it. 'I once did a cameo role as a favour. They gave me top billing and the film received disastrous reviews with the blame laid squarely at my feet. I learned a lesson from that one. I will never appear unless I can take full responsibility for the performance.'

He felt much the same about television, still refusing to do it for money. Only when he had a film to publicise would he go on to the small screen. However, since he was always making a new picture that needed publicity, his reluctance presented few problems for talk show hosts. When Barbara Walters offered him the chance to plug *The Man Who Would Be King,* he taped five segments for her *Not For Women Only* show. To him it was just part of the business.

Twenty-Three

California Suite

People were beginning to ask: Will success spoil Michael Caine?

His closest friends would testify to the fact that he didn't appear to be spoilt up to now, but the question was a reasonable one. He continued to earn, but he also continued to spend, and prodigiously. He spent like a boy from the Elephant who had won the lottery: he wanted everything that had once been denied him and wanted it now in case it wasn't there tomorrow.

The difference was that it was no lottery, he had earned every penny and tomorrow was always there, with as much work earning as much money as he could possibly need, even if some of the films were rotten. Or as he put it: 'If you have a very high standard of living, you sometimes have to make a very low standard of movie.'

'If I said I wanted a yacht in the South of France, I'd have to go out and make six pictures, wouldn't I? I don't want a yacht, so you can all rest in your beds. I do what is necessary at the time to do what I want to do. I don't care what anyone says about what I want to do.' The Caine philosophy on the great films and the crap. Now that he had made *The Man Who Would Be King,* and with *Sleuth* a very recent triumph, it didn't really matter that much.

Mention today the name *Peeper* and it barely gets a flicker of recognition. In the picture he played a British private detective down on his luck in Los Angeles. It was full of shades of Philip Marlowe but without any of the subtlety (*Variety* called it 'flimsy whimsy'). But again Caine's attitude to actors lower down the scale created an impression that was totally unusual in the business.

Michael Constantine worked with him on the movie. 'We were in the Bradley Building,' Constantine told me. 'The director, Peter Hyams, called out: "Great, but cut out the pauses." The truth was that we didn't know there were any pauses. So we did it again, this time at great speed. The director again called out, "Great. But cut out the pauses." The great thing about Michael was that he took it all in his stride and didn't mind the director's comments at all. He just went ahead and did it. That takes a wonderful professional.'

It wasn't a wonderful movie. But in this case it really didn't matter. Very few people even knew it had happened. It was one of the difficulties of just doing too much.

There were four Michael Caine films in 1975. The last of them was *The Eagle Has Landed,* in which he played the leader of a group of German paratroopers who disguise themselves as British soldiers to take over an English village as part of their plan to assassinate Winston Churchill. The picture, directed by John Sturges, was another of the better Caine vehicles and had people queuing outside local cinemas for weeks.

Michael wrote in his book that he only wished that another director had made the film. It would have been better, but Sturges had an arrangement whereby he didn't have to spend any time on the editing. Once the movie was finished, he just wanted to go fishing.

Richard Schjickel wrote in *Time,* 'There is not another leading man on screen today who so consistently exudes a sense of decency and honour without being stuffy about it.'

The next project was *Harry and Walter Go To New York*. The film could only have been made because Michael Caine wanted to extend his patio, build a new tennis court or change the engine on his Rolls Royce. It was directed by Mark Rydell, who should have known better and was to do much better (*On Golden Pond,* for instance). It dealt with the idea of carnival entertainers who find themselves involved in both big robberies and the suffragette movement. Elliott Gould and James Caan starred with him, along with Diane Keaton. Perhaps they all needed new tennis courts. As *Sight and Sound* magazine noted, this was a 'charmless mishmash'.

Caine was back in uniform in Richard Attenborough's *A Bridge Too Far,* a film dealing with the British disaster at Arnhem – one of the few defeats after the success of D-Day – when the paratroopers hoping to get a foothold in Holland were routed and their supplies landed behind the German lines. Caine had all the charm and bravery one expected from the officer class. He was very much an officer and a gentleman. It was only a cameo part, but it made a big impression.

He liked military roles, which were a kind of revenge for his treatment in Korea. Now he was either telling 'them' what 'we' wanted in a way he could never have done when ordered to sunbathe on the troop ship, or he was bravely doing the things that officers were supposed to do. He liked that, too. 'I think my attitude towards military life was best projected in *The Man Who Would Be King*, but the experiences that men have in wartime – both good and bad – are the most memorable moments of their lives.'

As so often happens, a memorable film like *A Bridge Too Far* was again followed by a film too far. *Silver Bears* was all about financial killings.

He wasn't having a particularly good run now. *The Swarm* tends to be spoken of in the same breath as Jack Benny's *The Horn Blows At Midnight* and Frank Sinatra's *The Kissing Bandit*; the definitive Caine entry in a compilation called *Movies I Wish I Had Never Made*. In this, he co-starred with 22,000 bees. The story of how it was made is a lot funnier than the movie itself which was about how the bees, all of them supposedly killers, fly over from Africa and threaten the sanity of every decent living American.

Caine himself told the story behind the story. 'They had 22,000 bees. They had Mexican illegal aliens sitting in little refrigerated caravans pulling the bloody stings out. Of course they missed a few and they were known as the hot ones.' Hot or cold, the bees had other natural functions to perform besides stinging. 'They didn't realise that bees don't make a mess in their own home. So they released five million bees [it was understandable that the number was exaggerated] and we had these white smocks on. Suddenly there was this haze and there was bee pong coming down. We only had an inkling [of what was happening] when the bees all crapped over me. What the hell do I know about bees?'

In London, *The Guardian* said of the film: 'You could pass it all off as a sick joke, except that it cost $12 million, 22 million bees and several years of someone's life.'

It was part of Michael Caine's life. He had decided to build a house in Beverly Hills and what he earned from the film would serve as the deposit. But he wasn't happy with the way things were being done in California. 'The builder gave me a choice of used bricks or "new used" bricks. Where else but California can you find such a thing?'

At home in Windsor, things had been even more difficult. An attempt to get planning permission for an extension to the Mill House resulted in a string of objections from neighbours who didn't seem to like the idea of the boy from the Elephant living in their midst. Or, from what

Michael says in his memoirs, the fact that he had an Indian wife.

Jerry Pam told me he had been telling the Caines for some time to set up residence in California. 'It all happened because of *The Swarm*. Irwin Allen who was the producer said it was very difficult getting a script to Michael and he had something he needed to see, but he needed an immediate answer. I told him that everything happened here and he needed to be on hand when a script came up that would suit him.'

There had been a perfect demonstration of that fact just a few days before. 'He phoned me and said he'd just read a script which he thought was terrific and would love to do it. I asked him what it was called. He told me and I started to laugh. He said, "What are you laughing at?" I told him I had been at the preview last week. He didn't know it had already been made. If he lived here, I said, he would know. I said, "When a producer gives a script to his agent and the agent sends it to you, and you take your time to read it, it's too late. They can't wait."

It wasn't enough to be able to phone him and send him stuff by air. By the time he got it and made up his mind it would be too late. It was the only thing he could do at that stage in his career.' The message was clear. 'I told him, "you are never going to be one of the very big stars in America unless you come to live here because they have this attitude. They want to be able to discuss things with you. Immediately. Face to face." '

So that was why he packed up his British home and moved to Los Angeles. At least, that was the official reason.

But to Joss Ackland, Michael gave a far more reasonable answer. 'He said,' Ackland told me, ' "Look, I've got this room, see. And I've got this billiard table, see. But the fucking room isn't big enough. Every time I hit the fucking ball, see, I hit the fucking wall with the cue. So I've got to move to another fucking country." '

Up to then, every time he came to California, he put up in an hotel, usually the Beverly Hills, with its banana leaf wallpaper. While those 'new-old' bricks were being laid, he made a movie about the hotel. (Although this time he stayed at the equally plush Beverly Wilshire; 'I didn't want to stay at the Beverly Hills all day and then come home to it at night.')

California Suite was an expensive movie, but it was worth it. Anything by Neil Simon usually was. His *Plaza Suite,* a portmanteau picture in which Walter Matthau played three different men in three different sketches all set in the same suite at New York's Plaza Hotel, was a smash. *California Suite* was set in the Beverly Hills Hotel and was as big a hit. Matthau was in this too, but in just one of the four sketches. Caine's part as the bisexual husband of an Oscar nominee, played by Maggie Smith who won an Oscar for her role, was one of those he can now paste on a board with a gold star next to it.

He never liked playing men whose sexuality was not as straightforward as his own. People might wonder about the research he had done for the role. 'Being in show business, I've been around a lot of bisexuals, so I didn't do any research at all.' After all, he said, the public had already accepted him as things that he manifestly was not, like a burglar and a murderer, so why should this be a difficulty? 'And, I played the character as a man with a dual sexual appetite rather than a limp-wristed loser.' Secretly, however, he did worry about it. He knew what his father would have said.

Frank Rich summed up the 1978 picture, describing it as 'by turns silly and thoughtful, tedious and charming, broad and delicate'. The Caine sketch was one of the best, on a par with Walter Matthau's, better than Jane Fonda and Alan Alda's, and a hundred times better than the farcical one that featured Bill Cosby and Richard Pryor. The big scene in the Caine sequence was the Oscar ceremony. 'I was in that scene,' Army Archard, the veteran *Daily Variety* writer, told me: 'We filmed it at the actual Academy Awards ceremony. It was the first time that the director of that ceremony had allowed it – or allowed a really funny scene.'

Michael was good at capturing the mood. He had been there as a nominee – for *Sleuth*. 'The producers flew me over, got me a suite at the Beverly Hills Hotel, just as in *California Suite*, and loaded it with flowers, chocolates and rare old cognac. I didn't win ... after the ceremony, I had to wait 20 minutes alone on the sidewalk for my car to pick me up. Only the losers are out there. The winners are all inside, giving interviews.'

Caine was giving quite a lot of interviews now, and not all of them were because of his acting. He was now a restaurateur.

Twenty-Four

Deathtrap

Peter Langan and Michael did their deal. They were going to take over the Coq D'Or restaurant near the Mayfair Hotel and turn it into a brasserie, modelled on La Coupole in Paris, 'large and noisy'. For Caine it was the fulfilment of an ambition.

He and Langan were not of the same stuff. His partner – Langan would have two-thirds of the investment, Michael got his third for £25,000 – was usually drunk and liked to tweak girls' legs as they sat at his tables. He had been known to approach them with the request: 'Let's see your tits', or to come up to other diners and lie himself down on their table. It wasn't that he was excessively rude, he was just always drunk. (Langan later died after setting fire to himself while in a drunken stupor.)

Michael said he trusted Langan completely when he was sober. The problem was that he wasn't sober very often. There was no doubt that he was much more dignified and he set about running the business as though it were his only interest in life. He needed to know what went on on both sides of the kitchen. He had to see the entire layout, know who would be sitting where – and eating what. And all the time, he enjoyed the work immensely. Sometimes, more than he enjoyed his movies.

He spent a lot of time in restaurants, had become very much a gourmet and knew his wine as well as he knew his scripts. As Jerry Pam said: 'He can't bear to be doing nothing. That's why having the interest in the restaurant became so important to him. Caine told Charlotte Chandler in *Playboy* that he saw 'an intimate relationship between nutrition and sex. The role of food and drink in romance and seduction cannot be overestimated.'

Langans was noisy, loud and offered huge portions. There was also no nonsense about certain conventions – he would make sure the place was never like the one in New York which hadn't let him in for lunch. He had arrived wearing a turtle-necked sweater under his overcoat. The *maitre d'* insisted that he couldn't come in unless he wore a jacket. So he kept his overcoat on and was admitted for his meal.

There were more restaurants as the bug bit deeper. They were not the indulgence of an amateur but a passion, and if he ever decided that there were too many bad movies and it was time to give up, he would become a restaurateur as involved and as dedicated as any holding Michelin stars.

Jerry Pam had seen the passion developing from reading about good food and wine to savouring and serving it. 'He's a very tough taskmaster because he believes that if you come in and pay for a meal, it should be really terrific. He wants people to be relaxed and enjoy what he does.' Others noticed that philosophy. It was not unusual for Michael Caine to be waiting at the door to welcome diners. Later, while he recommended the house salad, he would sign autographs. Pam noted: 'He went to France and to every three-star restaurant in the country. His chauffeur went to the annexe – so the chauffeur ate pretty well too.'

But nothing *was* going to stop or even slow his interest in the films. Some of them were hard work with only financial reward. *Ashanti* in 1979 was certainly one of those.

It was about the wife of the head of the World Health Organisation being kidnapped in West Africa. The director was Richard Fleischer, whose memories of the whole thing are a great deal happier than those of the people who paid good money to see it.

Fleischer hadn't really wanted to make the film in the first place. A Swiss consortium brought him in when another director was sacked. There was a deal. If he could make *Ashanti*, they would give him another picture to follow it, *Tai-Pan*. As things turned out, he didn't get *Tai-Pan* and had to be satisfied with *Ashanti*. And he only did the film because he heard that Michael Caine was going to be starring.

'It was a very, very difficult picture,' he remembered for me. 'It was just a waste of my time. Nothing happened with the picture. It never played anywhere. But I don't know why. It was as good as most pictures that are made.'

And Michael wasn't a waste of time. 'One of the reasons why I'm glad I made the film, was because I worked with Michael. We spent a lot of time together shooting the picture, socialising, having dinner almost every night with his family. We just liked each other.'

Peter Ustinov liked Caine too. He also thought the younger man was a good actor and respected him for that. Both would afterwards dissolve when they remembered one of the lines in the film. Ustinov, the slave trader who had disposed of the Caine character's wife, confesses: 'If I was not short of money, I would not have sold her.'

'Michael contributed great believability,' said Fleischer. 'I think that was because he is British. British actors are so well trained in their repertory theatres and most American actors don't have that. He took direction beautifully. He never threw his weight around. He told show business stories and he talked about being poor.'

But a happy picture? It was never that. And considering the locations in which they had to shoot, it was hardly surprising. As in Finland in mid-winter, making *Billion Dollar Brain*, Michael was suffering from the weather. This time it was the heat that caused the problems. The locations had been selected by the sacked director. Africa in the rainy season; Israel in the summer – when it was 130 degrees. 'The locations themselves were all right, but I would never have selected them at this time of the year,' said Fleischer. 'It was murder.'

The house in Beverly Hills was now very much home – 'not that he was here all that much,' said Jerry Pam. 'He was always working – and usually away, out of the country.' Nevertheless, it had been the right thing to do. Producers and directors were instantly in touch, just as Pam had predicted.

For Caine this was now regarded as home – and the people treated him as one of their own. The actress-socialite Ruta Lee told me: 'We always, right from the beginning, regarded him as part of the Hollywood community.' Jerry Pam disagreed. 'He had to be living here all the time to be regarded as part of Hollywood. When he was here, that was how they treated him.'

He himself felt there were few prejudices against him. Yes, he had once been called a 'fucking limey pinko fag' yet Hollywood didn't hold back on offering him work. But only up to a point. He admitted that the 'prestige' roles would still go to Paul Newman, Robert Redford or Dustin Hoffman before they came to him. But he accepted that as a fact of movie life. 'I'm extremely rich, extremely happily married and I live like a drunken gangster as we used to say when I was a kid.'

He had felt at home straight away, although he missed his mother. But when she came to Beverly Hills, she enjoyed it as much as he did. To his friends she was 'Ma'. As for her, she had long stopped calling him Maurice. Michael was his name and Michael was what she called him. She was 80 years old and for the first time able to enjoy all the things that she had never dreamed of having. 'She's got a colour TV with remote control, her cigarettes and chocolates,' he said. 'For her, that's paradise.' But she never referred to his success. She was too proud for that, he told journalists. If that meant that she never thought of Maurice Micklewhite junior either, he was glad. 'There's nothing of Maurice left,' he said about his original name. 'That was a completely different person' – and not one known in California.

Niki came too and loved the life. It could have been a difficult time for her. Her mother Pat, who had been Mrs Michael Scott, had just died of cancer. But Michael made Dominique feel at home and very much his daughter. On her first trip to California, he showed her the town. Sight-seeing was on his mother's agenda too. He took the whole clan to Las Vegas and made sure they were all treated as if they were the Royal family – which is perhaps how some Americans thought of them.

At home, he was on the Hollywood 'A' list, feted with the Gregory Pecks, the Billy Wilders and the Kirk Douglases. In New York, Betty Comden, the songwriter and playwright who has had a long professional partnership with Adolph Green, loved having him as a dinner party guest. 'He was so funny that we begged him not to leave when the evening came to an end,' she told me.

There were also the matrons who were not part of the celebrity community. He was standing in the Beverly Wilshire lobby one day, talking to Cary Grant, when a woman rushed over to him. 'God!' she said, 'I've been in this lobby trying to spot a movie star and couldn't see one. You're the only one I've seen.' The woman turned to Cary Grant. 'Terrible, isn't it?' 'Terrible,' he responded. But Caine has said, 'The people who are most likely to come up to me on the street are middle-aged women who are married to guys with blondish, curly hair and dark-rimmed glasses who have been told a million times they look like me.' That sort of recognition was what film stars worked for, whether they liked it or not.

But was Jerry Pam's reason for his settling in America the real reason? In his memoirs, Michael now admits what he had previously denied – that he had left Britain because of its tax regime. The decision was finalised in his mind when the Chancellor of the Exchequer, Denis Healey said he was going to tax rich people 'until the pips squeaked'. He was squeaking himself – with indignation. 'But it wasn't a case of tax avoidance,' Jerry Pam told me. 'He came here and paid his taxes. David Niven didn't do that. He moved to Switzerland where tax wasn't nearly as high as here.'

He couldn't afford to live in the country that he loved. So he sold Mill House for £750,000 – it would be worth four or five times that now – to Jimmy Page, of Led Zeppelin. He claimed he was broke because the California house left him with only £100,000 in the bank. He had used those 'new-old' bricks to extend what had originally been Barbara Hutton's property. The Woolworth heiress had bought it for her son Lance Reventhow's twenty-first birthday. To get into the house, you had to pass through forbidding, electrically-controlled iron gates. The house stood in nearly three acres – a lot in an area where, as he said, 'real estate is measured by the inch.'

There was never any need to leave the house, he thought. 'Tennis court, pool, garden.' But when he did travel, he did it in style – first class all the way; Concorde when he could. Three-star Michelin restaurants in France. That was what his money was for.

It was all par for the course on which he now played. His 'poverty' was only relative. 'When I was poor, people would say, "Money won't make you happy". But now I'm rich and perfectly content I sleep like a baby.' Except when he contemplated his debts. He owed a million dollars on the mortgage he had taken for a house that was guarded night and day by a security force.

He bought a large Alsatian in case the armed security men weren't enough and settled down to enjoy the garden. This was another of his great pleasures. Except seeing snakes in the grass didn't help him settle down as quickly as he might otherwise have done (which is perhaps surprising: his business was full of snakes in the grass).

He chose his own plants and asked for them to be delivered. 'When do they have to be planted?' he asked the man in the nursery. 'When you get home,' he was told. That is not necessarily the advice given in England where the seasons dictate what grows where and when. 'In California you step back and it's up your nose.'

But he tried to remain English – to the point of liking the comment of a fellow expatriot. He was told, 'Have a nice day.' 'I have other plans,' said the man – although Michael acknowledged that he couldn't see anything wrong with having a nice day.

He became an American sports fan, much more than he had ever been a sporting enthusiast in Britain. 'I'm now a baseball and football buff. I learned the rules for both sports. Now I go to Dodgers and Rams games. But I wouldn't bet on any games.' The memory of the older Maurice Micklewhite was too strong for that.

He still liked much about England. He wore English clothes – although he preferred American casual outfits – and wanted to know what was happening 'at home'. Every day, he went to the centre of Beverly Hills – the place that fascinated him because he once saw Fred Astaire buying sandpaper and Danny Kaye buying nails at a hardware shop – to pick up copies of the *Daily Mail, Daily Telegraph* and *The Times*. He had to keep up with the news; even lying on a beach, he'd have his radio switched on to the BBC World service news programme.

Oh yes, he drove *himself* to the newspaper stand. Almost 50 years old, he decided that the time had come to learn to drive. After six lessons in California, he took a test and passed. Now *he* could be at the wheel of his champagne-coloured Rolls Royce.

He went home whenever possible – but as a tax exile he was limited to stays of no more than 90 days a year. 'I still love Britain but I also love LA. It's laid back and I like that. The older I get the further back I lay.'

That was the sort of sentiment that satisfied the British-American Chamber of Commerce in Los Angeles, who immediately named him their man of the year. It helped him to consolidate the position he had now taken for himself – as 'British Ambassador to Los Angeles'. Just what a difficult task that would be took slightly more time to register. There were discussions with visiting cabinet ministers. Jerry Pam was at one meeting with a visiting British minister. 'He really let him have it – the Government wasn't doing enough to help the British film industry. That sort of thing.' So it wasn't easy being an ambassador. Like all ambassadors he had to welcome people who were his social inferiors and make them feel as though the difference in their social status didn't matter.

But nothing compared to the visit of the Queen to Los Angeles. Since LA is a kind city, it arranged to make Her Majesty feel totally at home. It rained – torrentially.

Jerry Pam tells a hysterical story about the party the Hollywood community gave for her: the Queen is sitting on a dais next to the most boring man anyone had ever met. He had paid for the party and had been seated next to her. But he didn't open his mouth. Protocol means you can't talk to the Queen till she talks to you, but she talked to this man and he wouldn't answer. 'In the end, Michael hears this little voice calling, "Mr Caine." No answer. "Mr Caine." Michael then realises that the Queen is talking to him. "Yes, Your Majesty?" he replies. "Mr Caine. Do you know any jokes?" '

Now that was not easy for the ambassador – who could be relied upon to know quite a few jokes, but none of them suitable to tell a Queen, and certainly not this Queen. But she was insistent. 'Try me,' she told Caine – and for the rest of the evening, listened to his stories. It was a wonder that after that he wasn't offered a real ambassador's job, but then that would have required Margaret Thatcher's approval and she wasn't famous for her sense of humour. He was also on record as saying that although he didn't like what Labour had done, the Iron lady was 'much too right-wing for me'.

Later, in 1984, the Olympics were held in Los Angeles. The British Trade Secretary, Norman Tebbit had said that you could tell people's true loyalties when you saw who they supported in international cricket matches. They don't play cricket in the Olympics, but the British colony in LA were asked to support 'their' team. Michael organised a group of British entertainers to perform in Hollywood – with all the money raised going towards the British Olympic fund.

There was a superb dinner at the Beverly Wilshire and the people whom Caine liked to think of as the 'cream' of the half a million Brits living in Southern California came. Guest of honour was Prince Andrew, who hadn't yet met Fergie or been made Duke of York. Michael said he thought he was 'a very genuine sort of bloke'. The Prince had already had one Caine connection. He had dated Niki. One newspaper asked if the Prince would call Caine 'Farver' – a question calculated to get the writer slapped with one of Caine's father's smoked haddocks. 'I'm regarded as a very fortunate semi-literate oaf,' he said – and resented the fact.

In 1981, Niki had married Rowland Fernyhough. It was said they met through a common interest – horses in general and showjumping in particular. Michael was delighted. He wanted her to have a good life. Which was why he tried to make up for those early years when he hadn't been a good father.

As for the Southern Californians themselves, they enjoyed having him among them. 'Here I am British without actually *being* British. I have a strange accent but a working-class attitude.' He was not, he maintained time after time, 'the no-chin, umbrella and bowler hat British' type. 'I judge a man by what he is, after I found out what he is.'

Journalists wanted to hear his views on politics – as though being a film star and earning lots of money made him a guru on international affairs. 'In the 1980s,' he told *USA Holiday* magazine, 'I think privilege will go out of the window. Our side of the world will go further left while the communist side will go further right.'

But for now, because of the boycott of Cuban goods he had to forgo his favourite Havana cigars, his passion since giving up the Disque Bleu fags to which he had previously been addicted.

Caine considered taking out American citizenship but he decided against it. 'Not just because I was homesick but because I wanted Natasha to be educated in Britain.' He still loved Hollywood, which he described once as 'a cross between a health farm, a recreation centre and an insane asylum. It's a company town and I happen to like the company.'

Californians were still fascinated by that accent, which he brought, lent but would not now sell to their country. Some people detected that it got more and more broad when the company he kept seemed to relish it. He worked on it, it seemed, the way Maurice Chevalier developed his own exaggerated French accent. 'But,' Jerry Pam told me, 'in films he had to learn to slow the pace, so that people would understand him.'

Some people could never understand why he made some of he movies that he did. *Beyond The Poseidon Adventure* in 1979 was one of those. It wasn't so much a sequel to *The Poseidon Adventure* of 1972 as 'an alternative ending' which sought to undo what had happened at the conclusion of the previous film. It had been about the sinking of a passenger liner. 'We're either going down in the ship or up in it since the ship's upside down,' Caine said at the time. 'It's a physically demanding role. You're walking on the ceilings and the light fixtures.'

He had to learn to scuba dive for the part, something he hadn't done in South London in the old days. But special effects kept going wrong and he claimed that he was almost killed twice. Insurance companies don't want that to happen to their stars.

The film marked a professional reunion with Karl Malden, the actor whose talent is too often submerged by the fascination people have with his bulbous broken nose. But the deformity has proved his fortune. Michael, however, liked him for himself – and for his talent.

It was through him that Karl got his part in the film. 'I had seen him one day in front of the William Morris building on Wilshire Boulevard in Beverly Hills,' Malden told me. 'I asked him what he was doing. He told me he was going into *Beyond The Poseidon Adventure* and then asked me if I were working. I said, no, not at that time. Then two weeks later I got a call. I've often thought that he was responsible. We never discussed it, but I think he told the producer that Karl Malden would be good for the picture.'

It was, as Malden put it with the memory of *The Billion Dollar Brain* behind him, 'another crazy film. It was a good idea, but we did crazy things in it. Michael is like that. He picks films like that. He's always fighting against the elements. He picks the hard ones, I think. But maybe they're the ones that he is asked to do. On the other hand, the basis for acting is truth. I have a feeling that it's a little of that in Michael. It's an innate thing. That's what I like about him.' Caine said he thought that the film was going to work, 'but I guess it didn't.'

What did work, however, was his own performance. As Karl Malden told me: 'In films, he could play a man who was mad with me. But there was always a twinkle in his eye. I loved that about him. Also his humour. He comes to work happy and I appreciate that. Happy without clowning around.'

And happy outside work too. He took his scuba diving equipment home to the Beverly Hills home and taught Natasha how to use it. 'I saw them,' says Malden, 'it was great to see such a happy family man.'

There was talk about Michael playing the spy Kim Philby in a second movie that was going to be made with Laurence Olivier, called *Jigsaw.* Philby didn't like that idea at all. He sent a message from his home in Moscow: 'The chap's a Cockney. How could he possibly play a person of class?' Caine wasn't sure about that. 'I think he'd end up liking me,' he said.

The picture hit financial problems after work had begun – there was no money to pay the cast. It was eventually made in 1985, now called *The Jigsaw Man*. 'I did it to work with Larry again,' he said.

'The final result is patchy to say the least,' said Leslie Halliwell. What Mr Philby thought about it has gone unrecorded.

The Island was another bad film – a stupid story about a journalist on a Caribbean island inhabited by cannibals who were the descendants of eighteenth-century pirates. Peter Benchley didn't think he had shocked people enough with *Jaws* and thought that audiences needed to be given an additional dose of fright. It was a film that United Artists should not have released.

Benchley himself said: 'Michael is tops. He's everything, co-operative, fun to be with, intelligent, articulate, almost a Boy Scout concept.'

Jerry Pam still thought so too: 'He invited me down to the Caribbean to join him. I said that I was only a poor press agent and couldn't afford all that. So he rented a place on the island and paid all the way.'

The only time he wasn't co-operative was when he refused to go into the water – because he had heard there was a shark out there in the blue. 'When did you last hear of a movie star being eaten by a shark?' asked Michael Ritchie, the director. 'I'm not worried about the last time,' Caine replied. 'I'm worried about the first time. I'm not about to be the first movie star to be eaten by a shark.' He held up production for hours until they were certain there was no shark around.

You had reason to be cynical as a movie star. He made the point that the only time a star was asked to do his own stunts was on the last day of filming – 'when they don't give a damn what happens to you.' As he said: 'What's the point of doing a stunt when there's a guy on the payroll who has spent his entire life doing stunts? Why put him out of work?'

The film was shot on Antigua, which meant that the cast enjoyed it. But *Variety*'s judgement was: 'Suspense gives way to gut-level sadism aimed at the lowest common audience denominator.'

The Hand wasn't any better, even though it was directed by Oliver Stone. Giving this particular horror film a miss would not have deprived anyone. 'Horror is hard work,' Stone said. 'You cannot imagine how difficult it is to get up in the morning, knowing you are going to decapitate someone.' The film was about a cartoonist who loses a hand – that's what happens when you leave it hanging out of a car window as another vehicle comes up from behind. What didn't usually happen was for that hand to take on a life of its own. He may have known it wasn't going to be one of the great ones. But that didn't mean he wasn't going to research the role. He heard about a nuclear physicist named Harold Goldwhite, who had lost a hand in an experiment and went to meet him – to see how he coped. It didn't much help.

William Wolf, an editor of *New York* magazine, thought that the game was over. Michael Caine's films, he said, 'are as disposable as Pampers.' Caine had said he would retire by the mid-80s 'because I have no desire to have my face lifted and wear a toupee.'

But the losing streak was coming to an end. *Dressed to Kill* was one of the sexiest movies he had ever made, although, no doubt much to his relief he was spared the sex scenes involving Angie Dickinson being seduced in a taxi.

In the film he played a psychiatrist who is also a transvestite murderer. The plot and the direction were on a par with the acting. David Denby in *New York* magazine said it was 'the first great American movie of the 80s.' It was directed by Brian De Palma.

Michael got on well with De Palma because he had allowed some of the worst excesses to be done by a double. 'If I had done the razor slashing scene myself, I would have objected. I thought it was completely gratuitous. I like Brian De Palma – technically he is one of the most brilliant directors in America – but his preoccupation with blood and stuff . . . it's incredible.'

Billy Wilder told me that he loved the film. 'I had met him at a party and told him I thought he was a very good actor – and said that that was not something you could learn. You are born that. I said at that time that I thought he was wonderful in *Dressed to Kill*. The gestures were all right. I was for a long time wrestling with myself to find a part for him, but unfortunately we never got to work together.'

Wilder was 92 when he told me that; I suggested that a Wilder-Caine partnership could still happen and should. Pauline Kael wrote in *The New Yorker* that Michael in *Dressed to Kill* 'brings finesse, precise shadings of ambiguity to the role'. I asked Angie Dickinson what she remembered of the film and Michael Caine's part in it. 'Too much to talk about,' she said. 'It would take days.'

Months, not days, were spent on the next Caine film, *Victory* (*Escape to Victory* in the United States). Once more, Michael was playing a British Army officer (the caps suited him wonderfully). And once more he was directed by John Huston, who encouraged him to improvise and rewrite his own dialogue (which would be better than anything that could have been scripted, said the director). In this film he was a prisoner of war and the movie was shot in communist Hungary.

The star with his name on the left-hand side of the top billing was Sylvester Stallone. Was this the writing on the wall? It began to look like it. And there was even worse to come. The honours were also shared by Pele, the Brazilian footballer. Michael himself played a footballer (the officer's cap was awarded to him on the field in recognition of his leadership qualities; at least that was the excuse for his promotion). Michael said he related to the character he played. 'He never believed he could become a captain; I didn't think I could conceivably be a famous actor.' Well, that was just another one of those things he contradicted himself about.

He had studied Pele and the way footballers lived their lives. He still watched people. 'I spend a great deal of time walking around, sitting on my own, just seeing how they behave,' he said at the time he made the film.

The film was about the Germans running the camp, deciding that there was propaganda value to be had out of getting the professional footballers among the prisoners to take part in a game against a Nazi side. Caine and the others found that it was a chance to organise an escape. But his career wasn't in need of an escape route.

Victory was better than many of the things he had done. But he was trying to get away now from his English image. He actually did fancy himself as another Cary Grant – not the kind of suave figure that Grant was but an actor whose nationality was never thought about. That seemed a tall order, but that accent was now merely a prop. He could discard it the way he could change his wardrobe from one film to the next.

Nobody talked about his Englishness in a picture called *Deathtrap*. It was based on a successful stage play, about a playwright hitting what might be called (forgive the pun) a bad stage in his career and who inveigles a young writer to his house with the intention of murdering him and taking his work for his own.

Caine was convinced that getting the role of the older writer proved beyond doubt the wisdom of his move to Beverly Hills. His agent was having a dinner party and invited the Caines. He also asked Jay Presson Allen, who owned the rights to *Deathtrap*. After dinner, Allen was determined to get Caine aboard. Had he not been living in America, he would not have been at the party and, as a result, would not have had one of his more interesting film roles. There was a worry, though. Michael had seen the play on Broadway. Would he not be influenced by how it was done on stage? No, he said, 'I'm such an opinionated ass about everything, including what I do, I wouldn't have listened to Winston Churchill telling me about the Second World War.'

The film was as much a fantasy as *Sleuth* had been, but unlike the earlier film it was virtually a stage play on film, and a play within a play at that. The picture was made in New York, in a huge warehouse which wasn't in the best part of town. But filming it was almost as exciting as the film itself. Michael renewed his friendship with Mia Farrow during this time. More than that, he was there when she met Woody Allen, a seminal occasion in the film business. Their romance lasted a long time but didn't really work.

Caine himself said much the same about his picture. 'Americans don't like that genre. It's too sophisticated for a mass American audience.' Perhaps that was unkind to the mass American audiences. It was a very entertaining production indeed. But there were complications. One of them was that Michael played a bisexual – again; and again it was not easy for him. He may have worried about making a habit of taking on such roles. In the most famous scene in the film, he had to kiss his co-star, a young and healthy Christopher Reeve, whom he liked very much, but didn't particularly fancy kissing.

'Two guys kissing each other didn't do us any good. Right now,' he said afterwards, 'I wouldn't touch a gay subject at all.' But he agreed that he had been in good company. 'Chris is so bloody good in the film.' He himself had wanted to 'dance around' the homosexuality but Sidney Lumet, the director, wouldn't agree.'

And nothing was left to the audience's imagination. As Caine explained: it was a 'full romantic kiss, as if I were kissing a woman.' Mind you, he said it was all a challenge. 'I had never kissed a man before – not even my father. Especially not on the lips.' Before they did the scene, the two actors shared a bottle of brandy and demanded that there would be only one take. There was.

Michael told a TV audience: 'I went back to London, and there was not a phone call, not even any flowers from Chris!' He *was* upset.

The preview audiences wondered about it. They sat stunned .... But at one early showing, the silence was broken by a woman shouting, 'It's such a waste!' He liked that. The link with *Sleuth* was there too. 'I find it extraordinary that in *Deathtrap* I play the part Larry Olivier played in *Sleuth* eight short years ago – the older man.' It surprised a lot of people. The critics liked it. One, Roger Ebert, remarked: 'It plays absolutely fair, more or less, and yet fools us every time, more or less.'

One of the two women in the film, Dyan Cannon, who played Michael's wife, said: 'What Michael brings is a sense of complete believability. If what you're getting is real and powerful it allows you to be all of what you can be. You don't hold back.'

He was not about to hold back now. Another one of those very big Michael Caine films was on the way.

Twenty-Five

Educating Rita

Willy Russell's *Educating Rita* would be an education all of its own. It not only showed how an unschooled girl could attempt, and succeed – at studying English literature via the Open University; it demonstrated just how an actor like Michael Caine could turn himself into a chameleon.

This was as different from the *Deathtrap* Caine as it was from *Alfie*. It was also as different from Michael Caine himself as anything he had ever done. But it was the chameleon that was most instructive. Put him in Liverpool as the setting for a picture and he became as Liverpudlian as the Beatles. Tell him he was a university lecturer who had to play drunk and you could almost smell the alcoholic haze in which he wallowed.

Yet the most interesting thing of all about *Educating Rita* was that for the first time, you weren't seeing the handsome Michael Caine who had had those female fans screaming for his attention or even for a chance to go to bed with him.

Shakira, of course, had changed his lifestyle and he was turning down every one of those chances. Not that some of his friends didn't wonder how long his fidelity would last. 'I'll tell you something,' said Jerry Pam. 'We were on location, 7,000 miles away and a couple of young girls walked into the place where we were. I said, "Look, we're 7,000 miles away and Shakira would never know." "No," he said, "but I'd know." ' She would have appreciated that.

But she probably didn't like the look of her husband in *Educating Rita* any more than he enjoyed looking in the mirror. His hair was long; he wore his glasses but you could see that underneath them, the eyes were puffy; the face was bloated; the stomach was bigger than any man in his early fifties would want it to be. Yet you were with him all the way. When he was describing the beauties of the English literary heritage to an uneducated Rita, played by Julie Walters starring in her first movie, you were drawn to want to sit at his feet and learn too. It was acting on a superb level. The puffiness wasn't just acting, however. He had to get in trim for the part – by eating all the meat, starch and fried things that he had been keeping away from for years.

But that was what he liked doing now, making every part as different as possible from the one before. 'I've always been just an actor who happens to play some of the larger roles. If you have a set personality, you hang on to it for as long as you can and then the world goes away from you. Up until *Alfie*, film stars had been unapproachable.' People didn't see him in the street and just point, as they did if Clint Eastwood walked down Beverly Boulevard. 'They say, "Hiya, Mike."' He liked that. 'A star is one who gets a persona and hangs on to it like grim death. But I became a star by changing all the time.'

Educating Rita was a change all right. People said that the play had overtones of *Pygmalion* about it. Michael had heard that himself. 'But I saw it, and played it, as *The Blue Angel*.

'He loves her vulgarity and the more vulgar she is the more he loves it. Not that I'm as good as Emil Jannings, but as I watched her, I grew more involved with her in the picture and my character descended.'

He said he based the character on two friends. The identity of one he wasn't revealing, but he has since admitted it was Peter Langan. The other was Robert Bolt, who had written *Lawrence of Arabia*. He said that Bolt's 'brilliance has put even arrogant men at his feet.'

It was the first picture Michael had made in Britain in six years – although he had been back and was keeping as close an eye as possible on Langans when he was in London. But now he had a part that earned him twice as much as the last part he played in Britain. 'I'd never have got that money if I was still living in England,' he said.

He was nostalgic. He liked being back home, but said he couldn't afford to stay there – or in Dublin, where a lot of the filming was done at Trinity College. (Ireland, of course, didn't count for the 90 days he was allowed to stay in Britain.) The picture represented a new opportunity to work with his *Alfie* (and *Carve Her Name With Pride*) director, Lewis Gilbert.

Gilbert had been trying to find an opportunity for a Caine reunion ever since *Alfie* had started to make a big impression.

'I didn't make a movie with him again because, frankly, he was always working and I always had something to do, too. Then came this film and I thought, "Michael would be good for that."'

'He was,' Gilbert told me, 'easier to direct this time. It was easier for him because he was well known now and British films were a lot more successful.'

'He jumped at the role,' said Gilbert. 'I rang him up with the idea and he said, straight away, "Of course. I'd love it." We were doing make-up tests and were just fiddling around with his make-up, his beard, that sort of thing. Somehow, it wasn't 17 years since we had last worked together. The chemistry was still there and it was wonderful to be back with him in that way.'

Playing the drunk was the hardest part of all. He played a real drunk, not a stage inebriate. As he had learned all those rep years ago, real drunks don't fall down or slur their words all the time. But they do sometimes – which is why you couldn't get a real alcoholic to play one. 'They're all over the place,' said Gilbert. 'Strangely, a blind person playing a blind person doesn't have that difficulty.' The Lowestoft director had been right, the director agreed, when he had said: 'You're an actor who's trying to walk crooked and speak in a slurred voice. Don't you realise that a drunk is a man who's trying to walk straight and speak properly.'

If he convinced as a drunk, others saw another side of Michael in the *Rita* role. His friend Bob Hoskins was to say: 'He played a poet. Poetry was dripping out of his soul.' The Caine generosity to other performers came to the fore. Said Gilbert: 'He was wonderful with Julie Walters whom he knew had never done a film.' After the first days filming, which was their first scene together, he told the director: 'My God, I've got to pull my socks up. She'll act me off the screen.' 'He was wonderful with her,' Gilbert told me. 'And afterwards he bought her a present – a camera. He was so supportive of her.'

Not that he usually gave his co-star problems. 'He doesn't worry over who his leading lady is going to be. He'll always tell you, "I'm like a doctor. They call me and I do the job."' And if some of his 'patients' weren't the nicest people around, well, he would say 'everyone hates me once in a while.'

On the whole, he had good reason to be happy with *Educating Rita*. The film won a BAFTA award for best picture. Michael was awarded the prize for best actor and Julie Walters, the one for best actress. They also won the Golden Globe, awarded by the foreign Press corps and traditionally the preview for the Academy Awards. Both were also nominated for Oscars, but they didn't win this time. Willy Russell was nominated for his screenplay, but he didn't get a statuette either.

Michael said that he wasn't surprised not to win. Four out of five of the nominees were British. He knew that the winner would be the only American who had been nominated. At times like that, the Academy of Motion Picture Arts and Sciences gets very chauvinistic. Robert Duvall won for his movie *Tender Mercies*. Coincidentally Duvall also played an alcoholic. Lewis Gilbert said that the Academy liked pictures about drunks – one reason he had recommended Michael taking *Educating Rita* in the first place.

People in Britain, however, seemed to accept the BAFTA view on both the picture and the performances. Not surprisingly, since everything about it was so British – even if the problems of the characters could have been mirrored anywhere in the world.

His old teacher-cum-adversary Joan Littlewood met him again at this time. She said she had seen the film. 'First fucking performance you've given in 20 years,' was the salutary opinion she offered. 'Thanks a lot, Joan,' he said. 'Don't worry,' she countered. 'I suppose you've made millions, not acting.' He assured her that he had.

He liked to think that he made people happy, something that came from his religious training – Catholic and Protestant parents, education at a Jewish school, marriage to a Muslim; he didn't pray, he maintained, he said thank you.

But he did lose his temper now and then. The angry restaurateur in him never comes to the fore more than when things aren't right when he takes friends out to eat at other people's restaurants. 'I saw him get very upset once in a restaurant,' Jerry Pam told me. 'We waited two hours for the first course. He just blew up with the manager and told him, "You are making me embarrassed in front of my friends." ' Michael Caine angry was not a pleasant sight. There was also the time that he complained to a neighbour about her dog biting Natasha.

Seeing Michael Caine and other stars together could be a formidable experience. At one party, Roger Moore did a strange walk and everybody laughed. It was an impersonation, he said. 'Of whom?' Michael asked. 'It's your walk,' said Moore. 'I didn't know,' he said. 'I've never seen it.'

At one time, it looked as though he and Moore were going to go into business together – with Sean Connery. They contemplated setting up their own production company. It would have been a 1980s version of United Artists, which had been set up by Charlie Chaplin, Mary Pickford and Douglas Fairbanks senior in the 1920s. It was the popular thing to do in the business. Barbra Streisand once buttonholed him at a restaurant. 'Oh, Michael,' she said. 'When are we going to do a picture together? I've just formed my own production company. But actually, I can't think of a name for it.' He looked at her, thought for a moment and then said: 'Why don't you call it "Re"?' 'Re?' she asked, puzzled. 'Yes,' he said, 'Re productions.'

That was not a story that got into the papers. He tried to keep publicity about himself confined to the work he was doing in his films. 'Everyone knows that Brigitte Bardot was once the most beautiful woman in the world, because everyone has heard of Brigitte Bardot. We all knew about Brigitte Bardot but most of us never saw all her movies. But everyone who knows me goes to see me in a movie.' But she publicised herself, not her movies. 'If you want to convince people about your work, you do it with less publicity about yourself.'

So he wasn't exactly a publicist's gift. The fact that Jerry Pam has been able to work with him says something about both men. They have talked over scripts before they become films and discussed the results, whether hits or flops. But Michael did need people to help get across his image.

'I find very few males like publicity and Michael is no different,' Pam told me. 'Females are different. My philosophy on publicity is that it creates a demand for his talent. He doesn't allow photographs of his houses, but he realises that he is in the public arena and that he has to do it. What he hates are the inaccuracies of the British Press – getting their facts wrong. Much worse than the Americans.'

In 1985 he was talking to English reporters about going back to live in England. He and Shakira talked it over, made a decision and almost immediately bought an Elizabethan house in Oxfordshire, again on the Thames like the one in Windsor.

The house, at North Stoke, Wallingford, was near Henley, home of the famous regatta. It was in a totally rundown condition, but the Caines saw its potential. They paid £380,000 for it – which in 2000 would just about pay for a three-bedroomed terrace house in Islington. But there would be at least that amount again to pay for all the adaptations they were going to make – new kitchens, converting big bedrooms without bathrooms into complete suites, pulling down a 1950s extension and clearing the undergrowth. The place was called The Rectory Farmhouse and it had long sweeping drives; both its name and its setting endeared it to them.

They kept on the Beverly Hills home for the time being, but the family's enthusiasm for the California life was declining. Shakira in particular wanted to return to Britain. She was quoted by the New York *Daily News* as declaring, 'They have much more time for you in London. LA people make friends quickly and they will drop you just as quickly if it suits them.' Those same LA people were into 'moneymaking and success', she said and Michael felt much the same. 'Everyone wants to know you when you are doing well, but God forbid if you are not. It's hard to keep your values straight out here.' Shakira knew that moving back was the right thing to do when she saw Michael alone in his study watching a children's television version of *Black Beauty*. 'Because he loved the scenes of the English countryside.' 'I could see from the light and the sun in the woods that it had been shot in March,' he told her. Shakira saw the writing on the wall: 'If you watched half an hour of children's television to see some trees,' she said, 'we'd better move back there and buy a house.'

So some things *were* more important than money. 'I don't want luxury ermine bed-socks or diamond-encrusted taps,' Michael said. 'I don't live like that. But I live comfortably and I am determined to retain that standard of living. My mother always said, "You're a long time dead." And I always wish every day to be as good and as happy and as much fun as possible.' And there was no reason to think that he could not get that in Britain.

He liked English houses. 'It's a way of living I love. The kitchen is the heart of the house, the bedroom the legs, the drawing room is the head and the wine is the blood.' He mightn't be on hand for the last-minute phone call asking him to do a film, but he did not need to worry about that so much now. There were sufficient offers on the table to keep him busy for a couple of centuries. 'If I'd have stayed in London, I'd have been almost forgotten,' he said, justifying his earlier decision. 'Somebody might have mentioned my name to a producer and he'd have asked, "Has he got fat?"' It wouldn't be like that now. *Educating Rita* apart, he hadn't got fat. But his career *had* expanded despite all the dud films.

The move back surprised a lot of people, but Jerry Pam told me he saw it coming. 'He's a native Englishman and that's important to him.' One of the first things he did when he returned to Britain was to write a book. He called it, appropriately, *Not Many People Know That*. Equally appropriately, the book was suggested by Peter Sellers. Sellers had discovered two things about him – that Michael wrote beautifully and that he had an enormous knowledge of trivia. Caine's own trivial pursuit now was to collate a huge mass of little facts and put them into the slim volume. As Jackie Collins had noted, 'He's always got something funny to say.' He was saying it in the book and when he came back to America on his next visit, he was saying it there too. Jerry Pam testified to that: 'I'm always being bombarded by American TV for him to do television here. He's a marvellous guest and can talk about anything.'

But it wasn't just the funny things he said. He was the great soother. Ms Collins remembered an incident that illustrated it perfectly. 'One of the big movie stars here was getting divorced. It was to Michael that she turned, to put her head on his shoulders and hear him say it would be all right.'

He was very generous, too. For years he had helped to finance an old school friend, Paul Challen, who was stricken with multiple sclerosis. Challen was the only 'mate' who had lent him money when he needed it. So now he was merely repaying an old kindness. That wouldn't surprise Jackie Collins. 'He's so unlike most people out here,' she says. 'An actor, pick up a check? Forget it. He always does. Always.'

He was doing it more and more at Langans, which was now claiming a larger slice of his attention. He was hoping to get a change in the English licensing laws (it would take time but it did eventually happen). 'I want to stay open like a proper brasserie,' he explained. The laws banning the serving of drinks in the afternoon 'strike me as paternalism'. It was as if someone were declaring: ' "Now, you working-class people cannot drink any more this afternoon." And I hate it when the bloody TV goes off at midnight.' (That would change too).

It was still true – with all his success and all his money, the one thing that couldn't be taken out of the boy from the Elephant was the class consciousness. It was really an inverted snobbery. 'America has class,' he said, 'but no *Khlass*.'

But now he returned to his roots. 'England is a good place for mild-mannered people because there are no extremes. And for all my brashness, toughness and outer personality, I am a very gentle man. That's what I have found out. But it took me 53 years.' It was a chance for him to act the English squire – and he never denied that that was how he now saw himself. If he could persuade the neighbours that he wasn't one of the puffed up *nouveaux riches* – as some would always believe him to be – everything would be fine. It was as if he were revisiting the one unforgettably and unredeemably nice part of his childhood, when he had lived with his brother and mother in the big house in Norfolk.

'Coming home for me means walking with Natasha through a rainy garden, smelling the earth when it comes to life again after the winter, seeing the first primrose of spring and feeding the swans on the river,' he told William Foster in *In Britain* magazine in 1986. 'Britain means Melton Mowbray pies and sausages that really taste of sausage. I've missed the smell of damp leaves on a smoky bonfire and sparks shooting up the chimney from a log fire in a pub, the sort with shiny horsebrasses on the wall. The fact is I'm fed up with the constant sunshine.'

It wasn't going to do his diet much good. He would miss the 'fabulous' American steaks, but English lamb was better than anything he could get in California – and then there were the breakfasts. 'In America I had only a grapefruit to start the day. But over here the cooked English breakfast is sheer temptation on a plate. I'm likely to have the full works – sausages, bacon, eggs and fried tomatoes and white bread and butter and tea with milk and sugar. There's no better way to start a day. But what happens when American producers, casting a new film, do say: "What about Michael Caine? Has he got fat?" The answer might well be, "Yes, he jolly well has."'

Once again he was the perfect host. They dined at the Compleat Angler in Marlow, one of the most exclusive restaurants outside London. But nothing was better than eating at The Rectory Farmhouse itself. 'He cooked roast beef, Yorkshire pudding, roast potatoes, like it was unbelievable,' remembered Jerry Pam. 'He had parties. People could go anywhere they wanted. He had an indoor pool and guests could go there if they wanted to. On Sundays, he had all the Sunday papers. You could read them and then fall asleep on a couch.'

Ellen wasn't sure she liked the new Caine house quite so much. In his memoirs, Michael tells the rather poignant story of how she thought her son was now down on his uppers. Why else would they now be living in a pub – the one where Shakira worked serving behind the bar? Even the parents of the very rich cannot escape the cruel effects of old age.

But being very rich made him a target – for other rich people. The Millionaires Club invited him to be a member. He turned down their invitation. 'What is this crap that would make me have to put on a coat and tie to go in?' he said, reprising his old hatred.

You didn't have to do that at Langans, which, besides fulfilling its function as providing good food for people who didn't want to wear coats and ties, was also a club for people who knew Michael Caine. It might not be the way to make a lot of money, but it was certainly a great way of entertaining friends. Dennis Selinger had his wedding reception there – with Michael picking up the tab. Ron Moody, famous for his portrayal of Fagin in Lionel Bart's *Oliver!* was there with his pregnant wife Therese. 'He saw Therese and put his hand on her stomach to bless the child. Daniel is ten now and I am sure because of that he is going to become an actor.'

It was packed to crushing point every night. Stephen Spielberg said he got in by convincing the *maitre d'* that he was Harrison Ford.

When Karl Malden came to London, he chose to go to Langans – without realising that Caine had anything to do with it. 'I was sitting there and all of a sudden Michael came up to me and said, "I'm so glad you're in my restaurant." I said, "You're kidding me." "No," he said, "it *is* my restaurant!" We had a good dinner – and he wouldn't let me have the bill.' It was a familiar story to those who knew him well. June Wyndham Davies bumped into him, rushing through Bond Street. 'Come to lunch,' he said and took her to a big new restaurant.

'"How do you like it?" he asked me. I said, "Darling, it's lovely. However did you think of coming to this place?" "I own it," he said.'

There were others getting a share of the proceeds, too. He organised 'Dine-A-Mite', a scheme through which he persuaded restaurants to donate half their takings one Sunday evening to the homeless. It raised over £500,000.

He had had too many bad experiences in restaurants not to want to make things work properly at his own. Jerry Pam was with Michael at a party held at the White Elephant on the river, which Harry Saltzman had owned. 'There wasn't space for me. Michael was furious. He said, that if I didn't sit, he wouldn't either.' No prizes for guessing what happened. It was a good party, said the publicist.

Being firmly re-established in Britain didn't mean that he wouldn't go backwards and forwards to America. He tried out Virgin Atlantic – because Virgin's entrepreneur boss Richard Branson asked him why he kept flying British Airways. But on arrival at London's Heathrow Airport, he was stopped. Fourteen suitcases belonging to him and Shakira were given a minute security check. He was furious. 'Don't you know who I am?' he asked the man frisking his bags. Yes, he was told, he did know Michael Caine and, of course, he loved his films. 'Do you think I'd try to blow up your fucking aircraft?' Caine asked. No, the security man said he was sure that he wouldn't. But orders were orders and he had to do a proper check on every tenth passenger. Michael had drawn the lucky number. When he returned, there was an angry phone conversation between him and Branson, who asked him how he enjoyed the flight. 'I didn't,' he said. He was furious. Branson apologised, said he would probably sack the man, but Michael wasn't pleased – and assured him he wouldn't travel Virgin again.

It was an unusual episode. Michael Caine doesn't often blow his top, but, as Jackie Collins had told me, 'he doesn't suffer fools gladly'.

He never denied having a temper to lose when the occasion demanded. Usually, he took out his anger in his acting roles. As Shakira said, 'it leaks out in front of the camera.' Michael himself said: 'Yeh. I have a temper that's so terrible I never lose it or use it – at least not more than once every three years. It's so bad it frightens me. But I'm not really angry any more. The anger has gone into the cinema roles or it's disappeared into my bank account. You could say I've buried it in money.'

But money wasn't the criterion for everything he did. And now he was giving people the benefit of his experience. To students at RADA, which he of course had never attended, he said: 'Listen to what I say – not how I say it.' Which is somewhat out of character for a man whose accent has proved to be one of his greatest assets. And then there was the BBC 2 master-class; he told them: 'When becoming a character, you have to steal. Steal whatever you see. You can even steal from other actors' characterisations. But if you do, only steal from the best.'

They would do better than to 'steal' from anything in the next Caine film, *The Honorary Consul*, which in America was called *Beyond The Limit*. It was the second picture on the trot in which Michael played a drunk, but that was about the only thing it had in common with *Educating Rita*. As he said afterwards: 'Two drunks. For a while, it was psychotics, then transvestites [that] they wanted me to play. I want to get back to comedy.'

He co-starred in this new film with his Cockney friend Bob Hoskins and with Richard Gere, fast becoming the hottest property in Hollywood. Hoskins told Michael that he was the reason he became an actor. He had seen that a Cockney could become a star in *Alfie*. They loved each other. But Caine and Gere weren't quite the same. He would complain that Gere was too unpredictable for him. One day the American would greet him with a kiss on the lips, the next he would completely ignore him.

Without a doubt, Caine preferred to be ignored – the experience with Christopher Reeve was not one he wanted to repeat; certainly not off screen.

The Honorary Consul was based on the Graham Greene story of a doctor in Argentina becoming involved in the kidnapping of the drunken British consul. It helped pay some of the bills for the new house, but was not a huge success.

But he did want to get back to comedy. And he did. *Blame It On Rio* was based on a French film. That should have been a warning. The French told stories beautifully on film if they involved sex and comedy in roughly equal proportions. This had equal proportions of sleaze, unsophistication, and boredom. Michael played a man who goes away to Rio de Janeiro with a friend and promptly seduces the man's daughter, who also happens to be the best friend of his own daughter. The girl he seduces was played by a newcomer called Michele Johnson, frequently called on to go topless on screen by the director Stanley Donen. The only interesting part of the film is the name of the teenager who played Michael's own daughter. It was Demi Moore.

Michael Caine celebrated his fiftieth birthday while working on the film. He was there with the jazz musician Quincy Jones, who was born on the same day. (He also shared a birthday with Albert Einstein, a fact that he liked to mention at least once a year.) Shakira and Natasha came to Rio too, to join in what turned out to be the only fun he experienced while the picture was being made.

If *Rio* wasn't so good – and considering it was written by Larry Gelbart, it was a bitter disappointment all round – *Water* was even worse. This film was supposed to be a comedy about the effects of checks on mineral springs in a Caribbean island. It was all very unexciting. *The Holcroft Covenant* was an unattractive name for a slightly better film, but again hardly worthy of the talents of a man still regarded as an exceptional actor. His description of the fate of the film? 'It went straight down the toilet.'

Hannah and Her Sisters, however, went straight into the movie history books. With this one film he had a new lease of life. It wasn't as good as *Educating Rita*. But this time it did win him an Oscar – if only for best supporting actor.

One of the real rewards of the film was working with Woody Allen. He said he took the part because he wanted to work with Woody, whom he appears to have enjoyed thoroughly and not found nearly as kooky as his reputation. Everything was meticulously planned, scripted and shot – even though sometimes the rehearsals became actual scenes in the film. There were sometimes nine or ten takes – compared with the two or three that were usual. 'Woody's a perfectionist,' he said. 'You work for Woody because of the writing, the uniqueness of the situation and because he has complete power over his films. He's like a dictator. He's someone who's written, who's acted, who's directed. So you know it's not going to be screwed up in the editing or the advertising. And he wouldn't let any of us be less than great, as he saw it.'

Caine asked him if he could wear glasses. Woody said, 'of course, but why do you want to wear glasses?' 'Because I figure I'm playing *you* in it,' he said. The story about the interweaving affairs of a family was always dominated by the wonderful Allen one-liners and the superb acting. When it was all over, it was clear this was a very special film indeed. Caine said it was 'Woody's warmest film. The warmth came out in me. It was entirely different from anything I ever did before. Woody gives you more freedom to do what you like than any other director I've ever worked with.'

His old *Ipcress* director Sidney Furie told him he thought it was a great performance. 'We wouldn't like that character, but Michael finds in him something you sympathise with. Michael finds that universal thing to feel sorry for a guy.'

Jerry Pam was the one who recommended that he try for the best supporting actor award, and not attempt to win the best actor Oscar that he had been aiming for. 'I said to Michael, "The actor all the way through is Woody Allen. Yours is just a supporting role." We talked and talked about it. It also looked as if Paul Newman would get the award that year. It was his time. I told him he could possibly be nominated for Best Actor, but that he wouldn't get it. After talking and talking, he agreed. We changed all the ads in the trades [the trade Press] and it was the best supporting actor he went for. I am glad – because he won.'

Variety called it 'one of Woody Allen's great films' and the writer-director won an Oscar for the best original screenplay as well as being nominated for best director. The film was also nominated for best picture. 'A loosely knit canvas of Manhattan interiors and exteriors,' declared *Sight and Sound*.

Michael saw some of those interiors and exteriors. Among them was Mia's own bedroom, where he is seen making love to her on her own bed while her lover stood behind the camera watching. What is more, André Previn, Mia's previous husband, was watching this scene as well.

He had chosen that day to come to see his children. 'I don't talk about anything connected with Woody Allen,' he told me.

After the triumph of *Hannah and Her Sisters*, Michael Caine was due for another flop. But *Sweet Liberty* in which he had a cameo role as an opinionated film star was good fun, mainly because it starred Alan Alda, who also directed. It was about the agonies of a college professor who sees his historical novel destroyed by the film company. Michael played a Revolutionary War officer. Once again, he was an officer who rode a horse. Once again, he fell off – this time into a lake. Marty Bregman, the producer of the film, said that working with Michael was 'like being with a combination of Laurence Olivier and Art Buchwald.' Alan Alda told him he had written the part especially for him. 'It's a conceited old film star – and you'd be perfect.' He'd been damned with faint praise before.

The picture introduced him to New York society's favourite escape centre – Southampton. It was nice there, but he didn't like the affectation all around. He hated the insistence on men wearing trousers and blazers – but no socks. It wasn't for him.

Nor were many of the things that people there thought about Englishmen. They had got most of it wrong in America, he thought. 'We have something I think might appeal to modern women. We were never a sort of macho bunch. It's no accident that Chauvin was a Frenchman. The English man has never been preoccupied with scoring – we don't have the word 'score' in England. A lot of the more macho types seem to make love to women as a punishment. The romantics always seem to be doing women a favour – you always feel a French or Italian will carve a notch on his belt.' Of course, he was speaking from past experience, very past. As a happy, married man he was now no more than an observer.

Half Moon Street was another of those pictures that Joss Ackland would call a 'crap' movie, this one about a woman Ph.D. who turns to prostitution. Signorney Weaver was his co-star, which was a mitigating factor. The truth was staring him in the face. He read somewhere that he had made more bad films than anyone else. 'That's only because I've made more films than anyone else,' he said, without denying the charge.

But around the corner, once more, was something much better.

Twenty-Six

Noises Off

Sometimes, actors have instincts about good pictures. They are going to do well and they want to be a part of them – even if the parts are small. *Mona Lisa* was one of those. Playing a gangster, he was subordinate to Bob Hoskins in the picture, but Hoskins wanted him on board and both benefited from this story of London's underworld.

Michael said he did it well because he knew people like his character in the Elephant and Castle. He had said that about *Get Carter* and if it worked as well for him as it had done before – even in a small part – he would be happy.

'I bet you never thought I'd do it, you cunt,' Hoskins said Michael told him. Michael said that the part was 'the only time I ever made absolutely sure I wasn't sympathetic. But it was a small part. If I was playing that guy in a story about him, I'd have to give him a sympathetic side, otherwise, you wouldn't go with him.' *Newsweek*'s David Ansen described his part as 'a pungent cameo of corruption.'

People asked Shakira what Michael was like when he came back home after a day playing a sadistic killer. 'He's just Michael, my husband,' she said.

Michael, her husband, was a contented man. He was asked if he didn't still want to direct. 'Yes,' he said, 'but I stifle it.' 'I've reached the stage,' he said in 1988, 'when if I have got some spare time, I'd like to fill it in at the Hotel du Cap in the south of France or somewhere. So the thought of getting up at 6 in the morning to direct a load of buggers like me is not as attractive as it was.'

He didn't even have a partner to worry about in the restaurant business. Langans was mostly his – there was another partner, but not Langan himself – even if the name was still that of the former owner. Things had not been going well for them for some time. They had a bitter feud when Michael refused to do an ABC-TV interview on the premises. Caine said he wanted $2 million for the appearance. Langan was so furious that he took away the table by a window that had been for Michael's exclusive use – and said that if he wanted to eat there, he had to sit upstairs. There was, though, the satisfaction that Michael's interest had gone up in value from £25,000 to about £1 million.

He was feted now wherever he went. He may have played truant to see films when he was a kid, but now he was an elder statesman in his chosen profession. In 1987 Michael Aspel hosted an ITV tribute to Caine, the first of many such occasions to take place on both sides of the Atlantic. He talked about himself as though he were at a dinner party. Actors who had worked with him, from June Wyndham Davies to Roger Moore, were there to pay him tribute. Bob Hoskins asked him if his accent had ever done him any harm. He said, 'I lost all the best parts to you.'

The trail of mindless Caine films continued. With Ben Kingsley in 1988, he made a terrible Sherlock Holmes movie called *Without A Clue* (he was Holmes, Kingsley was Watson). Everyone knew why he made the picture, and why, the year before, he'd made *Jaws: The Revenge*. Everybody knew his talents. But still, why make such unadulterated rubbish? 'For the money, why else?' he answered, 'and to be able to get the hell out of Hollywood.'

Dennis Selinger was still sure that he had been wise in advising Michael to work, despite the quality of the movie. 'But it has been his own decision,' he told me. 'I think it was always a matter of his background and the need to make money while it was still there.' Caine's admission that he would make the money and then skip Hollywood was doubly frank.

The kindest thing to be said about the *Jaws* film, the fourth of the series, is that no one really noticed it was there. Michael Caine had to be a good actor to be able to survive such ridiculous attempts at movie making and still be revered and quoted as he was. What was more, directors still wanted him to work for them. Jack Gold, one of the most eminent British movie and TV directors of the period, told me: 'I've met him a few times socially. We've often talked about a project but it has never happened. I should like it to. He's always very affable, friendly and jokey. A lovely guy.'

Ben Kingsley said he enjoyed the Holmes film. 'We rehearsed scenes with the crew and got a lot of laughs because we're a good double act,' he said.

There was a two-part TV play at about the same time in which Caine crossed the private eye barrier and became a Scotland Yard officer, Inspector Abberdine in *Jack the Ripper.*

Working on TV might have been seen as a kind of surrender – and an indication that he was going to start absenting himself from the big screen. Not a bit of it. There were two new thrillers – *The Whistle Blower,* in which he played the father of a spy, and *The Fourth Protocol,* based on the Frederick Forsyth novel, in which he played second fiddle to Pierce Brosnan. But he was co-producer of this picture and invested $705,000 in the $11.3 million budget. Forsyth himself put in $1.5 million. It wasn't worth it. The picture was too wordy, 'a talking picture, not a moving picture', Caine himself agreed. *Variety* said: 'There is an uneasy feeling that the whole affair could have been better made into an excellent mini-series.'

He made a comedy with Sally Field, called *Surrender.* He enjoyed comedy and played it subtly. 'I learnt not to solicit for laughter,' he would explain. 'Once an actor has his begging bowl out, they don't want to know.' Rather foolishly, he allowed one reporter to quote him as saying that it was the best picture he had ever made. It was also the only one that was actually booed in a theatre. The producer Aaron Spelling told him, 'It's funny how often the audience guesses wrong.' The *New York Post*'s Roger Ebert said it was 'an astonishing case of a movie that can do no wrong for its first half and a little right thereafter.'

The release of the picture meant that four new Caine films opened in American theatres in four months, generally accepted as a record. It was an improvement. As he said, 'I used to do four movies in five minutes.' It seemed like that. 'I was a late developer,' he explained.

Of *Surrender* Caine said, 'It's always a disaster when I like a film,' and he liked this one. 'I thought it was funny,' he said of the picture in which, once more, he played a writer with a bad reputation.

On the other hand, he should have realised that the depression that was obvious on the set of *Dirty Rotten Scoundrels,* in which he and Steve Martin played a couple of con men working on the French Riviera, was a good omen. No expense was spared. It was shot where it was supposed to be – 'the best location I ever worked in.'

The picture was a remake of a 1964 flop called *Bedtime Story,* which had starred David Niven and Marlon Brando and which the *Daily Express* in London had described as 'the most embarrassing film of the year'. Michael reported that when they showed the movie for the first time to the cast, 'everybody was pissed off and depressed.' But audiences who paid to see it were not.

Once more, the cards were turned and he had found a Jack, if not a king or an ace. Michael was extraordinarily good in the David Niven role – actually looking like the older Niven, complete with double-breasted blazer. He was a combination of mad Viennese psychiatrist – he runs after Martin with a stick – and a prince from some Ruritanian-type country. Martin was an inept American who tried to get on to his pitch. The picture was his best since *Hannah and Her Sisters*. The humour was almost as subtle and Steve Martin was an exceedingly good partner. He said he learnt a great deal from Caine – like how to order in restaurants.

'I knew that Martin was going to be crazy and I ostensibly was going to be the straight man,' Caine said. 'But there's no straight man in comedy. If you're working with someone who's comic, they're going for laughs without reality. So you become more and more real and you get the attention as well.' Had they made more movies like that, Caine and Martin could have been a 1990s version of Lemmon and Matthau. Alas, to date, they haven't.

And so the quest for good roles went on. Sometimes, he tried and failed. In 1987, he said he was offered the role of William of Baskerville in the film version of Umberto Eco's dark tale of monastery life *The Name of the Rose*. But the part went instead to Sean Connery.

He and Sean were involved in another case at this time. Between them, they sued Allied Artists for money which they said they were owed from the takings of *The Man Who Would Be King*. Sean said that for the money they got, the company only deserved to have had *The Man Who Would Be Prince*. They sued for $100,000 each. Allied Artists, in turn, sued the two men for libel – for the accusations they made about the company. The two men won on both counts, but then Allied Artists went out of business, Sean and Michael were left with their own legal costs to meet and no damages.

It was, to quote the title of Michael's 1990 film, *A Shock To The System*. In that picture he played a loser of a business executive who tries to solve his problems by committing murder. Simon Brett, the novelist whose book the film was based on, told me he was flattered to think that Caine was going to perform his work. That was what having Michael Caine in a movie did. It flattered the people whose efforts were now being filmed. Andrew Klaven, who wrote the screenplay, told me: 'It was amazing to see him in the part, reciting the words that I wrote for him. It wasn't the interpretation I had imagined but it was right. On the other hand, neither Simon nor I thought that the film came out well. It used too many camera angles. Much to our surprise, it has a cult focus these days.'

But not at the time. The public stayed away, as the expression goes, in droves. Once again, however, his bank manager must have approved – as did the people who sold him properties, which was where he was putting most of his money these days. He had more faith in bricks and mortar than he did in stocks and shares. He also liked money for money's own sake, but he knew there were more sensible things to do than just keep it in a bank – or look at it.

He wasn't going to make a huge amount from his second 1990 movie, *Bullseye*, in which he again played a con man. 'I didn't want him to do it and tried to talk him out of it,' said Jerry Pam, 'but he was determined. I think what he really liked was that it was a chance to work with Roger Moore. I wished I had prevailed.' But it was fun to see the two, in Highland dress, making off on a motor bike. Prince Edward, now the Earl of Wessex, appeared to enjoy it when it had a Royal premiere in aid of the Variety Club.

It was also an opportunity to work with Michael Winner, who directed him with pleasure as well as skill. 'I think Michael's my dearest friend,' Winner told me. 'He's very professional, a very solid citizen, a man who knows the values in life, as well as being a very sensitive actor who's a delight to work with. He knows the medium, but then he's been doing it for 90 years! He's not neurotic in any way. You know when you start work on anything with him, you are going to have a nice time.'

It sounds like a good school report or a testimonial, but it appears to be most people's view. The British film industry handed out a similar judgement. In 1990, the Los Angeles Chapter of BAFTA made him the recipient of the first 'Britannia' award at a ceremony at the South Coast Plaza Hotel in Orange county, the centre of all that was posh and right-wing in America, much more Reagan territory than Caine. But it was in aid of two important charities for children and he was delighted, as always, to accept tributes from his peers.

The Governor of California, George Deukmejian sent him a message of 'sincere congratulations'. 'Throughout your career, your performances in the many productions in which you have participated have been received by audiences with great enthusiasm and joy. Your international acting achievements have earned you widespread critical acclaim as well as the respect of your colleagues and the loyalty of countless fans worldwide.'

The City of Costa Mesa made a proclamation. 'Whereas Michael Caine, for 30 years, has made a brilliant contribution to the film art in both the United States and Great Britain .... Whereas he has, through his performance in both American and British films and the great box office impetus given these films throughout the world, he could bring the national film industries of the two nations together in one great English language film community....'

The whereases continued until it came to the 'delight' of the mayor, Peter Buffa, in being able to host the evening. Tom Bradley, the Mayor of Los Angeles added his own tribute. Roger Moore hosted the evening and the award itself was presented by Princess Alexandra. But had Michael done anything to upset Her Royal Highness? When it came to the moment when the crystal trophy – in Tiffany style, his own favourite – was about to be presented, she got up from her seat and, to quote *Variety*, 'thrust' it into Caine's hands without saying a word.

Sean Connery and Steve Martin were nicer to him and a note from Elizabeth Taylor said: 'Of all the things you have achieved, being one of the nicest and sweetest men in the world must have been the hardest.' It was rather a backhanded compliment but it was taken as meaning well.

Meanwhile, BAFTA in England gave him their Lifetime Achievement Award. He deserved respect. In his film *Mr Destiny*, co-starring with Jim Belushi, he played God.

Perhaps that accounted for the fact that Margaret Thatcher invited the Caines to lunch at her weekend residence, Chequers. But there was a price to pay. Perhaps she told her Chancellor of the Exchequer Nigel Lawson that Mr Caine looked very well and prosperous that day. Almost immediately afterwards, the Inland Revenue got in touch, with another invitation – to pay £1 million in back tax. He didn't dispute it, merely decided he had to make another couple of pictures. He did a new TV version of the Dr Jekyll and Mr Hyde story, *The Strange Case of Dr Jekyll and Mr Hyde*. 'What I remember about that picture,' Joss Ackland told me, 'was that Michael walked around dressed up as a potato.'

But things were changing. In December 1989 the news had come that he had secretly been dreading for years. His mother had died. Ellen Micklewhite, who had struggled so much in her early years and who had stood in the crowd to get a better view of her son at that first film premiere, was gone. She had been in a nursing home, smoking, drinking and eating more than was good for her and then quite suddenly, died. She was as old as the century, 89. He had wept when he had seen her body, he said. 'Ma' had played a huge part in every stage of his life.

It was a time to reassess his life. He decided that although he looked like his father, his mother's personality was much more his. His father had been a Micklewhite. He was Michael Caine. That was the name he would have on his tombstone. 'I have been Michael Caine much longer than I was Maurice Micklewhite,' he said. And life had to go on. He was going to pay more attention to his diet, cut down on his cigars. As for drink, Shakira had weaned him off most of the hard stuff.

In 1992, he made *Noises Off*, in which he was the producer of an American company putting on a British sex comedy. Carol Burnett, Denholm Elliott and, once more, Christopher Reeve were his fellow performers. *Variety* got it about right when they said that the adaptation of the Michael Frayn stage play (the screenplay was written by Marty Kaplan), 'serves plenty of laughs and in many ways it stands as a model transfer of a play to the screen'. Unfortunately, the public didn't think so, or if they did, they didn't tell anyone. The picture flopped, but it was not one of those films that could have damaged the Michael Caine career but never did.

Blue Ice, another product of 1992, *was*, however, one of those. He produced this picture himself for Home Box Office. It cost $6 million. 'We don't have $30 million to spend on stuntmen and explosives like they do on the *Lethal Weapons* or *Die Hards*. So what we have to spend our time on is imagination.' But the imagination was stretched too far. It was a sort of poor man's Harry Palmer movie, with a former secret agent turned jazz club owner asked to find his mistress's former boyfriend. That was not enough to whet anyone's appetite – or, as Sheila Johnston wrote in *The Independent*, it was a picture 'that belongs to that familiar genre, the bad British thriller.'

He was in the midst of a thriller himself at that time. Totally out of the blue had come a story published in *The People* newspaper in London. They had discovered a Michael Caine brother – not Stanley, but a man called David. He was only a half-brother, but one his mother had kept quiet about for more than 65 years. Her husband had known no more about him than had Michael. He was 67 when Michael went to visit him in the nursing home. He had been living there ever since the asylum where he had spent most of his life had been closed down. That institution, Michael revealed in his autobiography, was Cain Hill. He said he couldn't help wondering what had gone through his mother's mind when she heard for the first time that Maurice Micklewhite junior had become Michael Caine.

For among the other discoveries that Michael now made was that Ellen had visited her eldest son every week since he had been taken to the asylum as a child – without ever telling either him, Stanley or their father about her trips. David, who was never able to talk, had been born illegitimate in a Salvation Army home. As soon as he established that *The People* story was true, Michael went to see his brother, a little old man who was epileptic and who had spent his entire life in a wheelchair. But he had always know that Michael Caine was his brother. He died not long after Michael made his discovery and his ashes were buried alongside those of his mother – in Michael's garden.

It really was a time for thinking about things. A time for Michael to realise how lucky he was and for those who had been so jealous of him to think again.

He was going into business to buy another restaurant, this time with the chef Marco Pierre White.

The film work load now slowed down. But film actors continued to pay him tribute. Most loved him. Maureen Lipman told me she was taken to a meal with him and thought he was 'very friendly, but I never understood how he could have been a sex symbol. I think maybe I was trying too hard.'

His third film of 1992 was by far the best. *The Muppet Christmas Carol* retold the Scrooge story using the most famous puppets in the world and was one of the best versions of the Dickens tale ever put on to the big screen. Michael looked as if he enjoyed the experience as much as the audience did.

Britain continued to recognise his work by doing more than sending him income tax demands. In 1992, 'for services to the entertainment industry' he was made a CBE.

He didn't mention the fact in the autobiography he wrote that year. The critics loved the book, which was as funny as it was informative, but one person did not. Olivia de Havilland, veteran of those Warner Brothers films with Errol Flynn and of *Gone With The Wind*, reminded people that she was still around by complaining that her name was taken in vain in *What's It All About?* That was what *she* wanted to know when he quoted her as saying things she now claimed never to have uttered, when she appeared with him in *The Swarm* – in particular, that she said Flynn had called her 'The Iron Virgin'. 'That was a cheap shot,' she said. 'It is simply not true. I didn't have lunches with Michael

Caine. I met him only once or twice during the entire making of *The Swarm*.... I've never heard myself referred to in that way.... and if it were true, which it isn't, I wouldn't describe things like that to a friend, much less to a stranger like Michael Caine. Caine', she said, 'is a very fine actor.... but he's turned out to be a disappointment as a human being.'

That was hard talk, but nothing to compare with Caine's other two big rows of the decade. The first was with Richard Harris. Harris wrote a letter to *The Observer* attacking Caine for being too big for his boots. Michael was furious because it came 'out of the blue; I hadn't seen him for 20 years.' But now the two would meet. Caine knew that Harris was staying at the Savoy in London, so he took himself off to the hotel to confront his former friend. 'What the fuck is all this about?' he asked him. 'Where does this come from? I don't know you.' At that point, said Caine later, Harris apologised. 'Oh, I just had a funny day, I'm sorry.' They parted with Caine uttering the immortal words, 'Well, don't fucking do it again.' Unfortunately, he did.

The other row was with Marco Pierre White with whom Michael had gone into business, opening The Canteen, Chelsea's most chic eaterie. They went on record, when the restaurant opened, as saying that they were virtually in love with each other. 'I really love him,' said Caine, 'like the son I never had.' But then in 1995, they split up – and so seriously that everyone concerned worried about the effects of the break. They signed a confidentiality clause which meant that none of them – including the third partner Claudio Pulze, godfather to White's son – was allowed to talk about the affair. Rumour had it that White refused to allow Michael's idea of serving fish and chips to go ahead at The Canteen. That wasn't Chelsea at all.

That same year the verbal fight with Richard Harris blew up again. The love and affection that had been there, stemming from the days when they were two of the out-of-work actors who gathered near Leicester Square, was seriously over. For the second time, Mr Harris chose a Sunday newspaper to attack Caine, although it's fair to say that Michael had got in first. In an interview with *The Sunday Times Magazine* in August 1995, he said he saw himself as the British Gene Hackman. Harris, he said, was like Burton, a drunk.

Harris responded: 'I take great exception to anybody who in print attacks his fellow actors. I loved Richard Burton, who is now dead. I am glad that some producer has decided to rep-surge Michael Caine's career by putting him back to work,' Harris went on, 'but spare us the inevitable flood of self-satisfied, self-congratulatory interviews that will follow this incipient actor's resurrection, rendering indigestible our morning coffee.'

He added later: '[Caine] was always guilty of self-elevation through association with his peers. An elevation his credits hardly recognise. He once claimed to be England's Cary Grant but time proved the evaporation of that prophesy, having neither the charm nor the required sex appeal.... Hackman is an intimidating and dangerous actor. Mr Caine is about as dangerous as Laurel or Hardy, or indeed both, and as intimidating as Shirley Temple.' Then he turned political. 'He failed to realise in his long eclectic sojourn in Beverly Hills that only the poor are forbidden to beg, remembering that he voted for the Prime Minister who put them there.' Then came the unkindest cut of all. Caine hadn't received a knighthood like so many others. 'He did achieve the title he had diligently worked for, "Farceur de Salon of Beverly Hills."'

But later, Michael did respond. 'When he did it again and pretended it was because I'd said he was a drunk, I was disgusted at him. But I couldn't say anything because I didn't want to take any notice of it.' Wasn't he hurt? 'No,' he said, 'because if something is irrelevant, it doesn't mean anything. Someone tells me that somebody got run over in the street. I say, "that's terrible". But I don't burst into tears or get upset.'

So he got back to work. He played former President De Klerk of South Africa in a mini-series; Sidney Poitier played Nelson Mandela. In *Mandela And De Klerk*, a slice of modern history was taken into the home, in what America dubbed 'Black History Month'.

History and Michael Caine seemed to go well together. He was also one of the three stars in a TV mini-series that never reached England, but made a strong impression in America. *World War II – When Lions Roared* was about the meetings between the 'Big Three', Churchill, Roosevelt and Stalin. Bob Hoskins played Churchill, John Lithgow was Roosevelt – and Caine was Stalin.

He was taller than Stalin ever was. And he said: 'Stalin was 5 feet 2 with long black hair and brown eyes. So they thought, "Send for Michael Caine."' He wore padded suits. But his acting and his make-up man achieved a credible facsimile of the original – even though Stalin had never spoken in English. Michael listened to records of Stalin's speech and then to a Russian translating them into English. As few alive now had heard the Soviet dictator speak, it didn't need to be an impersonation but the words he used actually came from Stalin's speeches. It was a *tour de force* and deserved wider circulation.

It was two years before another Caine movie, a record interval. *On Deadly Ground* was one of his least pleasant experiences. He and the director Steven Segal did not hit it off at all. 'He is the only man he would never want to work with again,' Jerry Pam told me. 'I remember seeing them together,' Jackie Collins told me, 'and it was not a good day.'

There were two other made-for-TV films, *Bullet to Beijing* and *Midnight In St Petersburg*. They were both filmed in a period of 12 weeks in the area around St Petersburg, at a combined cost of $9 million, peanuts in the Hollywood he used to know. What those who didn't see them on television never knew was that in the films he was once more Harry Palmer, a much older Harry Palmer of course, who was now a private investigator. Caine apart, the acting was poor, the direction even worse. As the woman in the cinema had said when he had kissed Christopher Reeve, 'what a waste'.

Then in 1996 came *Blood And Wine*, which seemed like more of the same. It was a small part but he said it was 'a labour of love'. It was the story of a man who steals a valuable necklace only to lose it to his stepson, but it co-starred Jack Nicholson and that made it more notable than usual. Derek Malcolm wrote in *The Guardian*: 'The film doesn't seem very significant. Everyone's good, but it's less than the sum of its parts.'

1996 was also the year of *Shadow Run*, another thriller perhaps best forgotten. Also in 1996, there was a four-hour TV mini-series version of *20,000 Leagues Under The Sea*. He played Captain Nemo. The series should have remained on the sea bed. *Curtain Call* the following year with James Spader and Maggie Smith was another forgettable Caine movie. People were now beginning to ask whether this was the end of one of cinema's most interesting careers. And then came the offer of a secondary role that was going to make things very different. Very different indeed.

He took the offer and once more, the name Michael Caine was shouted from the rooftops – if with a *Little Voice*.

Twenty-Seven

Little Voice – and beyond

Voices have always played an important part in Michael Caine's life. As Ron Moody told me: 'He's very quiet when he's going to kill you. But he shouts at all other times.'

In 1998, he was speaking with a very soft voice indeed – although the *Little Voice* in the movie of that name was of a young girl, not of Michael Caine himself. He was once again in a subsidiary role, very much so. He was always in the picture but his was not by any means the biggest part. Yet he was the one who made the impression.

The picture was about a young girl who is virtually a recluse. But in the quiet seclusion of her own room, with only the LP records left her by her late father to console her, she comes alive. She impersonates voices and sings like Judy Garland and Shirley Bassey so perfectly that Caine, a down-at-heel theatrical agent, sees her as his salvation.

The girl, Jane Horrocks, repeating her stage role from *The Rise And Fall of Little Voice* (which was originally the film's title) was wonderful. Her mother, Brenda Blethyn, over-acted but did so brilliantly. But it was Michael Caine who was the real star. And the British film industry. It was one of those 'boutique' British films which, along with *Four Weddings And A Funeral* and *Brassed Off*, were making the world sit up and take notice of an industry so often written off. Anyone who had been writing off Michael Caine had to take stock, too.

In some ways, this was the tutor from *Educating Rita* taken ahead a generation. With a gold medallion around his neck, the professor was now trying to mould an unknown kid into an entertainer – the kind that he had prayed for all his life and had never found. Like his earlier self, as Ray Say he was unkempt and fat – but more greasy and pot-bellied than he had ever been seen before. Seeing him in *Little Voice* you would never have known that he had once been a handsome sex symbol.

There was little that was Cockney about this agent from Scarborough, but he sounded right just the same. 'I preserved this working-class identity', he told Megan Gresidder in *The Sunday Times*. 'It worried me when I was young and wanted to be an actor'. Now, he pointed out, he kept the image because there was 'some altruism in it'. It was for everyone else.

He got right under the skin of the character. He said it was 'sort of my revenge against all the duff agents who turned me down over the years'.

The critics loved him for it. 'Caine is brilliant, particularly when belting out Roy Orbison's *It's Over*', said Anne Bilson in the *Sunday Telegraph*. Antonia Quirke in the *Independent on Sunday* said: 'Caine's trashy impresario is thrillingly heart-proof.' And James Christopher said in *The Times*: 'Caine steals the film. Cruising the streets of Scarborough in a bright red Chevy, gold medallion and a truly horrific collection of Hawaiian shirts, Caine, the Joe Bugner of Hollywood heavyweights, hasn't looked so perfectly in his element for years.' But in *The Guardian* Derek Malcolm said that he didn't like the film that much. 'Only once does *Little Voice* change into a more reflective gear, when the con man sits on the girl's bed and tells her a children's fantasy in an attempt to persuade her to escape her mundane existence. Here, Caine, calling on his considerable experience, justifies his presence beyond any doubt. It is the film's one indelible moment.'

The Foreign Press Association in America gave them the Golden Globe award. Caine was there to receive it – a fact which he said worried him because it made him look as though he had no work to do. 'Oh what a shock! My career must be slipping. This is the first time I've been available to pick up an award.' The award was for best actor in a comedy film. It was his second Globe – the first had been for *Educating Rita*.

He was nominated for an Oscar but failed to win – to a chorus of angry comments from other British artists who thought he had been denied his just deserts.

The old Caine friends and admirers came to his aid. 'I was stunned. I thought it was the most wonderful thing I had ever seen him do,' said June Wyndham Davies. 'He is now one of the great actors. He was always a star.' 'A marvellous part,' said Joss Ackland. 'He can do those bizarre parts and retain complete believability. There are times like this when he really comes across.' And his ever-loyal Jerry Pam: 'I never met actors who don't think Michael is terrific, [forgetting Richard

Harris's outburst], from the bright to the not so bright.' Michael Winner agreed with all that. 'A chap with great wit and a serious human being – which is more than you can say about most actors.'

Now in his late 60s, he was still saying that he didn't want to grow old on screen – 'become an old fart' – but there are plenty around who hope he will. Lewis Gilbert told me: 'He's changed with the years. He has moved into middle age and later. If he lives to be 90 he will play 90-year-olds.'

There are still more restaurants – Shepherds, specialising in old-fashioned English food and said to be a favourite with MPs; Odins; and Langans Bistro in Marylebone.

And he knows he's succeeded. 'I'm married to one of the most beautiful women in the world, literally. It's like *The Picture of Dorian Gray*. I get older and older and she just stands there and nothing happens.' They have been a wonderful example to others in show business. As for Michael Caine himself, he's a pretty good example too – an actor with no side to him; a Cockney who may not have been one literally, but who never considered himself to be anything else. And if he worked too much, wasn't that what was expected of a working man?

Thirty years ago he said that there was an old dictum that you had to keep on going 'until your hat floats'.

Filmography

Director's names are given in italics

1956 A Hill In Korea
Julian Amyes

1957 How To Murder A Rich Uncle
Nigel Patrick

1958 Room 43
Alvin Rakoff

1958 Carve Her Name With Pride
Lewis Gilbert

1958 Blind Spot
Peter Maxwell

1958 The Key
Carol Reed

1959 The Two-Headed Spy
Andre de Toth

1960 The Bulldog Breed
Robert Asher

1960 Foxhole In Cairo
John Moxey

1961 The Day The Earth Caught Fire
Val Guest

1962 Solo For Sparrow
Gordon Flemyng

1962 Wrong Arm Of The Law
Cliff Owen

1963 Zulu
Cy Endfield

1965 The Ipcress File
Sidney J. Furie

1966 The Wrong Box
Bryan Forbes

1966 Alfie
Lewis Gilbert

1966 Gambit
Ronald Neame

1966 Funeral In Berlin
Guy Hamilton

1966 Hurry Sundown
Otto Preminger

1967 Tonight Let's All Make Love In London
Peter Whitehead

1967 Billion Dollar Brain
Ken Russell

1967 Woman Times Seven
Vittorio de Sica

1968 The Magus
Guy Green

1968 Deadfall
Bryan Forbes

1968 Play Dirty
Andre de Toth

1969 The Italian Job
Peter Collinson

1969 The Battle Of Britain
Guy Hamilton

1969 Too Late The Hero
Robert Aldrich

1970 The Last Valley
James Clavell

1971 Get Carter
Mike Hodges

1971 X, Y & Zee
Brian G. Hutton

1971 Kidnapped
Delbert Mann

1972 Pulp
Mike Hodges

1972 Sleuth
Joseph L. Mankiewicz

1974 The Destructors
Robert Parrish

1974 The Black Windmill
Don Siegel

1974 The Wilby Conspiracy
Ralph Nelson

1975 Peeper
Peter Hyams

1975 The Romantic Englishwoman
Joseph Losey

1975 The Man Who Would Be King
John Huston

1975 The Eagle Has Landed
John Sturges

1976 Harry and Walter Go To New York
Mark Rydell

1977 A Bridge Too Far
Richard Attenborough

1978 Silver Bears
Ivan Passer

1978 The Swarm
Irwin Allen

1978 California Suite
Herbert Ross

1979 Ashanti
Richard Fleischer

1979 Beyond The Poseidon Adventure
Irwin Allen

1980 The Island
Michael Ritchie

1980 Dressed To Kill
Brian de Palma

1981 The Hand
Oliver Stone

1981 Victory
John Huston

1982 Deathtrap
Sidney Lumet

1983 Educating Rita
Lewis Gilbert

1983 Beyond The Limit
John MacKenzie

1983 The Jigsaw Man
Terence Young

1983 Blame It On Rio
Stanley Donen

1985 Water
Dick Clement

1985 The Holcroft Covenant
John Frankenheimer

1985 Hannah And Her Sisters
Woody Allen

1985 Sweet Liberty
Alan Alda

1986 Half-Moon Street
Bob Swaim

1986 Mona Lisa
Neil Jordan

1986 The Whistle Blower
Simon Langton

1986 The Fourth Protocol
John MacKenzie

1987 Surrender
Jerry Belson

1987 Jaws: The Revenge
Joseph Sargent

1988 Without A Clue
Thom Eberhardt

1988 Dirty Rotten Scoundrels
Frank Oz

1989 A Shock To The System
Jan Egleson

1989 Bullseye!
Michael Winner

1990 Mr. Destiny
James Orr

1991 Noises Off
Peter Bogdanovich

1992 Blue Ice
Russell Mulcahy

1992 Muppet Christmas Carol
Brian Henson

1993 On Deadly Ground
Steven Seagal

1994 Bullet To Beijing
George Mihalka

1997 Blood And Wine
Bob Rafelson

1998 Little Voice
Mark Herman

INDEX

A Bridge Too Far 195–6, 240
A Hill in Korea 65, 67, 71, 239
A Shock To The System 228–9, 241
accents
  Cockney 1–2, 73, 95, 99–100, 105, 206
  other 32, 53, 72, 88, 131, 210
Ackland, Joss 76, 87, 114, 133, 184, 197, 230, 237
acting
  childhood days 16, 35–6
  early ambitions 28–30, 31, 32, 42–4
  first film roles 65, 66
  master-classes 1, 191, 221
  repertory companies 45–56, 57–8
  The Stage 42, 43–5, 57
  Stratford Theatre Workshop 68–9
agents
  Dennis Selinger 86, 89, 188, 226
  Jimmy Fraser 65, 67
  Josephine Burton 68, 70, 71
  publicity 119–20, 151–2
Alda, Alan 198, 223, 224, 240
Aldrich, Robert 149, 167, 240
Alfie 77, 86, 98, 99–108, 109–12, 239
Allen, Irwin 197, 240
Allen, Woody 210, 222–3, 240
America
  first visit to 116–23
  home, Beverly Hills 196–7, 201–6
  popularity 98, 107–8, 123, 155
  return to Britain 217–19
Amyes, Julian 71, 239
Archard, Army 198
Ashanti 200–1, 240
Asher, Robert 239
Attenborough, Richard 195, 240

BAFTA awards 214, 229–30
Baker, Stanley 67, 80–1, 84–5
Baksh, Shakira 169, 170–3, 179–80, 191, 216–17
Bardot, Brigitte 122, 146, 216
Barry, John 73, 160
Bart, Lionel 77
The Battle of Britain 147–8, 239
Belson, Jerry 240
Beverly Hills 118–19, 196–7, 201–3, 216–17
Beyond the Poseidon Adventure 206, 240
Beyond The Limit 221–2, 240
Billington, Michael 145, 187
Billion Dollar Brain 138–9, 239
Black, Don 146
The Black Windmill 183–4, 240
Blame It On Rio 222, 240
Blind Spot 239
Blood And Wine 235, 241
Blue Ice 231–2, 241
Bogdanovich, Peter 241
Booth, James 82, 85, 102
Buckley, Jimmy 33, 34, 104
The Bulldog Breed 239
Bullet to Beijing 235, 241
Bullseye! 229, 241
Burton, Josephine 68, 70, 71

Caine, Michael
  anger 215, 220–1
  birth 6, 7–8
  childhood influences 15, 20, 22–5, 29
  Cockney origins 5–15, 31–2, 48–9, 78, 81
  glasses 2, 8, 91, 92–3
  half brother discovery 231–2
  health 8, 41, 55, 57, 93
  image 1–3, 110–11, 119, 142, 216
  impact of success 123–7, 128, 137
  memory 156–7
  name changes 48, 70
  parents 3, 6, 7, 9–13, 26, 62
California Suite 197–8, 240
Canby, Vincent 108, 178
Cannes Film Festival 100
Carve Her Name With Pride 69, 239
The Case of Mrs Barry 51
CBE 232

charity work 157, 205, 220, 230
children
  Dominique (Niki) 58, 59, 60, 71, 109, 133, 137, 184, 202, 205
  Natasha 173, 174, 179, 184, 206, 207, 215
Chimes 68
cinema
  ambitions 54
  early influence 9, 15, 32
  early jobs 38
  first roles 65, 66, 79, 80–8
class system 11, 31, 33, 73, 218
Clavell, James 240
Clement, Dick 240
Clubland 7, 35
Collins, Jackie 97, 143, 152, 171–2, 180, 218, 221, 235
Collinson, Peter 239
Comden, Betty 202
The Compartment 78
Connery, Sean
  background 23, 72–3
  production company 215
  Requiem For A Heavyweight 74
  Shalako 146
  The Hill 92
  The Male of the Species 158
  The Man Who Would Be King 188, 190–1, 228–9
  The Name of the Rose 228
Constantine, Michael 194
Crist, Judith 96, 168
Curtain Call 235

The Day of the Jackal 183
The Day The Earth Caught Fire 74, 239
De Palma, Brian 209, 240
De Sica, Vittorio 135, 136, 239
Deadfall 141–2, 239
Deathtrap 210–11, 240
Deighton, Len 91, 95
The Destructors 183, 240
Dickinson, Angie 158, 208, 209
directing 153, 225
Dirty Rotten Scoundrels 227–8, 241
Dixon of Dock Green 71–2, 76
Donen, Stanley 222, 240
Dressed to Kill 208–9, 240
drinking 158–9, 169, 214, 231
The Dumb Waiter 77

The Eagle Has Landed 195, 240
Eberhardt, Thom 241
Ebert, Roger 211, 227
Educating Rita 212–15, 240
education 16–17, 23–30, 36, 37, 156
Egleson, Jan 241
Elstree studios 158
Emmy award 157
Endfield, Cy 81–2, 239
Equity 44, 47, 70
Escape to Victory 209–10
evacuation 17, 18–26

Farrow, Mia 122, 210, 223
Feliciano, Minda 149, 151
filmography 239–41
Finney, Albert 72, 76
Fleischer, Richard 200, 240
Flemyng, Gordon 72, 239
Fogel, Alf 95
Fonda, Jane 130, 132, 198
Forbes, Bryan 114, 115, 141–2, 144, 239
The Fourth Protocol 227, 240
Fox, Alwyn D. 46, 47, 48, 50, 55–6
Foxhole In Cairo 239
Frankenheimer, John 240
Fraser, Jimmy 65, 67
The Frog 75
Funeral In Berlin 126–7, 239
Furie, Sidney J. 91, 95, 97, 167, 223, 239

Gambit 117, 120, 121, 123, 239
gambling 11–12, 62, 158
Gelbart, Larry 114, 222
Germany 38, 127
Get Carter 164–7, 240
Gilbert, Lewis 69–70, 97, 98, 101–5, 133, 176, 213–14, 238, 239, 240
Gold, Jack 226
Golden Globe awards 214, 237
Graham, Sheilah 149, 151
Grant, Cary 117, 121, 155, 202, 210
Green, Guy 239
Grey, Edgar 46, 47, 55
Grosvenor Square 124–5, 152–3, 171
Guest, Val 74, 239

Haines, Patricia 58–9, 60–1, 65, 76, 109, 202
Half Moon Street 224
Halliwell, Leslie 87, 145, 207
Hamilton, Guy 127, 147–8, 239
Hamlet In Elsinore 86
The Hand 208, 240
Hannah and Her Sisters 222–4, 240
Harris, Richard 233–4
Harry and Walter Go To New York 195, 240
Hawkins, Jack 85, 168
Henson, Brian 241
Herman, Mark 241
Hodges, Mike 167, 240
The Holcroft Covenant 222, 240
Hollywood
  first visit 118–20
  home 196–7, 201–3, 216–17
  popularity 143, 144

Hollywood—*contd*
Queen's visit 204–5
homosexuality
in actors 31, 35, 46, 47, 49, 53–4
roles portraying 197–8, 211
US view of British actors 85, 116
The Honorary Consul 221–2
Horrocks, Jane 236
Horse Under Water 139
horseriding 83, 114–15, 160–1, 224
Hoskins, Bob 112, 214, 221, 225, 226, 234
How To Murder A Rich Uncle 69, 239
Hurry Sundown 130–2, 239
Huston, John 188–91, 209, 240
Hutton, Brian 240
Hyams, Peter 194, 240

The Ipcress File 89–98, 125, 139, 239
The Island 207, 240
The Italian Job 146–7, 239

Jack the Ripper 227
Jackson, Glenda 185, 186
Jackson, Gordon 95, 168
Jaffrey, Saeed 185, 191–3
Jaws: The Revenge 226, 240
Jewish influences 24–6, 156
Jigsaw 207
The Jigsaw Man 207, 240
The Johnny Carson Show 157
Jones, Alwyn *see* Fox, Alwyn D.
Jordan, Neil 240

Kael, Pauline 107, 164, 169, 178, 193, 209
Kidnapped 168–9, 240
Klaven, Andrew 229
Korea 38–41, 65, 125

Langans restaurants 185, 188, 192, 199–200, 218, 219–20, 225–6, 238
Langton, Simon 240
The Lark 70, 71
Las Vegas 172–3, 202
The Last Valley 160–1, 240
Lee, Ruta 201
Les Ambassadeurs 90, 92
Lewin, David 128, 238
Lipman, Maureen 232
Little Voice 236–8, 241
Littlewood, Joan 68–9, 215
Lloyd, Sue 91, 95
The Long And The Short And The Tall 75–6
Losey, Joseph 186, 240
Love From A Stranger 51–2
Lumet, Sidney 210, 240

MacKenzie, John 240
MacLaine, Shirley 118–21, 135
The Magus 144–5, 239
Malcolm, Derek 235, 237
Malden, Karl 26, 138, 156, 159, 206–7, 220
The Male Of The Species 157
The Man Who Would Be King 188–93, 228–9, 240
Mandela And De Klerk 234
Mankiewicz, Joseph 177, 178, 240
Mankowitz, Wolf 74
Mann, Delbert 240
marriage
attitude to 122, 129, 135, 142–3
Patricia Haines 58–9, 60–1, 76
Shakira Baksh 172–3, 179–80
The Marseille Contract 183
Martin, Steve 227, 228, 230
Matthau, Walter 197
Maxwell, Peter 239
McKenna, Virginia 69
Merchant, Vivien 1, 100, 113
Merv Griffin Show 157
Micklewhite, Dominique (Niki) 58, 59, 60, 71, 109, 133, 137, 184, 202, 205
Micklewhite, Ellen Frances Marie
death 230–1
Hollywood visit 201–2
motherhood 7, 9, 11, 13, 14, 231–2
own house 161
Paris visit 135, 136
rescues evacuee sons 21
support 63, 65–6, 125
work 11, 13, 22, 54, 66, 96, 111
Zulu premiere 87
Micklewhite, Maurice, Snr 7, 9–12, 21–2, 27, 54, 61–2
Micklewhite, Maurice Joseph 5–48
Micklewhite, Natasha Halima 173, 174, 179, 184, 206, 207, 215
Micklewhite, Stanley 14, 17, 20, 22, 65, 125, 187
Midnight In St Petersburg 235
Mihalka, George 241
Mill House 152–3, 171–2, 180, 196, 203
Millionaires Club 219
Mills, John 87–8, 114, 115
Mona Lisa 7, 225, 240
Moody, Ron 220, 236
Moore, Roger 23, 73, 78, 94, 215, 226, 229, 230
Morris, Ossie 177–8, 189, 190
Moxey, John 239
Mr. Destiny 230, 241
Mulcahy, Russell 241
The Muppet Christmas Carol 232, 241
music 25–6, 53, 95

The Name of the Rose 228
National Association of Theatre Owners (NATO) 141
National Service 38–41
Neame, Ronald 239

Nelson, Ralph 240
Neville, John 77, 86
New York 116–17, 210, 222–4
Newley, Anthony 97, 102
Newman, Nanette 114, 115
Next Time I'll Sing To You 78, 81
No Hiding Place 75
Noises Off 231, 241
Norfolk 22–6
Not For Women Only 193
Not Many People Know That 217
nude scenes 117, 160, 186

Olivier, Laurence 33, 52, 76, 148, 157, 169, 174–8, 207
On Deadly Ground 235, 241
One More River 74
Orr, James 241
Oscar nominations 113, 178–9, 214, 222, 223, 237
O'Toole, Peter 75, 76, 234
Owen, Cliff 239
Oz, Frank 241

Palmer, Harry 91–4, 125–7, 138–9, 235
Pam, Jerry
  best man 172
  on Beverly Hills move 196–7, 201–4
  on Caine character 215, 220
  on Caine return to Britain 217, 219
  Grocers school 24, 156
  Hannah and Her Sisters 223
  The Island 207
  Little Voice 237
  The Man Who Would Be King 191, 192
  publicist 119–20, 151–2, 155, 165–6
  restaurants 199, 200, 215, 220
  Tonight show 178
Paramount 87, 101, 103, 105, 108
Paris 63–4, 136
Parrish, Robert 240
Passer, Ivan 240
Patrick, Nigel 69, 239
Peeper 194–5, 240
Phillip, Prince 84, 121
Pickwick Club 89, 97
Pinewood studios 144
Pinter, Harold 75, 77, 100
Play Dirty 145–6, 239
Plummer, Christopher 86, 102–3, 148, 191
Poitier, Sidney 184–5, 234
politics 34, 70, 125, 145, 162–3, 205–6
Preminger, Otto 130, 131, 132, 239
production 144, 153, 164, 169, 180–2, 227, 231
publicity 119–20, 151–2, 216
Pulp 169, 240

Quinn, Anthony 145, 183

Rafelson, Bob 241
Rakoff, Alvin 66, 239
Rectory Farmhouse 216–17, 219
Reeve, Christopher 15, 210, 231
religion 26, 215
repertory companies 44–56, 57–8
Requiem for a Heavyweight 74
restaurant business
  The Canteen 232, 233
  Langans 185, 188, 192, 199–200, 218, 219–20, 225–6, 238
  Odins/Shepherds 238
Richardson, Ralph 114, 115
Ritchie, Michael 208, 240
Rolls Royce 112, 204
The Romantic Englishwoman 185–7, 240
Room 43 69, 239
Ross, Herbert 240
Russell, Ken 138, 139, 160, 239
Russell, Willy 212, 214–15
Rydell, Mark 195, 240

Saltzman, Harry 89–90, 92, 93, 125, 127, 138, 147–8, 220
San Sebastian Film Festival 149
Sargent, Joseph 241
school days *see* education
Scott, Michael 48–70
Segal, Steven 235, 241
Selinger, Dennis
  agent 86, 89, 151, 188
  Langans reception 220
  marriage guest 172
  work advice 132, 141, 226
Sellers, Peter 136, 217
Shadow Run 235
Shaw, Robert 67, 75, 86, 148
Siegel, Don 183, 240
Silver Bears 196, 240
Sinatra, Nancy 121, 122, 123
Sleuth 52, 174–9, 240
Smith, Maggie 1, 197, 235
smoking 159, 205, 231
Solo For Sparrow 72, 239
Sparv, Camilla 121–2, 144
spectacles 2, 8, 91, 92–3
Stamp, Terence 72–3, 75–6, 93–4, 102, 233
Stone, Oliver 208, 240
The Strange Case of Dr Jekyll and Mr Hyde 230
Stratford, Theatre Royal 68–9
Sturges, John 195, 240
Surrender 227, 240
Suzman, Janet 184
Swaim, Bob 240
The Swarm 196–7, 232–3, 240
Sweet Liberty 224, 240

Taylor, Elizabeth 167, 230

The Teitelbaum File 95
television
  charity work 157
  in dressing room 177
  early roles 70, 71–2, 74–5
  talk shows 158, 193, 218
  tribute programme 226
  US interviews 117
Thatcher, Margaret 205, 230
theatre
  Lowestoft Repertory Company 57–8
  Stratford Theatre Workshop 68–9
  The Long And The Short And The Tall 75–6
  Westminster Theatre Company 44–56
Today 157
Tonight, Let's All Make Love in London 135, 239
Tonight show 178
Too Late The Hero 148–9, 151, 240
20,000 Leagues Under The Sea 235–6
The Two-Headed Spy 239
typecasting 92, 109, 123, 126, 146

Ustinov, Peter 201

Victory 209–10, 240

Walters, Julie 112, 213, 214
Wannamaker, Sam 74–5
wartime 16–17, 18–26, 27
Water 222, 240
Wayne, John 117, 192
Weaver, Sigorney 1, 224
What's It All About? 232–3
The Whistle Blower 227, 240
White Elephant Club 152
White, Marco Pierre 232, 233
Whitehead, Peter 135, 239
Why The Chicken? 77
The Wilby Conspiracy 184–5, 240
Wilder, Billy 209
wine 12, 23, 30, 158–9, 192, 199
Winner, Michael 78–9, 229, 238, 241
Winters, Shelley 1, 100, 105–7
Without A Clue 226, 241
Woman Times Seven 135, 136, 239
women
  admiration by fans 49, 52, 76
  attitude to 104, 106, 119, 128–9, 142–3, 180
  Chinese 150–1
  early experience of 30, 33–5, 49
  girlfriends 85, 109–11, 121–2, 134–5, 143, 149–50
  love scenes 132
  marriage 58, 172–3
Women In Love 159–60, 185
Wood, Natalie 121, 122
work
  see also acting
  attitude to 133, 139, 141, 159, 183
  early jobs 37–8, 41–2, 59–60
World War II – When Lions Roared 234–5
writing 182, 187, 217, 233
Written In The Sand 153
Wrong Arm Of The Law 239
The Wrong Box 114–15, 141, 239
Wuthering Heights 55
Wyndham Davies, June 26, 45, 46–55, 75, 79, 220, 226, 237

X, Y And Z 167–8, 169, 240

York, Susannah 148, 167
Young, Terence 240

Zee and Co. 167–8, 169
Zinnemann, Fred 183
Zulu 79, 80–8, 239